Puppy
Zen

RANDOM HOUSE

UK | USA | Canada | Ireland | Australia
India | New Zealand | South Africa | China

Random House is an imprint of the Penguin Random House group of companies, whose addresses can be found at global.penguinrandomhouse.com.

Penguin
Random House
New Zealand

First published by Penguin Random House New Zealand, 2019

10 9 8 7 6 5

Text © Mark Vette, 2019
Photography © Rachael McKenna (except as credited below), 2019
Other images: page 10 Dreamstime/Dragonika; page 28 Vette family; page 31 Shutterstock/Kulanun Chutisemachai; page 46 Dreamstime/Holly Kuchera; pages 75, 90 top, 111 top, 198–199, 215 top and bottom, 240 top and bottom, Garth Badger/Thievery Ltd; page 89 bottom Shutterstock/Ksenia Raykova; page 130 top FCB New Zealand/SPCA/Mini; page 130 bottom Norbert Steinke; page 142 Dreamstime/Nancy Dressel; page 255 Dreamstime/Iuliia Zavalishina; page 416 Mark Vette.

Design by Cat Taylor © Penguin Random House New Zealand
Cover photograph by Rachael McKenna, Henry and George Ltd,
www.rachaelmckenna.com, www.henryandgeorge.com
Prepress by Image Centre Group
Printed and bound in China by Toppan Leefung Printing Limited

A catalogue record for this book is available from the National Library of New Zealand.

ISBN 978-0-14-377405-1
eISBN 978-0-14-377406-8

penguin.co.nz

Puppy Zen

Eight Weeks To Train Your Pup and Create a Lifelong Bond

Mark Vette

AS SEEN ON TV

RANDOM HOUSE
NEW ZEALAND

Contents

To Kim, my biggest cheerleader, advocate and muse, who can carve a story out of the wilderness. Together we birthed Dog Zen and Puppy Zen — thank you for mothering them into being.

I would also like to express my deep gratitude to my Zen Master and life-way teacher, Thich Nhat Hanh, who helped me find the 'zen' in Puppy Zen and taught me that 'love is understanding'.

And finally, to Hercules, the most amazing, intelligent and deeply bonded dog I have had in my life, who taught me how dogs can love and just how intelligent they can be.

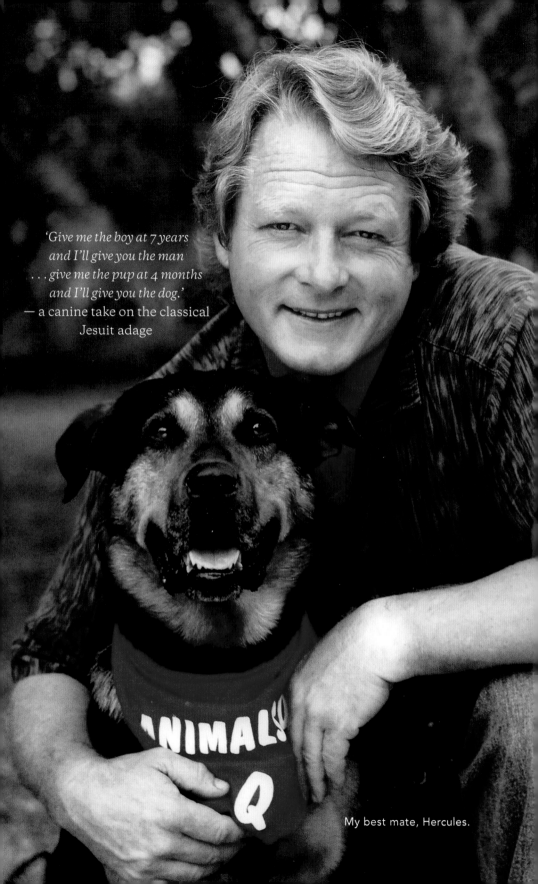

'Give me the boy at 7 years and I'll give you the man . . . give me the pup at 4 months and I'll give you the dog.'
— a canine take on the classical Jesuit adage

My best mate, Hercules.

Preface

There are two contrasting stories that are at the very heart of this book: a story of possibility, love and success, and another of missed opportunity, lack of knowledge and desperate tragedy. Both broke my heart in different ways. The former through true love and the grief of losing a very special friend, the latter through the deep despair of not being able to save all of those dogs who don't get the right start in life. While these stories are based on true experiences, some of the names have been changed.

These stories illustrate what an extraordinary life a dog can lead when given an educated start, and how awful it can be when we don't get it right. In the end, what both of these stories truly show is just how significant — no, critical — the formative period of a puppy's life (3-16 weeks of age) is, and how 'doing the right thing at the right time' makes all of the difference. The sage advice that 'Prevention is better than cure' definitely holds true here.

HERCULES THE STAR: THE BEST BEGINNING AND THE MOST EXTRAORDINARY LIFE

My relationship with Hercules, my handsome Huntaway–Rottweiler cross, is undoubtedly one of my most defining and heartfelt relationships with a dog. He bonded with me in such a deep and meaningful way, and our shared language was subtle and sophisticated. With nearly 150 commands and shared words, Hercules could discriminate hundreds of items, from toys to household items to movie props. He could get a beer out of the fridge, and when he'd visit me in the bath he'd close the bathroom door behind him. He was a great mate.

Hercules was best known for his prowess as an actor, with hundreds of commercials and movies to his name. The famous Toyota 'Bugger' advertisement won 15 international awards and he became Australian

Charles — so much potential.

Dog of the Year. Even as I write this, I see one of our national newspapers referencing that ad and Hercules 20 years on. It seems he wasn't only my dog — the whole nation fell in love with him, too!

He began life with my son Bodhi and me when we chose him to be the pup for the TV show *Hercules*. The noisy, complex environment of a film set, and learning to perform many behaviours in a very short time, is challenging for a pup, so it was critical we got Hercules at the right time: the start of his formative period after leaving his mother (7 to 8 weeks old).

Hercules' ongoing ability to learn and to adapt to new situations was profound, because he had 'learned to learn' at the right time, when he was soaking up new information like a sponge. More than his ability to learn and achieve great things was the deep and subtle bond that my family and I developed with Hercules as he grew. It was extraordinary the way I knew he kept an eye out for the kids, even pulling my youngest, Koan, away from the pool edge by his nappies when Koan had managed to escape my notice. I was amazed and grateful for another pair of eyes; he was such a significant member of our family.

How sad I was when he died, a true hero's death — educating children in the middle of a film set. Thirteen years old and in full stretch, he dropped dead of a heart attack — no warning, so unexpected. The national newspaper ran a full, blacked-out page with just a simple phrase in the centre — 'Bugger!'; and the TV news ran a story of farewell for him while playing Sting's 'Fields of Gold'. To this day that song makes me cry, good tears honouring a life well lived and with gratitude for having had such a good mate.

Although he had an extraordinary life, there wasn't anything innately special about Hercules: he just had the right start, which created a very special bond, and was a dog capable of learning and coping with life's complexities. His story is one of possibility: you, too, can create such a deep bond with your dog if you do the right thing at the right time with your pup.

CHARLES THE WEIMARANER: GONE WRONG SO EARLY

Charles's story is much sadder and more difficult, needlessly going down a tragic path. It is not an easy story for me and my team to tell, but we know people need to understand just how critical the formative period of a puppy's life is, and what the consequences can be without the right start for a pup. Over 40 years of seeing thousands of these cases makes the grief even greater.

Charles was a handsome, pure-bred Weimaraner, young, full of vitality and very close to his family. He bounced into Jane and Lex's lives at 12 weeks old, later than the ideal 8 weeks old, and just within the formative period. He was the centre of their lives. They hadn't yet had children, although they were planning for them in the near future.

Unfortunately, they were advised to keep him under a strict at-home regime until his vaccination programme was completed. This resulted in Charles not leaving their property until he was 4 months old, meaning that as a young pup in the critical formative period he had led a far too limited life. He had met very few dogs and people, and had not been exposed to much novelty and change. Research shows that if pups don't have much or any socialisation by 12 weeks of age, they will most likely be mal-socialised (not socialised to your extended social group) later in life, as was the case with Charles.

Early on, Lex and Jane had noticed the odd growl from their pup, and they had trouble with him growling and snapping when they tried to get him off the bed or tell him off. This problem continued to escalate over the months, until finally Charles bit his beloved owners several times. By 18 months old a further problem started manifesting: a wariness of strangers, both at home and elsewhere. By the time he was 2 years old, a complaint had been made to the council that Charles had bitten someone, so the family ended up at my clinic.

When I met Charles, and with a baby about to join their family, his fear-induced protective aggression and dominance aggression were already well established. Dominance aggression is one of the 10 different forms of aggression we treat in our clinic. It is characterised as aggression primarily towards family members, and can be very distressing and frightening. It indicates a malformed bond, where a dog is competing aggressively for resources with other members of the family. (Most often this is directed at those the dog perceives to be the more subordinate family members, but it can extend to all family members, as in this case.) His protective aggression made Charles wary of strangers, due to his not knowing how to meet and greet people. He started barking at and threatening visitors, although when you watched him you could tell it was fear-induced, and only got more offensive (direct) as his ability to displace people was rewarded by their retreating.

He was a challenging case in clinic, but after our standard 3-week residential stay he had all of the training tools and techniques established. We were happy that, if the owners could follow through effectively, things should go well at home. We transferred this work to the home and the owners, and for the first few months things went well. Unfortunately, it didn't last, and Charles started to revert to his old ways. With such difficult cases, the long-term prognosis relies heavily on the owners' ability to follow through effectively and consistently with complex techniques, which can be challenging even with the best of intentions.

Over the next couple of years, we would visit and try to support the family to settle things back down. It was a long and painful couple of years, and ultimately we discussed and recommended euthanasia, as the risks were rising with their son now becoming a toddler. They couldn't bring themselves to do this, so we all battled on, trying to make it work. Can you imagine the internal conflict within this family as they sought to protect their beloved son, their beloved dog and themselves? We felt for them dearly.

Eventually, the call came. He had threatened their toddler a number of times. They had tried re-homing (even though we hadn't recommended this), and each time he was returned for either threatening or biting his new owners. They brought him back to us to assess, and after some incidents with my highly experienced team we knew he wasn't a dog that could safely go to any home.

It is a brutal part of our work. After working with Charles for so long, we had become very attached. Yet part of our role is to help a family make difficult decisions, weighing up the impact on the dog and the family, as well as risks to the community. It isn't easy, and I don't wish it on anyone. We didn't have the resources to have him stay with us (which ones do you save?), and we knew he wasn't safe in the community, so we had to support the family to humanely euthanise him.

We held them as close as we could, had Charles on our property for a play-filled final week, and supported him as we lay him to rest in a sunny spot by our river with a ritual of care and love. How deeply we wished it could have been different for him, and it could have been with the right knowledge and understanding when he was a pup.

I loved that my TV show *Pound Pups to Dog Stars* gave me the opportunity to save dogs that had such terrible starts in life, but it also made me wonder about all of those other dogs that hadn't been so lucky. It is this drive — to stop the needless suffering of not only dogs and their owners but also the professionals that support them and the communities they live in — that is at the heart of this book.

In our clinic, we see the worst cases of aggression and other behavioural problems. It is heart-breaking knowing that this is often due to the foundations not having been put in place during the formative period, for example through a lack of understanding and poor advice about isolating the pup. How preventable this all would have been if the right thing had been done at the right time.

This book is dedicated to those dogs that helped us learn so many harsh lessons in order that you can have the happy path: a life with a stable dog and a lifelong, harmonious relationship.

THE BIG IDEA — PREVENTION IS BETTER THAN CURE

I believe we can transform dog behaviour in our communities in 10 years by doing the right thing at the right time in a puppy's life. We can prevent thousands of dog bites and anguishing behavioural problems if only we socialise and prepare our pups in their critical formative period. US research shows that 80 per cent of euthanasia in the first 3 years of a dog's life is due to behavioural problems not medical problems. While there are very few, if any, societal issues that can be transformed in our lifetimes, I believe this is one of them.

Dogs are such extraordinary beings. They have co-evolved with us over 40,000 years to form one of the most profound relationships we have with any species. They play so many critical roles in our communities — from beloved companions to service dogs like guide dogs, police dogs, epilepsy assist, cancer detection, sheep dogs and much, much more. They are also often some of the last vestiges of Nature in many of our increasingly concrete, screen-focused, out-of-touch worlds.

Yet we are at risk of pushing our beloved dogs into the margins of our communities as we focus on how to 'stay safe' around dogs, and how to 'manage' them. How awful if we are the generation that fails to

As dog owners we play a critical part in our dogs being welcome in our communities.

marvel at and protect this extraordinary relationship. Let's change the conversation from managing our dogs to *integrating* our dogs into our communities. Let's ensure these beings are celebrated and welcomed into the very heart of our communities.

Of course, as responsible puppy owners we play a critical part in this. Pups don't innately know how to live in our modern world. It is up to us, as their loving mentors, to help guide them. The wonderful thing about pups is that doing the right thing at the right time is easily achievable. But do we truly know what our pup needs to live safely and happily in our world? It is up to us to find out, and it is the purpose of this book to offer you this understanding. So let's begin.

What we do when pups
are young matters.

Introduction

Puppies are so cute, and when our oxytocin (bonding hormone) starts to flow we become weak-kneed and vulnerable to an overwhelming sense of love. This is what is called 'biophilia', the love of living things. We especially love things that remind us of babies (which is called 'neotony' — the love of baby-like animals).

Historically, we have thought of ourselves as rational beings that feel, but science shows we are emotional beings that think. You are going to feel deeply about your puppy, which is so important and a wonderful thing. But we are asking you to think, too. With Puppy Zen, we show you that you must use your mind, not just your heart, when you choose and raise your pup. We must love our pups with all our hearts, but also remember that they are not our human babies but our dogs, with their own specific needs and requirements that we must learn to understand.

Puppy Zen grows that understanding. It is the art and science of rearing and training your pup, and is at the heart of dog behaviour and training. In this book, we build our understanding of our emotional experience of puppies, and what we need to do to grow them into stable, happy dogs that we can have a lifelong, harmonious relationship with.

However, we are not so mean that we aren't willing to tickle your puppy addiction with some beautiful photographs from world-renowned animal photographer Rachael McKenna to help illustrate and grow this understanding!

MAKE OR BREAK YOUR DOG — THE CRITICAL IMPORTANCE OF YOUR PUP'S FORMATIVE PERIOD

If there is only one message you take from this book, then it is the critical importance of the puppy's formative period (3–16 weeks of age). Over 70 to 80 per cent of a pup's brain connectivity develops during this period, so what you do at this time really matters. If you don't do the work, then you will head down the path of behavioural issues, which creates a lot of suffering and requires a lot more work to fix.

In this formative period, the pups are in *tabula rasa* (like a clean slate), where they are able to be shaped very easily. Little learning (or wiring of the brain) has gone on yet, and the brain is only just beginning to wire its social and other developmental behaviours. This is when you must start all of the necessary exposure and training required to develop a well-rounded pup and later dog. Exposure is the operative word here!

Although pups and dogs are naturally attuned to bond to us and live in our world, these behaviours do not automatically switch on. You must activate or switch on these ancient pathways during the formative period. Ideally, these behaviours should also take place in a certain order. In science this is called *cascading* — the important sequencing of behaviours that need to be switched on or put in place. Think of it like building a house: first we need to put the piles and foundations in the right place, then the floors, the walls, the ceilings and finally the roof. If things are not put in place in the right order, the building can easily fall down.

The puppy's remarkable formative period is Nature's extraordinary window of opportunity to adapt and integrate our pups into our complex human world. In that time, we must:

O create a strong, healthy bond to us and the home site
O socialise them broadly with humans, dogs and other species (cross-foster)
O expose, habituate or desensitise them to the environment you are going to live in
O teach them the shared language (including family rules) so you can communicate.

Do these four things in the right order and in the right period and your pup is beautifully prepared to live a happy, harmonious life with you in our complex modern world. If not, you head down the more challenging path of mal-socialisation and adult behavioural issues.

In *Puppy Zen*, we show you how to switch on these ancient bonding pathways (or behaviour systems). It is principally a step-by-step, 'how to' book that takes you through what you need to do in each stage of your puppy's development. We hold your hand through the why, when and how.

In Part A, we grow your understanding of your puppy, and how a dog became a dog. We identify the defining features inherited from his ancestors that we use to grow your bond and train your pup. In particular we will look back at the origin of the pup's formative period, and how hugely significant it is in a pup's development.

In Part B, we look at the significance of our bond with our pups, and how it is the foundation of everything. We outline the nature of that bond, and how we mimic natural systems to develop the bond. From there we build a shared language and teach the family rules, so we can communicate and explore the critical role we have as our pups' mentors. Dogs, better than any other species, can bond with us intimately and integrate into our world. Our super-intelligent cousins, the primates — such as the chimpanzees, orangutans and gorillas — while being social and intelligent like us and dogs, can't bond with us as dogs do, having not lived intimately with us for the tens of thousands of years it has taken to co-evolve and grow this unique and astounding bond.

From there, in Part C, the training foundations, we explore pups' intelligence, how pups learn, and the importance of the learning state in training. We then take you through all of the necessary tools and basic commands you need to build your shared language to bond with and train your pup. The magic of the clicker is taught here too.

In Part D, we turn from the theoretical to the practical, introducing the most important techniques you will use with your pup through the formative period, bringing together building the bond, the tools and the basic commands learnt in Parts B and C.

In Part E, we help you prepare for getting your own pup, including the all-important matching of the needs and strengths of various breeds and individual pups to your own needs and lifestyle.

In Part F we pull it all together and outline what to do as you raise your pup, taking you step-by-step through their critical developmental stages. *If you were to do nothing else in this book, this is where you should go.*

While *Puppy Zen* focuses primarily on the puppy's critical developmental stage of the formative period (3–16 weeks of age), we also include information on pups up to 24 months old, which is the end of puberty and the sub-adult phase. We do this so you can get support through the critical and at times challenging adolescent and puberty stages, where the more dominant and protective imperatives start to take effect. This is when the growing pup starts to build his confidence and outward focus, and can become distracted by the world. From 8 months on, sex raises its head and the pup can lose his focus somewhat, so this is the time to really consolidate and proof (bed in) what you have taught him already.

We aim to hold your hand through this wonderful period of puppy-raising, helping you get through this sometimes overwhelming stage by growing your knowledge, and providing you with a clear to-do list to encourage you. Remember, from 3 weeks of age until 16 weeks, you and your breeder have about 3 months to create 15 years of joy, rather than 15 years of frustration. What you do during this time is critical.

RESCUE DOGS AND OLDER PUPS — AN IMPORTANT NOTE

Of course we aren't always so lucky to get a pup in that critical 3–16 weeks of age period, and not every pup and dog gets the best start in life. I highly encourage people, if they have the confidence, ability and time, to offer their love and homes to rescue pups and dogs, and give them a second chance. It is a very rewarding and loving thing to do — all four of my dogs are rescue dogs.

As I showed in *Dog Zen: Everything you need to know to transform your dog*, we can undo inappropriate coping behaviours by using sophisticated learning techniques to 'take them back to the den' and re-create the learning conditions that are inherent in the young pup. While this is a different, more complex learning and training process for both you and your dog, it is possible to effect change. It just takes more time, skill and patience.

If you do get a pup after the formative period, then the information in this book is still very useful, and we explain in Part F how you can use that section for these pups, too. We provide trouble-shooting advice throughout the book to help you resolve any issues that might be emerging. However, if you do find that your pup needs further support with emerging issues go to our trouble-shooting resources on www.dogzen.com/puppyresources. I would also like to offer a subscription to our online program (30 how-to videos) for just $1 for the first month (use code DogZen1)

We will give you step-by-step instructions about how to train your pup.

PART A

The Puppy

Oh, how we love our puppies — I'm sure I don't have
to explain that to any reader who has found their
way here. Cute beyond words, soft and vulnerable,
they strike at the centre of our highly social hearts.
Yet there is so much more to these cuddly beings that
share such an ancient history with us. Together we
have built one of history's most amazing cross-species
bonds, a relationship based on trust, co-operation,
honesty and love.

Chapter 1

For the love of a puppy

How is it that we have such a deep connection, which is not even replicated by our closer cousins, the highly intelligent and social primates? To help answer this, here we explore why we love our puppies and dogs so much, how the wolf became a dog able to live in our living rooms, and how we make use of the wolf's greatest gift to us — the pup's formative period — to enable this extraordinary, heart-warming relationship.

Both dogs and humans are highly social animals and share a need for connectedness and relationships. For us, this expresses itself as a penchant for pets and sharing our lives with other species (biophilia). Research has found that humans even have specialised brain cells (neurons) in the amygdala (one of the emotion centres of the brain) that respond preferentially to animal images.

We particularly love animals that are neotonised (show more puppy- or baby-like attributes). As we will see later, a significant part of the co-evolution of the dog has been the juvenilisation of the wolf, resulting in dogs taking on some of the characteristics of wolf pups.

OUR MUTUAL SEARCH FOR CONNECTION

Studies show that the dam-to-pup attachment relationship is almost identical to the attachment relationship between the human mother and her infant. Dogs have similar hormones to humans. Like us, they produce oxytocin, vasopressin and other hormones that enhance the bond between humans and dogs. For example, studies found that when women were shown images of their own children and dogs, and then images of unknown dogs and children, a very similar response in the brain was produced, suggesting that maternal feelings might extend to animals. Thankfully, this is a two-way street, as dogs also

We can have the same emotional physiological response to our puppies as to our human loved ones.

live for social fulfilment and connectedness, and recent research has shown that a dog's central focus is us, even over and above his own species.

Studies reveal that the emotional bond between dogs and their owners is proven to bring many benefits, such as decreasing stress, improving longevity, and fulfilling our emotional needs in distressing situations. Healthy relations with us offer the same benefits to dogs. We both enjoy the interactions, derive support, and co-operate at an unusually high level. I know from being with my own dogs how I love throwing the ball, going for walks and swimming in the ocean with them. It is fulfilling, joyful and calming to all of us. Such unconditional love, joy and relaxation brings me back to Nature and my own inner peace.

How remarkable it is that we can have the same emotional physiological response to our dogs as to our human loved ones. You can see why the mistake is so easily made in treating dogs like humans. However, it is critical that we treat and guide our dogs as dogs — in ways that are helpful to them, and from their perspective. Guiding them to live in a human world like humans will not help them, but will cause them confusion, fear and stress.

So this is our challenge: to love them with all our hearts and treat them the way these animal beings need us to treat them. To do that we must understand them, and this is the purpose of the first part of *Puppy Zen*. What really is a pup that becomes a dog, and how do we help them live in our lives harmoniously?

Chapter 2

Becoming the dog

To truly understand what pups are, what they need from us, and how we can best rear and train them, we need to look into their ancestral roots to see what has shaped their evolution. From looking at the dog's ancestors we can determine the defining features that make a dog, and how we can utilise these in our bonding and training processes.

Our understanding of the dog has evolved incredibly in the past 10 or 15 years, yet there is still a lot of debate around the exact ancestral pathway dogs took to become dogs and join up with humans. Nevertheless, let me outline my view informed from the current wealth of research.

Cat- and wolf-like species diverged from their shared ancestor (the *Miacis* genus) about 50 million years ago (mya) to form the earliest cat-like and wolf-like species. The very first Caninae subfamily appeared about 34 mya, and around 11 mya these canids (mammals of the dog family) diverged into three separate forms: wolves, jackals and foxes.

Eight million years ago, the Beringian land bridge between Alaska and Eurasia formed, allowing some of the early canids to cross over and begin to populate Eurasia. From here, the Eurasian wolf diversified into many different habitats all over Eurasia, and became the most successful predator of the time. The wolf and other canids also returned back to North America about a million years ago. The dog, however, evolved from the Eurasian grey wolf, and the American clade (branch of the original shared ancestor) did not contribute to the modern dog until much later, through hybridisation once humans brought dogs to America, about 10,000 years ago.

Most importantly, the Eurasian wolf was in the areas where early humans entered Europe, from North Africa via the Levant, around Israel. We believe that the wolf and our ancestors met and began our extraordinary co-evolutionary process about 30,000 to 40,000 years

ago, possibly in northern Europe and southern Asia, with the Asian clade taking over the European clade.

Emerging science shows us that a now-extinct sister to the modern grey wolf was present in Eurasia 40,000 to 50,000 years ago, and it is she who was the historic progenitor of the pariah and village dogs, and hence our dogs. With the sister wolf now extinct, it leaves us with only the modern grey wolf to help us understand what the wolf has brought to the dog. We do, however, believe that they were very similar.

Some of the key contributions the wolf gave the dog derived from its evolution into a kin-related pack animal. Through its early evolution, the wolf began to form into kin-related packs, driven by the selective advantage of exploiting the untapped niche of hunting large prey. The social co-ordination needed to hunt such large prey was the likely selective pressure that grew their sociability and their social brains, making them more intelligent, with a greater behavioural plasticity (flexibility) and adaptability than the more solitary species of canid (like foxes).

The kin-related wolf pack is made up of the dam (mum), the sire (dad), and the pups and uncles and aunts. The pack centres on a mating pair in a monogamous bond, which breeds first in a whelping den, and then shifts to a rendezvous den over the first 4 months of the pups' lives. The whole pack settles temporarily for that 4-month period, in order to raise the pups. This is the important formative period: a short, intense time of optimum learning for the pups, which is critical to their development into stable pack members. The 3-12-week period within this time is known as the *critical or sensitive period for socialisation*, and although the wolf pup's formative period is for 4 months, most of its social behaviour is established by 12 weeks (or less). You will see later how the dog has extended that ability to 16 weeks (if the right foundations are put in place by 12 weeks of age).

By the time the pack is on the move again, the pups' formative period has closed down, their having learnt everything they need to know about their world — who is in their pack, who isn't, and the key skills for survival. This formative period is an important contributor to the dog, however, it's worth noting that wolves start and end primary human socialisation earlier than dogs and are more suspicious and anxious generally. The juvenilisation and domestication of the dog has effectively delayed and potentially extends the socialisation period in the dog, calming the dog pup and leading to a calmer temperament in dogs.

The older siblings normally disperse to form their own packs from around 1 to 4 years of age, but before that they become the very important helpers in the pack. Their role is to help raise their younger siblings to adulthood. They mentor the young — a bond that is very important in aiding the pups' learning and social integration. It is this critical *helper bond* that our bond with our pup mimics, and it contributes significantly to the evolution of our relationship with them.

PROTO-DOG AND SELF-DOMESTICATION

The wolf gave the dog its sociability and social brain, the formative period and that all-important helper function, but what created the titanic shift of the wolf's attention away from its own kind to humans, and put in place the beginnings of the dog?

Research suggests that wolves started congregating around hunter-gatherer settlements about 30,000 to 40,000 years ago, attracted — just like seagulls, pigeons and rats — by the opportunity to pilfer and clean up our food and faecal waste. The latest, most convincing research suggests that the wolf then self-domesticated to take full advantage of this waste and other resources.

It is speculated that the more courageous, confident wolves started to scavenge during the daytime, when humans were around. It is thought that these wolves, which could eat near humans and not get too stressed (which would stop them eating), had a selective advantage. With their growing awareness that the critical food resource came from humans, their focus concentrated more and more on us, until ultimately humans became more important to them than even their own kind. It is this shifting focus from hunting to scavenging, and hence from their own kind to us, that established the proto-dogs, and then dogs as a separated subspecies (*Canis familiaris*).

Research shows that this increased docility, paired with smaller adrenal glands, would have produced less of the fight–flight hormones, and created a more friendly, confident dog. As they became more docile, the emerging proto-dogs stayed in an extended formative period, allowing the pups a longer period of brain growth and peak learning (the critical period of socialisation extended from 12 to 16 weeks, as noted earlier). As their brain capacity increased through greater connectivity, their intelligence and their ability to learn increased. This enabled the proto-dogs to build even more complex relationships, learn to read our gestures, and cross-foster (bond and include in the family) with even more species. Essentially this was one of the primary processes that led to the dog: the juvenilisation of the wolf. In other words, the dog is a 'puppy-ised' wolf.

A significant finding was made in France, where, 33,000 years ago, a hunter-gatherer boy's footprints were preserved in ancient mud, with ash from the fire torch he was carrying also evident — and beside him ran the footprints of his mate, a large wolf-like proto-dog. Fearful of people and fire, a wolf would not have been that close to a human boy or to fire. How evocative it is to imagine these companions, not so very unlike ourselves, exploring the world together. I remember as a young boy exploring the wilds of my local neighbourhood together with Scott, my large German Shepherd companion, so that ancient scenario doesn't seem so hard to believe.

One of the 850 million village/pariah dogs — the true ancestor to the dog.

Village and pariah dogs

Around 12,000 to 15,000 years ago saw the beginning of agriculture and the creation of permanent villages. During this time, we start to see a huge increase in the numbers of proto-dogs and human populations forming. These proto-dogs slowly evolved into the dog we see in the village, the wild (pariah) and dump dogs of today. Leading behavioural ecologist Ray Coppinger says that these are the direct ancestors of our dog.

The pariah and village dogs are not a migratory hunter anymore; instead, they are scavengers and/or hunters of small animals. Their food is generally found in the village surrounds, concentrated in areas like dumps and latrines, and its availability is regular. They can, and do still, hunt small prey but, critically, not as a pack like wolves hunting large prey that is dispersed.

The wolf's social structure of a family pack with a monogamous pair of wolves is therefore no longer necessary. Instead, village dogs now form loose packs that don't protect territories like the wolf, and are promiscuous or form short-term pairings. They are much more tolerant of having a large number of unrelated dogs around, although they can compete over a short-term or scarce resource. They also don't seem to have the strict wolf-like hierarchies or social structures, but are still highly social beings.

Feral dog studies have shown that the leaders of these packs, far from being the dominant despot that was once proposed, are instead the most liked, and are connected with the most friends. They are often very aware that humans are the source of the resources they need, and so humans have become a focus of their attention. They are capable of bonding with humans, and often actively 'adopt' humans, if possible. I certainly remember fondly one or two who have adopted me on my Pacific and Asian holidays, which I might have encouraged . . .

Interestingly, because food resources are smaller and more discrete than a large kill, dogs don't share food like the wolf — rather, possession is nine-tenths of the law. As the value of the resource goes up, so does the protectiveness. This is called the resource holding potential (RHP), a hypothesis that helps explain how dogs might resolve conflict when they don't have a linear hierarchy. Dogs have conflict over resources (resource guarding), so, according to RHP, each dog judges who wants the resource more, and they assess the risk of a fight. While fighting is uncommon, threat displays are used to displace other dogs. This is largely signalling and posturing, and the more strongly motivated dog normally wins the interaction.

Due to their human orientation, dogs' attachment relationships are especially focused on the caregiver (mentor), compared with the wolf, whose attachment is more generalised onto the whole pack. As wolves move to a new pack after puberty, wolves, and therefore dogs, have an ability to redirect their attention and affiliation onto new individuals outside of the group. This keeps their ability to change and adapt open much longer, and enhances their ability to learn and re-bond as their environmental and social context changes — a great attribute in our highly variable modern world. We use this attribute of the dog to build our own bond with them as their mentor, and it also allows us to re-establish the bond with rescue dogs later in life if needed.

Finally, the dog's unique capability to cross-foster onto other species while retaining their sexual preference for their own species — and so continuing to breed and evolve into *Canis familiaris* — was also a defining attribute that allowed dogs to live with us so successfully.

Most other species that cross-foster onto another species during the formative period lose interest in their own species (e.g. sheep imprinting onto humans). If done in the formative period, dogs can cross-foster with other domestic species, like chickens, pigs and sheep, which if they had continued to predate like their wolf forefathers would have quickly ensured a one-way ticket out of the village!

Ray Coppinger and his colleagues have estimated that there are 850 million village, pariah and dump dogs in the world today, compared with 150 million pet dogs, demonstrating just how successful a niche human waste has been for dogs. These village and pariah dogs are living examples of proto-dogs: advanced and evolved, yet not pet dogs (although they could become one if gotten at the right age). He also says that the small 10- to 15-kilogram tan dog with a curly tail is the naturally selected form of the dog in the wild. In time dogs return back to this form, even if domestic breeds get into the wild population. This natural dog is the ancestor to all of our dogs.

HUMAN-LED DOMESTICATION AND BREEDING (DESIGNER DOGS)

By 10,000 years ago, humans had started to shape the dog through domestication. Different from self-domestication, which is a natural process, domestication is a variant of evolution that is driven by human need and desire. We are effectively designing the dogs we want or need. For the first 9000 years there might have been 30-plus variants or breeds. In the most recent 150 years, we now have between 170 and 400-plus breeds, depending on whose categorisation we use. What an incredible influence modern man and woman have had on the dog.

Through this period, we started to differentiate dogs for different purposes. To start with, most of this would have just been by selecting for size, colour and behavioural traits — what could be seen and observed. By 5000 years ago, breeding was much more deliberate, and we start to see the ancient breeds emerging, giving us our modern classes or basal (the base from which others came) breeds, such as the Basenji, Chow Chow, Saluki and the Spitz breeds.

Initially, it would have been very utilitarian: the breeds would have been bred for practical reasons — sheep dogs, sled dogs, guard dogs, scent hunters, sight hunters, and so on. However, fast-forward to 2000

Line breeding or pure breeding is only about 150 years old as a generalised practice, but has had a big impact on the dog.

to 3000 years ago into the homes and castles of the élite in Europe (and in China even earlier), and we see the emergence of companion dogs and small lapdogs. Over the next 1500 years further specialisation and the rising of all different types and breeds of dogs occurred.

Line breeding, or pure breeding, is only about 150 years old as a generalised practice, as by that time we were able to properly fence off and segregate our breeding dogs. This now provides us with near complete control of breed selection. However, dog eugenics — the strict and fanciful selection of appearance traits — may have contributed to the loss of the functional purpose of owning a dog. With a strong focus on looks, this is starting to compromise the dog. As health and behaviour lost their priority to appearance as the most important traits, we entered a worrying time for the dog's health and wellbeing.

We are now seeing major inbreeding depression, manifesting as physiological and behavioural aberrations that are infiltrating the breed genetics, to the point that some breeds are almost completely dysfunctional. This can manifest in heart, eyes, hips, joints and nasal problems, cancers and much more. Problems can also manifest behaviourally, such as genetic fearfulness, hyper-aggressiveness to other dogs and/or people, and excessive gaminess (full of fight, plucky, willing to persevere despite threat). Hybrid vigour refers to the physical and behavioural benefits of out-crossing these lines, something we may miss in our line breeding (or pure breeding) of today.

These faults are a result of aberrant human choices, and they are threatening the central place of dogs as our best friend. We must not let this happen. By far the most important priorities in our selection criteria should be docility and responsiveness to humans, and dogs' health and welfare. Anything else invites the wolf's worst attributes to return.

Particularly in the case of fighting breeds, we are compromising behavioural safety mechanisms, which can lead to a loss of the critical signalling of dominance and subordinance, and reversing what wolves evolved to minimise — fighting and death in the pack. When we select for fighting to the death, we are breeding out of dogs their innate inhibition caused by submission (that is, when a dog submits, they stop fighting). This safety mechanism, inherited from the wolf, has allowed large predators to live together and not attack and kill each other. Hence, the dog has been selected by Nature to be docile and friendly.

Breed groups

The latest genetic research undertaken by Bridgett vonHoldt and colleagues found 10 genetically distinct groups of dog breeds, based on their genetic signatures and relatedness: spaniels, scent hounds, working dogs, mastiff-like dogs, small terriers, retrievers, herding dogs, sight hounds, the ancient and Spitz breeds, and toy dogs.

These groupings allow us to make generalisations about their traits and temperaments, which is useful when you are considering what breed you should get. In Part E, we go through the 10 breed groups and outline their general characteristics, so that you can get a general sense of the type of breed that will suit your lifestyle. While the 10 groups are helpful, be aware that there can be significant differences within a group, and even within breeds. Do plenty of research to help your decision.

DEFINING FEATURES OF A DOG

Below are summaries of the key attributes the dog has derived from the wolf, proto-dogs, and pariah and village dogs. This is the raw material we have for rearing a pup, and, in particular, for building our unique relationship.

Key attributes from the wolf

O Its anatomy, sensory capacities and behaviour systems, such as retrieve, hunt, sexual behaviour and play.
O Its intelligence and behavioural plasticity, especially its ability to learn.
O The formative period (3–16 weeks).
O Its social brain, sociability and greater brain connectivity.
O Its sophisticated peer-to-peer social communication system of signals, vocalisations, intonations and pheromones.
O Its helper function — the ability to form a social bond with the mother and helpers.

Key attributes from the village and pariah dogs

O Its docility and juvenilisation — the wolf became a pup again, in order to become a dog, so to speak.
O The extended and delayed formative period, giving the pup more time to socialise and learn.

O Its tolerance of other non-related dogs.

O The human focus, which is the core of our relationship.

O Its ability to bond with humans, similar to our own attachment relationships.

O Its ability to cross-foster onto other domestic species, such as cats, sheep, birds, fowl, etc.

O Its heightened confidence and ability to habituate to novel stimuli.

O Its ability to stay in a learning state longer, and to switch more easily — a critical difference between the dog and the wolf.

Chapter 3

The formative period — the wolf's greatest gift

Prevention is better than cure. The most important message in this book is to do the right thing at the right time. Miss that period and your pup will be mal-socialised, which can create terrible suffering — both for you and your pup.

It is important to realise that the puppy is like a whole different species compared with the adult dog, with the extent of change similar to that which takes place from a caterpillar to a butterfly. However, this maturation depends on what genetic and epigenetic switches are turned on (or not) through exposure to various stimuli. Pups don't just adapt to the human world by themselves: it is our critical role as their mentor to offer them the appropriate exposure at the right time. Puppy Zen looks closely at which behavioural switches we need to turn on and when, to guide the raising and training of our pups in the most effective, loving way. We use this information in Parts D and F to guide our training.

If these behavioural switches are not turned on, we begin the difficult and traumatic path of behavioural issues and mal-socialisation — dogs that don't know how to be social, and instead are anxious, fearful, aggressive and compromised. The importance of getting this right is highlighted by the American Veterinary Society, which in a paper on puppy socialisation states that behavioural issues are responsible for 80 per cent of euthanasia for dogs under 3 years old.

We can be so captured by our pups' cuteness that we forget that love also requires understanding. Resist the urge to purely mother or father your pup. Also grow your understanding, ability and commitment to do what your pup needs you to do. We have to bring our hearts and minds together: love with all our hearts, and grow our

The puppy is like a whole different species compared with the adult dog.

knowledge with all our minds. Just as we do for human babies, taking the time to prepare for your pup's arrival will help enormously in successfully raising him. A critical part of this is understanding your pup's formative period and what needs to be done during that time.

THE DEVELOPMENTAL PATHWAY OF THE PUPPY

There are eight key periods the pup goes through on his way to adulthood.

- **0-2 weeks: Neonatal period** — milk, mum, filial imprint. The most important primary function in this time is maternal care. The newborn pups are born helpless and dependent on their mother (dam). Our main focus at this time is on supporting the dam, plus providing touch and smell for pups.

- **2-3 weeks: Transition period** — awakening of senses (calm, relax, quiet). This sensory transitional period is characterised by significant changes and neurological development. During this stage, the pups' senses are opening and they are becoming aware of the world around them.

- **3-16 weeks: Formative period** — establishing our pup's future. This is a critical development stage for pups, where much of their behavioural foundations will be established (or not). This is where we, as dog owners and breeders, have the most significant influence on our adult dog's future behaviour and ability to live harmoniously in our lives.

- **4-6 months: Juvenile** — entering the world. The critical period of socialisation is completed and the pup's sympathetic nervous system has developed. The sponge-like learning state of the formative period has slowed or shut down. Compared with the previous three stages, the juvenile period is one of gradual change, mainly involving the maturing of established motor capacities and behaviour. The pups can be outwardly focused and easily distracted by new external stimuli. This is also the beginning of the fourth fear-imprint period, also known as the *flight instinct period* (4 to 8 months). This period can last for a few days or several weeks. This period is also called the fear of new situations period, which is present to protect the young wolf cub as it moved out into the big world to hunt. Similarly, the dog pup is moving out of your home to your everyday world.

○ **6-12 months: Early puberty** — hormones, hormones, hormones. This is the onset of puberty (6-8 months), where the period of rapid growth is complete, and the pups are approximately two-thirds of their adult size. Sex and dominance order can become an important and sometimes distracting focus. This period is also punctuated by the fear impact period (6-14 months), which seems more related to the internal issues of coming into puberty, and so becoming a potential sexual competitor to the mating adults. It has similarities to the previous period, which can manifest as new fears of new or old things, and so requires alertness to sudden changes in confidence. See Part F for full description.

○ **12-18 months: Late puberty** — becoming an adult (sex). Your dog may start to challenge the dominance of the other pack members in this later stage of puberty (especially if entire — not neutered). It is important to maintain control of resources through continued training and bond work. The territorial drive starts to kick in at the end of puberty, too, so make sure socialisation and meet and greets continue, particularly around the dogs' own territory, including the car. They are growing strong and confident now, so channel that into constructive activities and give them a purpose.

○ **18-24 months: Young adulthood** — establishing their role in the pack/family. They are growing to full size over this period, and in the wild would be moving into more adult roles like breeding and directing their family, so they are beginning to need some responsibility and purpose in their life (such as agility, canine good citizen, flyball, competitive scent work). They are wanting to guard the territory, so again do controlled meet and greets with new people at the gates and entry points. Teach discrimination, so if they alert you to a stranger they don't get aggressive. Good generalised socialisation and a strong bond with the mentor who is keeping control of resources will help. Dogs are at their optimal peak at this time, so are eager to learn and are likely to be physically fit. Again give your dog a purpose where possible.

○ **24 months onward: Adulthood** — responsibilities are established in the world. By now you should have all of the basics established for a mature, stable dog that is well connected and bonded to you. You know this if your dog exhibits focus on you, and keeps close but is relaxed. Commands and shared language are now more a conversation, and routines and rituals are established.

ABOUT THE FORMATIVE PERIOD

My understanding of the formative period is largely informed by the work of John Paul Scott and John L. Fuller, as well as by contemporary findings from research and my own clinical experience. John Paul Scott wrote *The Genetics of the Dog*, and was an early mentor of mine. He is considered by many to be the father of dog behaviour and genetics, in particular for his and Fuller's in-depth research on the timing and specificity of the critical period of socialisation. While this work has been refined over time, it is still the basis of our understanding of puppy and dog development, and his theories fit well with my own clinical experiences.

What is the formative period?

The formative period is between weeks 3 and 16 of a puppy's life, where critical development occurs, establishing the foundational skills needed for adult life. The formative period is the pup's optimal learning time, and plays a huge part in the future adult dog's ability to learn (hence why it is called 'formative').

The formative period is a time of enormous brain growth. Puppies have their full complement of neurons from approximately 6 weeks of age, but the number and complexity of the connections between these grows rapidly up to 4 months of age. The extensive brain expansion that occurs in this time (70–80 per cent increase in volume) is primarily triggered by social relationships and an environmental enrichment.

Transitions, fear-imprint periods and critical periods

During the 3–16 weeks formative period there are also various transitions, fear-imprint periods and critical periods. Again we use the wolf as our model to understand these.

Within the formative period pups gradually emerge from the whelping den into the world through four developmental transitions, which are regulated by fear-imprint periods (peak periods of sensitivity to fear). These transitions are seen at approximately 5 weeks of age (the start of weaning), 8 weeks of age (with the move to the mentor and family), 12 weeks of age (the closing down of socialisation in preparation for joining the big, wide world) and 16 weeks (heading out into the world). As these times are key periods of expansion (broadening horizons) and newness, they come with increased risks, and so Nature has wisely associated them with an increase in fear (the fear-imprint period) to ensure the pups are suitably cautious for a period of time while they learn and adjust to a new environment. Remember, fear is an ally in these times, as it automatically alerts the pup to threats.

Throughout these transitions there are also a number of critical periods where specific behaviours develop. These are periods of time in which pups are evolutionarily designed to best learn or develop specified behaviours or behaviour systems. Some examples include critical periods for socialisation, noise, curiosity and communication. Understanding the timings of these critical periods helps guide us in when and what we train.

Cascading — switching on a pup's behaviour

Cascading is the unfolding of behaviour through a series of interrelated stages and steps necessary to a pup's development. It is like putting down the foundations of a house first, and then the walls, with the roof going on last. If one of these steps is missed out, it can create difficulties in the next stages as the necessary foundations haven't been put in place. While it is possible to go back and fill that gap, it is harder and more complex, and requires a different form of learning (counter-conditioning and desensitisation — see the discussion in Part D). It is much easier to ensure we do the right thing at the right time — remember, prevention is better than cure.

Critically, pups' developing behaviours do not automatically turn on: they have to be deliberately switched on during this crucial formative period. This switching on is triggered by multiple social relationships and exposure to enriching stimuli. What gets switched on depends on the pup's environment and experiences. Enriching experiences that involve touch, socialising, sound, movement, light, texture and motor activity, help switch on these switches and grow a pup's brain connections. Our bond is also critical. If the pup has a secure attachment to us and her location, she is less anxious, and so has an increased ability to learn.

We have to expose our pups to a variety of experiences.

What (if anything) gets switched on determines the behavioural direction a pup heads in. If we don't socialise and expose a pup broadly to life during this period, we can limit this process and learning. If pups don't get exposed to stimuli — such as trucks, other races of people, kids, ducks, old people, men, cats — before 12 weeks old, then they will either be aggressive to or fearful of them after the formative period. This lack of appropriate experience is largely the basis of behaviour issues and possible euthanasia in adult life.

Guiding our training — bringing it all together

Understanding cascading, and how these transitions, fear-imprint periods and critical periods come together, helps determine what socialisation, training and exposure we should do, and when. This will guarantee our training is in tune with the critical development steps of the pup, supporting her optimum development. Training at this optimum time means we can make considerably less effort now to get results than if we did it outside of the formative period. Hopefully that is enough incentive for you to do the right thing at the right time!

Based on a pup's developmental pathway, we have created eight training activities to help organise our training efforts. We outline these later in this section, and use them extensively in Part F as we create our training plan.

Before doing this, let me first bring this complex talk of a pup's development to life by telling you the story of the wolf pup, our dog pup's ancient ancestral roots that have evolved over millions of years. Here we follow the wolf pup as he pokes his nose out of the whelping den to join the pack and his mentors, learns who his extended family is, and then moves out into the big world of hunting and pack life. By doing so, we can see how this informs the development of our own beloved pups and how it guides — actually, dictates — our training.

THE GREATEST GIFT FROM THE WOLF

The formative period is the ancestral wolf's biggest gift to the dog and us! It is the period when wolves hunker down and stop their migratory hunting to raise their young in a safe place for a short period (4 months).

Imagine the tiny wolf pup as he starts his life in the maximum safety of the whelping den, which is dug deep into the dark, secure earth. Mum is there fearlessly protecting her pups, while the pack protects the wider den area outside. The pup is vulnerable and helpless; deaf, blind and dumb, although already with a highly evolved sense of smell. He has no need yet for a well-developed fight–flight sympathetic nervous system (fear), as in here there is absolute safety. All the pup needs to do (and can do) is suckle and grow.

At around 2 to 3 weeks the wolf pup's senses start to develop, as does his bond with mum and his litter mates. At around 5 weeks of age weaning begins, and the pup starts to briefly explore the outside world, poking his head out of the den to seek solid food and contact with the pack outside. This comes with increased risks, so Nature in her wisdom has also created the pup's first fear-imprint period to remind the pup to be a little cautious while his understanding grows. This is only a minor fear-imprint period, which sometimes may not even be noticed, but it is there. This is the start of the pup's sympathetic nervous system developing. Over the next 2 to 3 weeks, this dance between the whelping den and increasing engagement outside the

The wolf pup's emergence from den to pack mirrors the dog pup's transition from den to family.

den grows the pup's experiences, which helps switch on the next developmental stage.

From 6 to 8 weeks the pup starts the next transition, moving away from solely mum and the whelping den to be with the pack outside. The young wolf pup moves his bond to the sub-adult wolves (helpers or mentors) and more broadly to the pack. The pup remains within the protective precinct of the rendezvous den. Again, in this transition slightly more risk occurs, and so the second fear-imprint period peaks at 8 weeks old to support the pup's transition.

From 8 weeks of age, the wolf pup is now firmly supported by the mentor wolves and the pack, learning rapidly about his extended family and the wider world. From 8 to 12 weeks, the pup's sympathetic nervous system is still undeveloped and is still relatively open, allowing the pup to socialise and learn. It is a critical time of socialisation; the time in which the pup will find out who is and isn't in his pack. He will engage with the various stimuli in his environment, which will help him develop emotional resilience to novel things and change. This is the pup's most critical time of learning, preparing him for when the pack heads back out on their migratory hunts when the pup is around 16 weeks old.

At 12 weeks, with only 4 weeks to go before the wolf pup starts running with the pack in the big, wide world, another fear-imprint period begins the slow closing down of this open learning state and critical period of socialisation. The pup now knows who his pack is, and over the next month further develops the teamwork and co-operation skills needed to hunt together. From 12 to 16 weeks the wolf pup's sympathetic nervous system will mature until it peaks at 16 weeks, with the final fear-imprint period that fully closes off socialisation before puberty. In this period the wolf pup must consolidate his foundations in preparation for entering the big world.

By 16 weeks of age, the pup is in the riskiest transition of all: leaving the rendezvous den to now move continuously with the migratory pack as they hunt for survival. This is a dangerous life, full of change and unknown risks. The pup must have all of the foundations in place (skills, knowledge, who to trust) to survive this huge leap toward adulthood. Given the scale of risk, this transition comes with the most important fear-imprint period, enabling the wolf pup to be alert to risks. The sympathetic nervous system is fully developed by now, and the adrenals are activated so that fear responses are heightened. This lessens the wolf pup's socialisation ability and pervasive sponge-like learning state, and heightens his sensitivity to novel things. Fight-flight responses are established so that the wolf pup is ready to deal with the uncertainty and risks of the outside world.

The dog pup

This story of the wolf pup helps us understand the basis of our dog pup's development. These stages are more subtle and less evident, because the dog is more juvenilised and has smaller, less reactive adrenals; nevertheless, they still exist. Understanding the meaning and purpose of each stage of a pup's development helps us understand what we need to do to support our pups.

For our dog pups, instead of going out into the wide world to hunt, they are heading out into our wider human world. The formative period's time of learning and safety, between 3 and 16 weeks of age, is our pups' opportunity to adapt to our world of people, traffic, other dogs and other species, which are unique to our lifestyle. To live in the human world, our pups' definition of pack (family) must be extended to include a broad range of people and dogs, as well as other species. However, socialisation at 16 weeks still closes down (and if not started by 12 weeks, shuts down even earlier).

CRITICAL PERIODS WITHIN THE FORMATIVE PERIOD

As noted earlier, our pups go through a number of critical periods that provide the ideal time to establish specific behaviours. The timing of the critical periods outlined below are approximations, with start (onset) and closedown (offset) periods being influenced if socialisation starts early. While all puppies develop to their own individual timetables, which can vary somewhat according to breed, the following timeframes are still very useful to help guide our training.

The critical period of socialisation (3-12 weeks) is the most important period of a pup's life. It is a peak period for learning and socialisation, and it is when pups learn who is in their family. The critical thing here is to broaden the concept of the pup's family as widely as you can, so he is friendly to all people, dogs and other species. In this period the puppy learns that he is a dog and how to be a dog. This is why it is very important that a pup is kept with his litter mates and dam in the early stages. A puppy removed from the litter before 7 weeks is more likely to become overly noisy, lack an inhibited bite reflex, or have other behavioural problems, including dog- or people-oriented aggression, as his behaviour has not been moderated by his dam and litter mates.

When the pups are 3 weeks old, mum starts licking their faces, and so begins the critical *communication and enrichment period (3-16 weeks)*. (Note that this is different from licking the pups' rear ends to encourage toileting.) We believe that this is the start of social signalling, pro-social behaviour and social communication. We get involved at this stage with our first gestures and cues, to start shaping our shared language. (Ideally, we do this with a marker, such as a clicker — a small hand-held device that makes a sound when a button is pushed — to identify and reinforce the appropriate response.) Reciprocal communication also starts between the dam and the litter. Play begins, with the pups giving and receiving invitations to play (play bows, and so on). They can ask (solicit) already, with pawing, facial licks and jumping up. They can show an emotional response to mum or others (e.g. tail wagging), and the start of the social order begins as they defend themselves by growling and fighting back. Their shared language of asking, being heard (us responding) and showing emotions has begun in earnest.

At 3 to 4 weeks of age, pups show no fear (as the sympathetic nervous system has not switched on properly), so this is a critical opportunity to activate and shape their *fear-recovery cycle* and *emotional resilience* through graduated exposure to environmental stimuli. Noise desensitisation is optimal from 4 to 10 weeks, so it is at this time that we start to desensitise noise by introducing the pup to low levels of sounds (using, for example, sound recordings off iTunes or YouTube) to habituate them to noise. Household noises can be gradually increased, such as the radio, dishwasher, TV, hairdryer and vacuum cleaner. At 4 weeks, when they are the least fearful, we can start some startle recovery work by dropping things, so that they startle and then quickly recover. This is important in developing the pup's emotional and sensory resilience.

At 5 weeks of age pups approach their first (minor) fear-imprint period, so we need to take care and make sure they don't have fearful experiences. Also at weeks 5 to 7 the *curiosity period* begins, and they are entering a peak socialisation period where they have the highest approach and the lowest fear. Now is the ideal time to introduce pups to as many people and enriching experiences, and as much learning, as possible.

From 7 to 9 weeks we have the *homing critical period*, where the pup should be leaving mum to go to his new home and pack (as he would in Nature). In this critical period for separation, the pup naturally has the ability and readiness to let go of his dam and re-bond to the mentor. However, 8 weeks old also coincides with the first fear-imprint period, so the correct methods need to be employed in this transition. A puppy is susceptible to long-lasting effects of fearful stimuli at this stage, so if the puppy perceives an event as traumatic, he may generalise it (extend it to other contexts), and it could affect him for the rest of his life. Care should be taken to avoid fearful reactions during this stage, so exposing pups to graduated experiences and desensitising them is important (see Part D). The more skilfully you do this transition, the better your pup is able to create healthy bonds. You need to ease your pup into the move and make sure the first week is calm and relaxing. Part E provides guidance on how to do this.

There is a bonus
socialisation period
from 12–16 weeks
if foundations have
been put in place by
12 weeks.

The environmental awareness critical period (9–16 weeks) is punctuated by the last stages of socialisation, the focus now moving to the environment as the pup adapts and learns about what else is in the world outside the pack.

Even though a pup's peak period of socialisation finishes at 12 weeks, there is still an additional (although decreasing) window of socialisation for another 4 weeks. This is called the *bonus period of socialisation* (12–16 weeks), and coincides with the pup's growing independence. If you get a pup after 12 weeks of age, you need to focus on his socialisation at this time with a concerted effort, particularly if you think the pup's socialisation up until now has been limited. Use a clicker and food rewards to help speed up learning, and fill in the gaps using desensitisation and counter-conditioning (outlined in Part D). If you have done what is needed up to 12 weeks, then this is the opportunity to round off your pup's (bonus) socialisation. This will ensure your pup's socialisation is well established, although more is needed for some time to consolidate good behaviour, particularly through the pup's adolescence.

The earlier we start and the more varied the experiences we offer our pups, the longer and richer and more successful their formative period will be. Limiting their experience early limits their formative period. Well-socialised pups exposed to a variety of general stimuli can extend learning beyond this offset period. In fact, the ability to keep them open and learning continues well into their first year in well-adjusted dogs, especially if you are using the right tools to train them. This highlights just how critical the role of breeders is, as what they do in those early weeks also impacts significantly on the pup — even so young. It is your role as their mentor to ensure that your pup is skilfully supported through these necessary stages, and builds the experience and skills he needs.

EIGHT KEY TRAINING ACTIVITIES

Having looked at the developmental transitions, fear-imprint periods and critical periods within a puppy's development, we now identify the key training activities we need to undertake to support the pup's optimum development. In Part F, I take you week-by-week through what you should do, and when, in terms of these activities. The eight training activities are:

o mentor bond (you and the extended family)
o socialisation (human, dog, other species)
o shared language (obedience, learning state, tools and techniques)
o fears and phobia prevention
o teaching separation
o house training
o bite inhibition
o enrichment, play and exercise.

Let me reassure you that none of this is hard to do, nor does it take that long, primarily covering the 3 to 16 weeks period. The breeder will have taken care of the first month or so, meaning a consistent commitment by you to your pup from 8 to 16 weeks is required, which can save a lifetime of suffering both for your dog and you.

Mentor bond
The critical period for socialisation runs from 7 to 16 weeks, peaking ·

at the age of 12 weeks.

The first role as a pup's mentor is to build a healthy bond that has the pup feeling secure and safe, looking to us for guidance, while also being able to enjoy being by herself for periods of time. From this place of trust, we then safely and gently introduce and habituate the pup to the things that will be in her life as an adult dog. Joining up is our signature technique that will be used often here.

Socialisation

Critical period is 3 to 12 weeks, extending up to 16 weeks if started early.

This includes socialisation to dogs, humans and other species, like cats, chickens, birds and stock (cross-fostering). This is the time when pups develop their bonds with their new family, so it is important to extend this as much as possible. Socialisation is one of the most essential tasks during the formative period. Weeks 3 to 12 are the most critical, with weeks 12 to 16 ideally reinforcing and generalising the previous socialisation. If there wasn't any or enough exposure by 12 weeks, mal-socialisation is likely.

Shared language

Critical period is 3 to 16 weeks, but extends longer in most pups if they learn to learn early. The earlier it is started and established, the better.

Building our shared language requires a shared social purpose within the dog–human relationship, such as co-operation, co-ordination, trust and love. We commonly refer to shared language as 'obedience commands', but it is much more than that. It requires us to read dog behaviour and then shape a shared language between us through gestures, eye contact, intonation, orientation and much more. It is a reciprocal language, and dogs have evolved the ability to read our gestures, look to us for direction, and ask and give. However, we need to lead this communication, because pups can see the world only through their own language and culture. Building this shared language is fundamental to our relationship and how our pup navigates our world.

The formative period is all about the learning state. Brain development is complete by 6 weeks and they are ready to learn. Pups are the most open and malleable in this time, as they are in a nearly constant learning state (parasympathetic arousal). Their brains are *tabula rasa* (a clean slate), a sponge-like state that is ideal for shaping (training) desirable behaviours. In Puppy Zen we influence a puppy's learning state by engaging his vagus nerve and parasympathetic arousal through the use of the clicker and 'sit' and 'Zen down' commands. It is only when the pup and his vagus nerve are relaxed that he can learn. It is one of the key reasons why the clicker and 'sit' (and, later, 'Zen sit' when the pup sits of his own accord) and 'Zen down' are such powerful tools and worth investing the time to learn how to use effectively.

Without early experience/habituation, a pup is more likely to have amygdala-dominant responses (primitive emotional responses). You want to encourage your pup to start using his pre-frontal cortex and make more measured and considered decisions and behaviours, which dampens the effect of the primitive brain. When your pup is anxious, use a lure (food in hand) and ask for a 'sit'. As he considers and then does the 'sit' (makes a decision), the pre-frontal cortex dampens anxiety, calming the pup and improving learning.

Fears and phobia prevention

Critical period is 4 to 16 weeks, peaking at 12 weeks.

The formative period has evolved over millions of years in the wolf to allow a safe period of 4 months for the pups to grow up in a secure environment (the whelping and rendezvous dens). By 4 months their fight-flight system develops fully, readying them for the big world where they need to know what to trust and not trust and respond accordingly.

During this peak learning, low-fear period, it is critical that pups are exposed to as many stimuli as possible, to help them become accustomed to novelty and change. After this period, pups can potentially become fearful of new or novel things that they were not exposed to during the formative period. Fear is the primary cause of behavioural problems later in life. To avoid this, we need to gradually habituate and desensitise our pups to as wide a range of novel stimuli as possible. Most pups will have a couple of things they are fearful of, so identifying any fear-inducing stimuli is critical, and the earlier the better, so you can desensitise your pup to them using the phobia-proofing techniques.

It is important that any exposure to a new object, person or animal is paired with a positive experience. (We mainly use the clicker and

See this beautiful
contact between
us as we read each
other's language.

food rewards in Puppy Zen.) If an experience is traumatic, you might be setting up your pup to develop an aversion and be fearful instead of calm. You need a good habituation/desensitisation schedule as described in Part D, and also enrichment learning activities, such as the games and training, to ensure the experiences stay positive. The majority of training at this puppy stage uses positive reinforcement, as we are shaping new behaviours as opposed to modifying old behaviours.

Below are stimuli your pup must be exposed to during this time. They are grouped into two categories to help establish priorities: home-related and outside the home.

Within the home, both breeders and owners (priority for 4-10 weeks)

O people, dogs, other species, noises, handling, surfaces, stairs and travel.

Outside the home (8-16 weeks, but start as early as you can)

O people, dogs, other species, movement (bikes, rollerblades, skateboards, flags), novel objects, novel environments and change

O roads and traffic awareness, and rules around and noise desensitisation

O vet and vet clinic (including procedures).

Teaching separation

Critical period is 6 to 10 weeks, peaking at 8 weeks.

This is teaching your pup to be able to be on his own without a fuss for periods of time. This is the naturally occurring time when pups leave the dam and join the pack most effectively. Separation distress is the result of your pup becoming overly dependent on you or your family, a weak bond, and developing a fear or phobia of separation.

House training (nest-site soiling inhibition)

Critical period is 3 to 16 weeks.

Puppies learn house training by generalising their nest-soiling inhibition. The dam licks up the pups' urine and faeces in the first 6 weeks, and then, as soon as they can, the pups head out of the den to toilet. They don't want to soil in the nest (nest-site inhibition), and use their ability to discriminate surfaces through their paws to know where to toilet. This means they don't want to toilet on surfaces associated with the den, but surfaces associated with outside are okay to toilet on. In house-training our pups we use this innate inhibition to toileting in the den, and the ability to discriminate different surfaces between the den and outside. We do this by establishing our house as the den, which is identified through its associated surfaces, and reinforcing the outside as the appropriate place to toilet.

Bite inhibition

Critical period is 1 to 4 months, and 4 to 6 months (when they lose their milk teeth).

Biting is a common problem in a pup, because they use their mouth like a hand, and it is natural for them to be very oral during this stage. Pups initially learn to not bite too hard from the dam and their litter mates, and then from the wider pack early on in socialisation. There is another period, at around 4 to 6 months when they lose their milk teeth, essentially going through a teething stage, which leads them to want to chew things (just like teething in human babies).

Enrichment, play and exercise

Critical period is 3 to 16 weeks, and beyond.

The latest research indicates that play has a critical function in a pup's development, by developing and practising segments of behaviour patterns that will be required later in life, such as hunting, conflict resolution and avoidance functions. In terms of intelligence, play helps grow a pup's ability to learn about the world and practise behaviours that will grow the puppy's brain through increased connections: *what they fire, they wire.*

We need to ensure that pups (and adult dogs) get opportunities to play — especially pups in their formative period. Interestingly, human-dog play is more co-operative, and dog-dog play is more competitive by nature. Pups need both.

Play also has an important role in socialisation. For example, the play context allows two very different-sized pups, and dogs with different temperaments, to interact at high intensity, rehearsing and alternating places in the relationship. This allows them to negotiate and understand relations without escalating into fighting. If they break a rule, we can see how pups apologise through posture, showing submission through rolling over, showing their bellies and licking the other dog's jowls. If they bite too hard in play, they may reprimand each other (growling, muzzle pinning — see the photos on page 58 — scruffing, biting) or apologise (through jowl licking and submissive gesturing). This cultivates tolerance and the learning of boundaries, allows all members to be involved in the games, and facilitates bonds within the whole pack.

Exercise can be an underestimated component of pup development and health. The demands for exercise increase with age, and exercise is very important for good physical development. However, be careful as you can overdo this if the pup is too young. Pups need to gradually increase their physical development as the joints strengthen and bones harden. It is important to understand that different breeds and even individuals will need varying amounts of exercise. For example, large and giant breeds are more vulnerable to damaging cartilage and joints if over-exercised. Do your research in terms of breed requirements.

A NOTE ON VACCINATION PERIOD

We cannot change this critical formative period in a pup's life, so, even though this time conflicts with your puppy's vaccination period and building immunity, you still need to find ways to socialise your pup in a safe manner. If not and your puppy is isolated, he could develop life-threatening behavioural issues later on (like Charles, introduced in the preface). We cover this in Part E.

Play helps pups practise new
behaviours (and it's cute!).

FINAL WORDS ON THE FORMATIVE PERIOD

We have just covered a lot of information on the formative period. I provided such in-depth information to help you fully appreciate just how significant the changes that take place in your pup during this period are. The role you and the breeder play are critical in wiring your pup's brain to create a stable, happy pup and adult dog. Using this information, in Part F we build a week-by-week plan on what to do and when for you and your pup.

SUMMARY

We have all experienced (or are about to) the profound and unique relationship with our beloved pups and dogs, one of the world's most astounding cross-species bonds. What a remarkable journey our dogs have made — from the wolf via the proto-dog and pariah and village dogs — to come into our living rooms and hearts. While the dog is 99.96 per cent wolf, that 0.04 per cent does make all the difference!

The dog is effectively a juvenilised wolf, with the wolf giving the dog its social brain, sociability, helper function and formative period. Evolution then shaped the proto-dog, through the wolf self-domesticating around our hunter-gather settlements — thereby moving from hunter to scavenger. This resulted in the dog's titanic shift in attention towards us, making humans more important to them than even their own species.

The most important attribute the wolf gave our dogs was their formative period, a significant time of learning and bonding, in which puppies grow 80 per cent of their brain connectivity. It is a critical time of socialisation, adapting to novelty and change, and the building of our bond. Get this time right and you have a stable, happy dog for life. Get this time wrong, and you head down the path of mal-socialisation and suffering.

What is so remarkable (and a true blessing) is that it is so easy to teach our pups the right thing at the right time. Two months of concentrated, committed action when you get your pup and you will have a loving, harmonious relationship for life. How could you not?

A Bond For Life

Dogs are born to live in relationships; their intelligence is augmented by sociability.

In this section we explore what lies at the very foundation of a happy, harmonious life with our puppies: the bond. Without it, nothing can be built between us. Here we discover the key parts of establishing a stable, lifelong bond by:

O understanding the nature of the pup-owner bond — the foundation to everything
O developing the bond by mimicking Nature's methods
O establishing family rules (agreement on how all will behave together)
O building a shared language, including basic commands (talk to each other)
O understanding the critical role of a pup's mentor.

Pups are important members of our families.

Chapter 4

The bond — the foundation of everything

Dogs love us and we love them, which, as we have seen, is scientifically proven! Isn't it extraordinary that we can form such an intimate bond with a very different species, one that not so many thousands of years ago was a feared predator and competitor?

Both humans and dogs share a need for relationships. The importance of relationships has shaped the dog throughout its evolution (as it has us). Relationships are critical to the dog, and we have evolved to play a very significant role in fulfilling that need. If you understand the dog's need and drive for relationship, you understand the dog and how you can adapt that need to forge a strong, stable relationship, which will be the foundation of your life together, including training.

HEALTHY BONDS

When you become your pup's mentor, you are the centre of her world. Your pup should be highly attuned to you, follow you, look up to you regularly, and study and to some degree mimic you to build her understanding of appropriate behaviour. Your puppy will be well adjusted, able to both be in contact with you and be alone for periods without suffering separation distress. Having a healthy bond gives your pup the security and trust she needs to feel safe in the world and to stay in a learning state. Steadiness, calm and trust are critical for training.

Through the formative period (3-16 weeks of age), puppies have an openness and fearlessness that make them ripe for learning and socialisation, so ideally the mentor bond will be built strongly during this time. Although dogs can bond later in life, in my experience you never quite create what you can by having your pup at the right time.

AVOIDING UNHEALTHY BONDS

A lack of appropriate socialisation, support when frightened, or understanding and empathy can create a weak bond that leaves pups uncertain of their place, role and safety in the world. Behavioural issues can easily stem from a poorly established bond between pups and their mentors.

The attachment relationship can also be over-developed, where the pup is overly dependent on you and has not been taught to separate properly, resulting in her not being able to tolerate periods of time on her own. This can lead your pup, and subsequently adult dog, to suffer separation distress. That is, your pup/dog displays anxiety, whining, destructive and/or soiling behaviours and other symptoms when separated from you for any length of time. The sensitive period for learning separation is 6 to 10 weeks, and so is the ideal time to learn. In Part D we will go through how to create healthy separation in your pup, to avoid separation distress developing.

CLARIFYING A MISCONCEPTION: THE OLD LUPOMORPH MODEL OF WOLF AS AGGRESSIVE DOMINATOR

It is worth touching on some old research that people often get confused about. Forty-plus years ago the world's imagination was captured by research on the wolf and how it related to dogs, and the now-discredited social order model developed. The Lupomorph model described wolves as if they are aggressive despots, tough leaders of the pack with strict linear hierarchies maintained by aggressive dominance.

This theory was based on observing unnatural zoo-formed wolf packs made up of older, unrelated wolves. However, in the wild, wolf packs are made up of kin-related family members. Within these egalitarian family packs, dynamics are mediated by threat signals with very little actual aggression, whereas interactions between separate, unrelated packs are often severe. Unrelated wolves will often attack or kill wolves they don't know. Without the ability to leave, as would occur in the wild, the social dynamics of unrelated zoo packs become disruptive and aggressive.

Puppy Zen doesn't use the 'leader of the pack' model, but instead the more relational mentor of the pack, where we are still guiding and leading, but are more like family members than a tough leader from the top calling the tune. Understanding, relationship and effective knowledge-based methods underpin our approach. This makes for a healthy bond without the anxiety or fear of a leader that can be seen with excessively assertive, dominant approaches to training that create unhealthy bonds.

THE NATURE OF THE BOND

Humans and dogs are very different species, yet we have similar ways of engagement and conduct, which allow us to live harmoniously together. Adam Miklosi, a friend and one of the leading canine cognitive scientists, says that dogs have a high level of social competence that depends on a number of factors, including the ability to form attachments, control aggression, learn and follow family rules, and help and participate in group activities. Canine ethologist Marc Bekoff, an early mentor of mine, says that both dogs and humans have relatively egalitarian societies that are 'other regarding' (considering the needs of others), with a suite of behaviours that regulate social interactions. These include fairness, co-operation, patience, forgiveness, understanding and mutual benefit, all of which are evident in the way pups and dogs play with one another. Research has shown that both dogs and humans have intrinsic honesty and a resultant trust that underpins our social orders. Like us, dogs can detect deception, so it is important that our signals are honest. Dogs pick up inconsistencies, excessive and unfair assertiveness, or if you are trying to trick or lie to them. Incorporating positive behaviours and attitudes in your engagement with your pup will help ensure your bond has a stable basis.

See the contact between these two — the softness of the body language reflects their relationship.

SHIFT IN FOCUS FROM DOGS TO US

As we have seen, a critical moment in our shared history was when the proto-dog moved from hunter to scavenger, and shifted their focus from their pack to humans. Fast-forward to today and we are central to our dog's world, clear and simple. They know that we are in control of the key resources of their life (food, contact, freedom), and so engage us to gain access to these needs, including their love for connection.

Recent research shows just how highly attuned to humans dogs are; they even prioritise us over a connection to their own. They find human contact very rewarding, and are motivated to please us. From this focus comes their intense ability to bond with us, be in our families and learn our family rules. They have family rules in their packs, too, so they understand that we have them and that they can learn them.

Dogs have a great ability to understand us, and are able to adjust seamlessly to family life because of their attentiveness and sensitivity to human communication, emotions and behaviour. They can read our gestures (such as nodding), as well as follow facial gestures, eye movements and pointing, even mimicking our behaviours. They can smell our pheromones, and therefore may know when we are anxious, fearful or happy.

Research shows dogs are very aware of where we look, what we are doing and where our attention is. Dogs not only attend our gaze, they gaze back and they are aware we are attentive of them (the bond gaze). Dogs look at us for direction, to recruit help, for reassurance and information, for direction to important resources, especially food, and just to please us. This ability to look us in the eyes is an unusual behaviour in the animal world, where (including the wolf) staring is often a threat. While intense and/or sustained gazing can be a threat to dogs, and us too, when a bond is established, holding our gaze becomes a defining feature of a healthy bond and stimulates oxytocin in both parties.

Be aware, however, that some pups and dogs will find sustained eye contact slightly threatening, so over time you will need to desensitise them to this. Notice how your pup responds to eye contact. If he seems wary, you can grow his confidence by using joining up and clicker training to reinforce the desired contact, and help your pup to relax into looking to you for direction. You click as soon as your dog does a desired behaviour, and follow with a food treat, providing positive enforcement. The use of the clicker is discussed in more detail in Part C.

Eye contact has subtle nuances in duration, fixedness and force. For example, you know how if you hold a stare with someone on the street for a second too long they disengage, or how a flirty stare may be held for a couple of seconds longer than normal. A good trainer uses eye contact to manage and communicate subtly with the pup. Firm up your eye contact to fix (hold) a pup in a 'stay' or 'wait', and relax eye contact or turn it off (look away) in the case of a recall (it is non-threatening, so draws them towards you).

Because pups look at our faces, follow our gestures, notice the things we touch, watch our hands (particularly if holding food), notice our postural signals and much more, we need to be very conscious of how to use visual cues to our advantage — and also recognise when we are giving unintentional cues. Using changes in our body orientation, posture, hand signals and gesturing helps create a bond and shared language with our pups.

Pups also are very good at recruiting help from us. They understand that we can help them get to their end goals — namely, access to some form of resource. This attentiveness and seeking help from us is a useful mechanism for training — however, care needs to be taken that your pup doesn't end up training you!

Chapter 5

Mimicking nature — developing the bond

Just because dogs and humans both live for relationships doesn't necessarily mean that we know how to automatically do it together. We come from very different worlds, so our relationship firstly needs to be built on understanding. In this section, we look at:

O key aspects of the naturally occurring dog bond, then
O how we mimic these to create the bond by joining up, using a clip station, and reinforcing that 'nothing in life is free'.

KEY ASPECTS OF THE BOND

Given the dog's natural inclination to relationships, we can use the innate mechanisms in a pup's development to help us develop a relationship. From years of study and practice in my clinic, I have developed signature techniques that simulate Nature. Three natural processes we mimic to create the bond are:

O the 'secure base effect' and the attachment relationship
O the helper or mentor role and bond
O the innate follower response, which is seen in most mammals.

Secure base effect

Research shows that the bond (attachment relationship) between dogs and humans closely resembles that of human mothers and infants. This bond is important, as it allows our young to safely explore and learn about the world. The result of this primary attachment relationship is called the secure base effect. For dogs and infant children alike, the secure base is the safe person or place from which they can venture out and learn about the world. If they feel secure, they can be calm and stay in a learning state. A healthy bond means that a pup will be a better learner and more readily able to adapt to our dynamic world.

The secure base has two aspects: psychological and spatial. The psychological component of a secure base is the pup's relational bond to you, the mentor. A well-established secure base relationship will have your pup looking to you for confidence and direction. It means your pup will stay connected to you, checking in to see where you are and get guidance if a new situation arises, such as meeting a new dog or person, or if there is an unexpected noise. The pup can trust that you are there to help navigate new experiences. This secure base also helps build resilience to stress.

The spatial (place-based) aspect of the secure base can be established by transferring the sense of safety and security associated with the mentor to a place and/or an object. It is what I call the *den effect* — Nature's safe place. In the wild, the wolf pups hunker down in the den, which is 2 to 3 metres underground, creating a sense of safety and security. We can re-create this by using the clip station (a mat and short clip lead to a fixed point) and the crate (see the toolkit section in Part C for more details). There are many purposes we can use the clip station and crate for, including teaching our pups separation and house training, as well as providing a safe place in our home, or at cafés or friends' homes, to keep them calm and able to learn even in new, unfamiliar locations.

Helper/mentor role

From studying wolves, we have learnt that as the pup transitions away from his mother (in the whelping den) towards the pack, he forms his first significant relationship (aside from mum) with helper wolves or, as I call them for our purposes, the mentors. The secure base attachment shifts or extends from mum to this mentor.

In the wild, this mentor is normally an older wolf sibling(s), and shows the pup the ways of the pack and the world. It will teach the pup what he can and cannot do, what is safe and what is not, and what the pup's role and position is within the pack.

By building this secure base relationship with a mentor, the pup can stay more often, and longer, in a peak learning state. He has confidence to do things when his mentor is around that he might otherwise be too

Creating the follower response with food lure and clicker.

anxious to do. This is evident in research that investigated whether dogs would play with a stranger, with and without their owner present. When tested with the owner present, the dog would play with a stranger; however, when the owner was absent, in the majority of cases the dog did not play with the stranger. This research was undertaken with adult dogs, so imagine the increased importance of the safety of the mentor for a growing pup!

For our pups, we are that next relationship after mum, the mentor who supports our pups as they move into their new pack — our family. It is our responsibility to become that mentor, guiding the pup, then dog, through life. What is also important to understand is that dogs can develop close relationships with all of its human family members. This is particularly so if all of the members participate in controlling and sharing the resources with the pup, and in his training and care. If only one family member does this, then the pup will build a stronger bond with only them. I highly recommend that as a family you ensure that you generalise your pup's socialisation with many family members and friends, so he has as large a sense of family as possible.

The follower response

Most mammals have a follower response to something they are 'imprinted' to (that is, become attached to in the immediate period after birth). Visualise a ewe trotting over the hill with her lamb at foot — the follower response. This response is elicited by Nature's signals (hormones, pheromones and vocalisations) that are species-specific and occur in the imprinting-sensitive period (for sheep, this is within 24 hours of birth). This same imprinting process occurs in pups, first to their mum and then to their mentor in the wild.

Because we don't produce Nature's signals, I have developed techniques that entrain this innate response using a lead, a clicker, a crate, a clip station and food rewards to induce a state of secure base. If you can do it in the pup's sensitive period of 3–12 weeks of age, it will be much more effective, powerful and long-lasting. Once this follower response becomes entrained to you, you receive the benefits of this mentor bonding process, thereby creating a bond for life (this can also be achieved later with the clicker).

TECHNIQUES TO CREATE THE BOND

So now we understand the importance and nature of the bond, how do we go about creating a bond across the species divide? In Puppy Zen we rehearse co-operative activities that strengthen the bond. We are re-creating the secure base, the mentor role and the following response, which all come naturally in the dog-to-dog bond. These are best demonstrated in key techniques: the joining-up technique, and the clip station and crate methods.

Joining up — building the psychological bond (safety)

Joining up is the natural process of bonding, and cultivates the following and 'look-to' responses to mum and the helpers that naturally occur in the wild world through pheromones, hormones, vocalisations and visual signals. As we don't have most of these naturally occurring features, we need to re-create them with other techniques.

Our joining-up technique shapes and rewards (with clicker, food and lead) the following responses through basic behaviours like 'heel', 'sit', 'down', 'Zen down' and 'wait'. This is a combination of moving with you, sitting and lying down when you stop, and moving off when you move, while looking to you periodically. This is subtly reminding the pup to stay engaged with you. Joining up encourages your pup to look to you for direction on how to act in any situation, and to follow you. Looking up to you and holding eye contact is an important part of training in Puppy Zen (bond gaze) to reinforce the bond. I call this 'contact', reinforcing the following response I expect the pup to have towards her mentor.

Altogether, joining up creates a ritualised sequence, almost like a dance, that entrains the bond. These basic behaviours trigger latent co-operative and social tendencies in your pup, mimicking the follower response. All in all, you are reinforcing contact, and encouraging your pup to look to you so she learns to focus on your signals. It reinforces the idea that safety is in your personal space, and is a technique you will use throughout your puppy and dog training.

Research has shown that oxytocin increases considerably when in close proximity and attending (including gazing) to a bonded individual. By also utilising the clicker and a food reward, we activate dopamine and other reward hormones that help to wire this behaviour in the brain. Go to Part D to see how to do joining up.

Building the spatial bond — establishing or re-establishing the den (safety)

The crate and the clip station are the spatial representations of the secure base or den. It is a way of taking puppies back to the den (the first and most fundamental secure base), which is a safe, contained space that allows puppies to be calm and therefore able to learn. This makes use of the neo-natal nesting effect.

This space will be associated with you as the mentor and inherit your safe influence. It re-creates the security and trust of having you, the mother or mentor (and her environment) around, which gives your pup the confidence to learn and do new things. It is important that the crate and the clip station always remain a secure base where the pup is comfortable and happy.

When you establish the crate and the clip station for your pup early, they continue to be the places your pup (and later as an adult dog) can retreat to and find comfort. You can also re-create these safe spaces in the car, or at a café or friends' places. They will also be a haven for your pup or dog when there is something potentially frightening happening, such as thunder and fireworks. Having a den space also decreases the risk of separation distress, as your pup or dog will always have a safe place to go back to even when you are not there (just like the wolf pups in the wild den). Slowly this space can evolve to your pup's sleeping site or mat as she grows.

The crate and the clip station also reinforce the learning state, the 'rest-and-digest' state inherent in the formative period. They allow your pup to be in an optimum learning state, and are a very handy tool for training, as you will see in Part C.

The best time to establish this den-site attachment with the crate is during the formative period. Ideally, breeders start introducing their puppies to a crate at around 4 to 6 weeks. We introduce the clip station at 3 months of age.

Research has found that the olfactory (smell) memory is primary in creating the bond, so we can use this naturally occurring element by ensuring that smells associated with the mentor are present firstly in the crate and later on the clip station (e.g. using a piece of the mentor's clothing). Spraying calming scents around, like lavender or canine appeasing pheromones, can also help calm pups.

The crate

With a pup, initially start with the crate, then from about 3-4 months introduce the clip station. The younger you start the crate training, the better, as you will be enabling the neo-natal nesting effect (love of the den) to continue; however, this does not last long, so start early. Not completing your puppy's crate training prior to 12 weeks will result in the loss of the neo-natal nesting effect, which will make it harder to establish crate training thereafter.

When you start using the crate early and correctly, your pup will love it. If you start it too late or introduce it poorly, your pup can sometimes become averse to containment, which means you will need to retrain your pup to enjoy the crate as a safe place — a harder process, so best to start young! Make sure your pup enjoys the crate by clicking and rewarding for calm behaviours and/or feeding your pup in the crate. (See Part C The crate.)

Another useful benefit of crate training is for house training, as pups don't generally soil in the den. (See the section on house training in Part D for details.)

Ideal set-up for house training. We are replicating the comfort of the den with the crate.

Creating the secure base effect with a clip station.

Clip station

The clip station is the next step after the crate: it mimics Nature in the move away from the den and the transition to the outside world; hence we start using it from 3 months of age. It gives your pup a growing sense of freedom (with some boundaries and control), while retaining a sense of safety in a controlled, quiet space. It also provides physical control, which allows you to settle your pup down and complete training sessions. Be careful when introducing a pup to a clip station, as we don't want the pup to get a fright and form bad associations with it. This place must at all times be a safe place. (See Part C The clip station for details.)

The clip station is an important starting point in teaching separation from you. You can use a clip station to keep your pup secure and in your vicinity (but separated) when you are spending time at home, by leaving your pup clipped up for periods of time while you are busy around the house — close for security and safety, but the beginnings of separation. It can also limit destructive behaviour, as the pup is secured. It is also a great place to facilitate house training, alongside the crate, as a pup won't toilet on the clip station (unless left for too long) as it is associated with the den and nest soiling inhibition.

To re-create the clip station elsewhere, just attach a lead securely to a table or chair leg, or even your own leg, making sure your pup can't drag or pull over what she is attached to. If you have a mat, that's also great, but it is not always necessary for this temporary arrangement.

A month or so after establishing the clip station, you can also use it as 'time-out' when your pup is misbehaving. After spending a little time in time-out, the pup is then allowed off the clip station, rewarding the calm, relaxed behaviour. However, care must be taken that negative associations do not get created with this place of safety. As with any time you are establishing new behaviours, don't use any corrections during the training phase — only positive reinforcement initially, so you don't switch the pup out of the learning state. This is why we don't use the clip station in the early stages for time-out. Only use it for time-out once your pup clearly associates it with a calm, safe place, so that when you do put her into time-out the effect is one of establishing or asking for calm rather than being punished.

Make training fun and bond with the family too!

Chapter 6

Establishing the family rules

Having clear, consistent family rules is essential for a bond of trust to develop. Our requirements for a safe and happy life are often different to a pup's natural inclinations, which they get from their wolfish roots. There are many risks in the human world that pups and dogs don't understand — cars are dangerous, aggression is largely inappropriate, killing stock and cats is unacceptable, and so on. Establishing what we want and don't want from our pups, and communicating that consistently is crucial to a harmonious relationship.

We have a shared sense of fairness, co-operation and a helping culture, which enables our pup or dog to be a family member and understand the importance of the rules in the pack (family), and therefore follow them. Through their ability to follow our gestures and learn by observation, pups can learn the rules and synchronise their behaviours with ours. Dogs want to please us, and they have the ability to understand 'yes' and 'no', which allows them to learn and follow the family rules.

It is important that the rules are established and agreed to by the whole family, and are implemented consistently, so you don't confuse and mislead your pup. (Remember the importance of honest communication with pups in establishing trust and a sense of security.) It is best to do this before your pup arrives home and the cuteness factor becomes distracting!

Of course the pup needs to be taught the family rules, and how you do this is covered in Parts E and F. What is important here is that you take the time as a family or household to establish these rules together. It might be helpful to create a list that you keep some-where handy, like on the fridge, as you undertake the critical and

No jumping up is
an important rule.

concentrated training during the formative period.

The family rules will be a mix of compulsory rules (considered the norm for responsible dog ownership in our communities) and conventions that you need to decide on together (things that you would like to see as they suit your lifestyle and preferences).

TYPES OF RULES YOU NEED TO PLAN FOR

Compulsory rules

- Have a strong bond with mentor and family.
- Be friendly, gentle and docile (no aggression to people, dogs and other species — except hunting dogs under control).
- Know our shared language (obedience and basic commands).
- Be clean (house-trained).
- Be quiet (don't bark unnecessarily).
- Be calm (not hyperactive or anxious, but able to relax and rest).
- Be aware and discriminating (in the learning state when

appropriate, and have the ability to discriminate a real threat).
- Have good recall ('come') and consistently respond to commands/cues.
- Be able to be handled around the collar, head and shoulders safely.
- Be able to tolerate veterinarian examinations.
- No jumping up (keep others safe).
- No eating from the table or your plate, or stealing food (so you don't encourage soliciting or competition).
- No barging through doors, jumping out of cars, etc., without a cue.
- No resource guarding (food, toys, beds or owner's space/lap).
- Be confident with loud noises, such as traffic, firecrackers, thunder, etc.
- Be confident on all different substrates (lino, tiles, shiny wood floors, etc.).
- Walk on the lead calmly, ideally joined up and in contact with you.

Conventions (examples)
- Who is responsible for feeding the pup and overseeing health/wellbeing?
- Inside or outside dog? (Dogs prefer to be close to you.)
- Where is the dog allowed in the house?
- Where will the pup sleep — bed, couch, inside, outside, her mat? (For more dominant pups and dogs, they should not be allowed on beds, couches and other high places.)
- Do you want your pup to be security-conscious/alert for strangers?
- Where will the pup toilet?
- How will you safely transport your pup in a vehicle, etc.?

The family rules are for your pup and everyone in the family. They ensure the family is clear on the requirements of the pup, and therefore the pup will get consistent messaging that she can trust. Although critical for a dog at any age, this is particularly important for a pup that is just beginning to learn the family rules and their importance in life, so you don't want to confuse your pup!

Chapter 7

Building a shared language

Building a shared language is a critical part of establishing our bond. Dogs have a different language and perspective of the world than we do. Yet they are communicating with us all the time, whether intentionally or unintentionally, as their posture and pheromones mirror their internal state. Dogs can't change the way they communicate by themselves: they speak dog language, and that's how they read us, too.

It is up to us to understand them and take the lead in creating our shared language. This will enable us to articulate to our dogs what we want from them and how we will keep them safe.

Creating a shared language involves:

O understanding what and how our pups and dogs communicate with us
O understanding how they read us, and what we are communicating, so we can adapt our messaging to ensure it is appropriate and consistent
O building our common language through our tools, basic commands and training.

UNDERSTANDING WHAT AND HOW OUR PUPS AND DOGS COMMUNICATE WITH US

Key attributes of dog language

Dogs are one of the hyper-social species, and they have a highly nuanced and sophisticated peer-to-peer social communication system inherited from wolves. Their peer-to-peer communication is much more sophisticated than those of solitary species like the ancestors of the domestic cat, which aren't social so don't need to communicate with

Jazmin helping her daughter, Nalu, build the reciprocal shared language.

each other as much. (Cats adapt their maternal and sexual behaviours to communicate, rather than having a peer-to-peer system.)

A shared language between our pups and ourselves comprises a number of elements, such as postural information, vocalisations (including intonation), scent marks and pheromones, not all of which we can sense. Each component can have many nuances; for example, a stare can vary from direct and active to looking away (on purpose), or it can be a 'targeting' stare that is lining up the other dog or prey.

Dogs are approximately 90 per cent postural communicators, so as their mentors we need to learn how to read their postures to understand what they are saying or meaning. Dog postural communication, like any language, is highly subtle and complex, and beyond the scope of this book to go into deeply. However, the basic postural components or shapes, and their behavioural and emotional meanings are explained here to give you the important basics.

This information on dog postural communication will not only help you understand your own growing pup as he becomes a dog, but just as importantly help you to read other dogs your pup might encounter, enabling you to respond appropriately (for example, allow your pup to happily play, or remove him from an escalating situation). While it is essential that your growing pup gets opportunities to meet and greet other dogs and to play, you also do not want to have your pup suffer any trauma associated with an aggressive dog or an overly boisterous, much larger pup. Reading these interactions early and correctly is critical. Later, in Parts C and F I will show you how to moderate an overly excitable pup's behaviour to facilitate a playful interaction at similar levels of arousal or excitement.

Reading postural signals

As dogs and puppies are mainly postural communicators, the main body parts you should look at to read a dog are the body, eyes, ears, lips, hackles and tail. In particular, whether they are signalling 'I'm big' or 'I'm small' or 'I'm out of here!' Pups' postures are often less exaggerated than those of adults.

Following are the six main behavioural states in a pup that you need to be able to read, and the signs you need to look out for. Remember, these reactions are intrinsic (innate) so will be honest (true). We also need to take breed differences into account when reading pups and understanding their predispositions and problems. (See Part E for details of breed group temperaments.)

1. Aggression/Dominance

As noted earlier, when I talk about dominance it is not in terms of the discredited Lupomorph model of aggressive, dominant leaders of the pack; rather, it is a relationship that is based on guidance from a parent or older sibling (the mentor). It is demonstrated through *big postures*, which dogs use to make themselves look bigger and more dominant. Pups almost always signal a threat before an attack, and there are often gradual build-ups, called *stacking* (increasing adrenalin). Reading these signals early will help you and your pup avoid direct aggressive situations.

O *Eyes*: Staring directly, with the gaze held longer than normal (fixed stare), pupils dilated (enlarged).

O *Ears*: Pinned forward, so they are able to pick up auditory information well if they have upright ears (pinnae).

O *Lips*: Fully puckered forward into a full, offensive snarl, or, as submission increases, they are retracted back (ventrally) into a smile-like gesture, or more of a gape if fearful and a conflicted response increases (less intense in pups).

- O *Body*: Strutting and standing over the neck and shoulders of another dog (the T-section). A dog on the verge of aggression may also stiffen up (standing-over tactics).
- O *Hackles*: Hackles (the hair along the back of the pup's neck and back, even to the tail in some cases) are raised (piloerection), which can indicate dominance or fear. (The difference is in the shape of the back — see the fear section on page 88.) This really signals arousal of the adrenalin-induced fight–flight state.
- O *Tail*: The tail will be held up high or at least level (12 to 3 o'clock position) Most pups don't wag their tail when they are aggressive, but some do, so don't rely on a wagging tail to identify a dog as friendly — look for other signals to confirm this.
- O *Tone*: Deep growling, especially if the aggression is intensifying. Barking is a lower tone, and occurs more when the pup is behind barriers or on a chain, as it indicates a level of conflict between approach and retreat, because the pup cannot get fully away as he is contained or restrained (less intense in pups).
- O *Body orientation*: The more direct, the more threatening.
- O *Approach*: The more direct, the more threatening, whereas circling behind shows an element of fear.

2. Confidence

This is demonstrated through *upright and relaxed postures*. This is the behaviour and posture we expect from calm, stable pups and dogs.

- O *Eyes*: Looking at the other individual, but not with a fixed stare.
- O *Ears*: Upright ears, pointing forward and relaxed, not on the alert.
- O *Lips*: Normal and relaxed.
- O *Body*: Upright, but not puffed up or out, strutting or lowered.
- O *Hackles*: Not up, or, if they are, this can be just arousal if there are no other aggressive signals.
- O *Tail*: Normal, relaxed height (4 to 6 o'clock position), could be wagging slightly.
- O *Tone*: Normal to higher-pitched.
- O *Approach*: Calm, with no strutting or lowering of the body.

The pup on the right is showing dominant signals: direct stare, hackles up slightly, and tail up. This shows how being on lead forces head-to-head meetings and can lead to trouble. The dog handshake defuses this.

Puppy (left) displays a confident posture, while the older dog watches its owner.

3. Playfulness

This is demonstrated by *play bows* and *play-soliciting behaviour*. Pups and dogs often use play to mediate and reduce conflict. Play behaviours range from subordinate through to dominant, although dominants will initiate play to create safe interactions with subordinates and relieve the tension of a social interaction. One of the main purposes of play is to rehearse various behaviours.

O *Eyes*: Happy (soft) eyes, not staring. Sometimes the dog will be staring in play threat when combined with a play bow.

O *Ears*: Relaxed, but can vary as pups mimic other behaviours in play at times.

O *Lips*: The playful pup will approach, lick the jowls of the other dog (or human), then run away, then approach and lick the jowls again, then run away.

O *Body*: The pup will do play bows, soliciting to play, but there are lots of other postures included in play, too.

O *Hackles*: Not raised unless they get a fright, which could turn into a dominance interaction or an apology, but generally hackles are not present.

O *Tail*: Wagging or relaxed, but variable.

O *Tone*: It will be an up intonation, a high-pitched bark or whining, or a play growl.

4. Affiliation (wanting to associate or get something; for example, security, support, food, play, contact)

This is demonstrated through similar types of behaviours to those of a submissive dog; however, submission is normally slower, more wary, lower-energy and precautionary. Affiliative is more active, so you will see more tail wagging, more licking and higher energy. Affiliative behaviours are more actively engaging of the recipient than submissive behaviours. They are not fearful. You will see them more in puppies, although adult dogs can exhibit them, too.

Affiliative greeting became ritualised in dogs' social evolution through rituals around the pack leaving to hunt and returning from the hunt. When the pack heads out on hunts, the pups go through a hyper-excitable departure routine, jumping up over the adults, and displaying affiliative behaviours that build bonds plus excitement for the hunt. On the return of the pack, pups solicit pack members to regurgitate food so they can feed by licking the older wolves' jowls. This is the origin of pups wanting to jump up on owners on their return: so they can lick their owners' 'jowls'.

5. Submission

This is demonstrated by *lowered positioning* to make themselves smaller, but they stand still, slightly approach or roll over rather than withdraw (which we see in fear). Submission is different from fear. The purpose of submissive posturing is to inhibit threat in the other dog by saying 'I give up!'

- o *Eyes*: Not looking at the threat, but actively looking away, although as the appeasement/soliciting element increases, the more the pup looks at the object.
- o *Ears*: Often back or flat.
- o *Lips*: The pup might have a 'smile' on his lips: the lips might be more pulled back (called 'ventral retraction'). The pup can be licking the jowls of the dominant from underneath.
- o *Body*: The body will be lowered. The back half might be lowering down towards the ground, or the dog might roll right over onto his back into a recumbent submission. A submissive pup might also urinate, actively affirming he gives up!
- o *Hackles*: The hackles will not be up unless the pup is very fearful.
- o *Tail*: Often the tail is low, but out from the body (5 to 6 o'clock position).
- o *Tone*: Whining and solicitous.
- o *Approach*: Submissive pup will slowly approach the other party (whereas a fearful dog will avoid the other party).

6. Fear

This is demonstrated by *lowered and arched back and/or withdrawal*.
- o *Eyes*: Pupil dilation is extreme.
- o *Ears*: Back or flat.
- o *Lips*: Sometimes fearful pups do a full gape and open their mouths, but the lips will at least be pulled back like they are in submission.
- o *Open mouth threat gape*: This is where they are snapping towards you in a defensive threat, in the hope that you will back away. Generally, this is display only, to ward you off. Only if you

Playfulness — the pup on the left is play bowing to solicit more play.

Affiliation, soliciting and appeasement are behaviours derived from food soliciting in the pack.

Recumbent (full) submission. Note the revealing belly, licking and 'I give up!' squint.

Fear — note the position of the tail under the body.

continue to encroach into their personal space might they defensively bite.

O *Body*: Lowered, but normally in fear they will not roll over unless caught.

O *Hackles*: Hackles will often be up in fear (not in threat) all the way down to the tail, and are more extended than in threat. This is adrenalin-induced, with flight dominant.

O *Tail*: Down or tucked fully under the body between the legs. (This is often the most obvious sign.)

O *Tone*: Quiet or high-pitched, whining or barking.

O *Approach*: They will be demonstrating extreme avoidance behaviour, trying to get out of the situation. They will not approach.

It can be fairly easy to confuse a submissive dog with a fearful pup (or vice versa), but it is important to know the difference, as a fearful dog can be dangerous if he feels cornered, and may bite in defence (fear aggression). A submissive dog isn't feeling as threatened, so is unlikely to turn fear-aggressive.

The noticeable differences between fear and submission are the indications of sympathetic arousal state (the adrenalin-induced fight-or-flight state), which a fearful dog will show, such as with his hackles up and pupils dilated. In fear, the back is also more arched, and the tail is forced right under the belly. Ears are often flat, and in extreme cases the dog may defecate or urinate, and/or evacuate their anal glands. A fearful pup will also be trying to escape or avoid the situation, whereas a submissive pup is likely to actively go up to the other dog or human that it is acting submissively towards.

Intonation and barking

In general, pups' intonation (if they use any) will be a high-pitched bark or whine if they are soliciting and happy, and maybe in fear, and low-pitched and growling in their full aggressive, threatening, dominance state. Sometimes they might be barking in a deep tone.

Barking in pups and dogs is a mix of tones influenced by environmental and emotional factors. Often pups and dogs that bark are in conflict, torn between a threat and a retreat. Normally they would probably prefer to retreat, but if contained they can't, hence they are in conflict. This is evident by the alternating frequency and tone of bark (from high to low, defensive to offensive). Dogs barking in yards, on chains and in houses are often conflicted, because if they were free they would stay silent and avoid the threat. Territorial and protective dogs are less conflicted and more offensive.

Understanding a pup or dog's motivation behind the barking is helpful, so you can either fulfil his need or resolve his conflict, or remove the threat or fear-inducing stimulus. Below are some of the different types of barking and their motivations.

O *Threat growl or low-pitched (low-frequency) bark*: This is when the sender is aggressive and wants the hearer to withdraw — 'Back off!'

O *High-pitched tonal signals like a puppy's whimper* (whine, lost call, play bark): These tend to be care-soliciting, appeasing or play-soliciting. It is not threatening, but is encouraging and telling the receiver it is okay to come closer.

O *Hunt or scent bark or yodel*: These are typical of the hounds, like Beagles, who produce a characteristic, loud, high-pitched and tonal cry: the 'scent bark'. The outcome of giving this tonal signal is that the whole pack, along with its companion human hunters, rallies together to follow scent.

O *Soliciting whine*: This high-pitched vocalisation is calling the recipient to pay attention or to come to the pup.

O *Separation distress*: This can be a bark or a high-pitched tonal cry, even a howl. The dog is attempting to call the owner back home. Wolves use howling to re-gather the pack after the hunt. It says 'I'm lonely' or 'I'm lost: come back to me.' We feel it!

O *Fear-induced bark*: This is paired with the fear postural signals and is conflicted. If the dog was free he would retreat, but since he cannot he gives a defensive threat bark, which has predominantly high-pitched vocalisations.

O *Retreat woof*: Wolves, and feral and mal-socialised dogs, do a single or a few low-tone woofs as signals of retreat — 'Let's get out of here.'

O *Stimulus-oriented barking*: This varies, depending on what the stimulus is. With cats on the fence it is a cross between the hunt bark and the threat bark. Hard-to-identify objects will induce a conflicted threat bark ('What is out there?'). They are questioning in a higher pitch.

Interestingly, humans and dogs use similar parts of the brain to read intonation and to understand the emotional content of the sounds. We, too, use low-frequency sounds for threat, and higher-pitched sounds to greet, care and solicit. Often when we talk to pups and dogs with our baby talk, we exaggerate this tonal sound, and as trainers we rely on this and use it to our advantage.

MEET AND GREETS — THE DOG'S SOCIAL COMMUNICATION SIGNALS

It is important that we, as our pup's mentor, understand the social signalling system pups and dogs use to meet other dogs and people, so we can ensure our pups learn appropriate greeting behaviour during the critical formative period.

Although dogs have a completely different way of greeting each other than we do, the principles aren't so different. Dogs meeting new dogs or people need a formal greeting just like we do. Usually, we humans would be introduced with a handshake, a hug, or perhaps a kiss on one or both cheeks, depending on where we are from. The way we are introduced to and meet other people forms the basis of our future relationship. If we receive a genuine handshake and a warm 'Hello, how are you?', we would generally expect that the relationship is off to a good start. However, if someone were to stare meanly at us across the room, refuse to shake hands or say hello, then I would expect we weren't going to be the best of friends going forward. Critically, with pups and dogs, the nature of their first introductions sets the tone for their future relationship(s). I can't emphasise this enough.

Doggy handshake

Greeting routines for both the ancestral wolf and dogs are very formalised and ritualised. The main elements of these routines are posture and pheromones. Both greet each other by sniffing the inguinal and anogenital area — the groin and the area underneath the tail. (I call this the 'dog handshake'.) This informs the dog about sexual status, age, the relative dominance of the other dog, and whether or not a female is in heat. There are also very important appeasing pheromones in this area that defuse possible aggression.

After they have checked out all of this crucial information, they will often then greet and sniff at the face end of the pup or dog, as there are pheromones there, too. When they are doing this natural greeting, they use signals and postures that say 'Hello, I'm not going to fight.'

It is interesting how often people think sniffing the rear end is inappropriate, because from a human perspective we don't like a dog greeting us that way. However, for dogs it is the proper way of introducing themselves. It diffuses aggression and calms them, due to the pheromones, so not only should we teach them to do it, we should actively encourage proper dog handshakes all the time.

Conversely, if dogs meet head-to-head and are standing staring at each other (see photo on page 86), this forces them into a dominance stand-off and can result in an aggressive interaction. This is not what we want to happen at all. However, often dogs on leads can inadvertently end up meeting this way, so we need to know how to avoid and/or manage these situations.

Ideally, in the first instance raising a highly social pup is the best way to avoid any difficult meet-and-greet situations. Young pups often greet the face first, but need to learn to do the dog handshake. Start teaching them early, as it is less threatening to older dogs. An adult dog that is greeting inappropriately is more likely to end up in aggressive situations, whereas a pup inappropriately greeting is likely to be more tolerated by another dog and only receive minor corrections if needed — a necessary part of a pup's learning. Teaching your pup a 'rear present' (you actively turning the pup's rear to the other dog) is a good way to diffuse another dog being aggressive, as well-socialised dogs will not attack from behind. (This is an innate dog rule, with the exceptions being fighting or mal-socialised dogs.)

Pups that are not correctly exposed to other dogs in the formative period do not get these intrinsic greeting behaviours switched on. That is, they haven't learnt dog social signals of affiliation and greeting at the right time, and so can give off inappropriate signals that can get them into trouble. This underlines the critical need for socialisation during the formative period, as they can learn how to appropriately meet and greet with the 'nicely' cue and greet much more safely.

Human meet and greet

It is also important that you teach your pup a formal meet and greet with people, so that the pup learns to look to you for assurance and stay

Pup at right sniffing anogenital area to read pheromones that have an appeasing effect.

The adult will normally threaten only, as this one is doing, but they can bite too. The pup needs to learn good meet-and-greet skills, so I use a moderating technique to manage the pup's behaviour.

in a learning state while greeting new people. Using the clicker and food rewards reinforces direct contact and sociable interaction with new people, teaching your pup appropriate discrimination and social responses. Having a formal greeting routine with a pre-established 'nicely' cue will allow you to manage and grow your pup's ability to meet people as she grows into an adult dog.

The most important thing to learn when cultivating good relationships between your dog and other dogs and people is how to read a dog's body language. When we know what our pups and the other dogs are saying, we can react accordingly to ensure we respond to the situation in a helpful way. For example, if you know how a dog looks when she is feeling happy or playful, you will be able to recognise this behaviour when your pup meets other dogs, and will know they are friendly with each other and are not going to be a problem together. Conversely, it is even more essential you recognise when a dog (or your pup) is showing warning signs of annoyance, fear or aggression, so you can moderate or alleviate the situation immediately, using the learned response to reduce the risk of escalating aggression into a dog fight. In Part D Meet and greet, we go through how to train the meet-and-greet routines.

RECOGNISING AND RESPONDING TO YOUR PUP'S BEHAVIOUR

As the bond with your pup grows, you will learn more about her individual personality and quirks, and how to predict and read her behaviour more accurately. This will help you understand how to respond to your pup, and guide her through any given situation and circumstance.

The better you observe and understand your pup, the earlier you can intervene and guide her behaviour. As you grow in understanding your pup's behaviour, you will understand when to get contact and control. Dogs and pups go through escalating signals of behaviour intent. The hierarchy of intent is:

O *Orient*: Pups will first orient to a stimulus (turn their heads and look).
O *Alert*: Their behaviour will be alert (adrenalin starts to flow).
O *Target*: Next they will target (fix on their 'target'). The pupils dilate

and adrenalin increases up to 4 times higher than normal, which initiates and influences the behaviour (starts the action).

O *Action*: Finally, they will activate the behaviour. For example, the pup will attack if it is aggression, chase if it is prey, or herd if it is herding arousal, like a Border Collie eyeing a flock.

The first three are the most important ones and I use the acronym (OAT) to remember them. As your pup's mentor, it is the time between your pup alerting and targeting her behaviour that is critical for you to recognise, so you can intervene at an early stage (acting as an interrupter). This is before your pup's adrenalin rises too much (stacks) and the primitive brain kicks in: by that stage you will have far less control. In this window of opportunity, you can make contact with your pup and get her focused on you, her mentor, so you can guide her towards the right decision — appropriate behaviour! Having your pup look to you is the key (bond gaze), as in most instances as soon as your pup looks to you, you can intervene effectively.

It is also important to understand your pup's *trigger points*. What are the early warning signs that your pup is going to behave in ways that are inappropriate? Understand how these might accumulate (or stack) in your pup — the final trigger might be small, but it has resulted from a number of other earlier steps that can build or stack up. The key is to observe and understand your pup's personal triggers, and identify whether they are stacking up and about to trigger your pup.

The combination of understanding what situations trigger your pup and how your pup signals her behaviour is a powerful means by which you identify what is going on, so you can intervene early to keep your pup safe and out of trouble. This is your critical role as mentor, and is how you can build her trust in you and your guidance.

HOW OUR DOGS AND PUPS READ US, AND WHAT WE ARE COMMUNICATING TO THEM

We need to be very aware of our posture and tone, as pups and dogs are highly receptive to human cues. For example, research shows that they follow our pointing, our eyes and where we are looking, and they watch our faces carefully, knowing when we are distracted or not. All that said, pups still come from a very different culture, and the ancestral meaning of many of their behaviours is different. Pups read our behaviour and language largely in dog terms — meaning they are using *their* language to interpret us. What you are doing doesn't necessarily mean what you think it means to your pup or dog.

Many of our social gestures can be the opposite of what pups would do. A prime example is if you hug a pup that doesn't know you. In your human mind, a hug is a warm and friendly greeting. However, to the pup it will normally be perceived as a threat (the neck and shoulders are the ritualised threat areas, where dogs bite in dominance interactions), so a hug can be a stressful and threatening experience for a dog. Remember this with kids, as they love to hug pups and dogs, which is not advisable if they don't have a bond or relationship of trust with the pup or dog. Surprisingly, a majority of bites happen between dogs and those they know or have met previously, but it tends to happen when they haven't been greeted properly, so I will show you how to desensitise pups to these human gestures.

Note: Relationship and context are important here. If you are well bonded to your pup or dog, he will experience these gestures differently,

Orient.

Alert.

Target.

Diffuse.

Understand your pup's orient, alert, target sequence, and you will be able to intervene early.

as you would have already taught him what they mean. By the time your own pup gets to know you, he will be able to reinterpret some of your behaviours based on what you have taught him they mean. It is most important to remember these guidelines for dogs you *don't* know.

HOW A DOG READS YOUR POSTURING AND BEHAVIOUR

Because pups translate your actions into dog language, they are looking for your *postural indicators*. Of course, you don't have all the right appendages (such as big ears and a tail), so instead they will be noticing:

- your eye contact (direction, duration, degree of fixation of stare, squint/open, pupil size)
- how you approach them, including speed and orientation, direct or indirect (three-quarters on)

O your height and stiffness of posture, and postural tone
O how and where you handle them
O your vocal intonation
O pressure/tension on the lead
O the context, because the meaning changes if it is with someone they know, or if it is near their territory or car
O the degree of freedom they have — whether you are holding their lead, they are chained up, contained or in a kennel, etc.

In simple terms, you will be gesturing threatening, neutral or friendly behaviours. As noted above, here I am talking in general about meeting new dogs.

Eye contact

One of the major threat gestures to a dog is direct eye contact. If you have a good bond with your dog and you aren't excessively assertive with him, then looking at your dog and him looking back can be subtle and encouraging (bond gaze). However, like humans, dogs can tell whether your look is a threatening stare or an encouraging contact. Don't stare in a fixed fashion, especially if you are approaching the dog, as he will feel threatened.

Approach

Moving directly into a pup or dog's personal space can be a threat, so when you greet a new dog, simply walking up to him can be interpreted as a threat. If you let the dog approach you instead, it is much less threatening. A pup has a personal space of about a metre, so once you get inside that personal space you can be directly threatening the pup. If it is your own pup, he won't normally worry, unless you are being overly dominant in other ways.

As a general rule, it is best to stop outside of this space and allow pups and dogs to approach you when you are meeting them. Stop a couple of metres back, and if comfortable crouch down, hold out the back of your hand (in a relaxed fashion) and allow the dog to approach; if comfortable, call the pup to you in a higher-pitched tone. If you are approaching, approach from the side, or present yourself with your shoulder (three-quarters on) rather than walking directly towards the pup straight-on.

In this photo, we are desensitising the pup to a child's touch. We use the clicker to teach the pup that the child is not a threat.

Height and posture

The directness and assertiveness of posture influence the dog, too. Be aware that height is a threat to a pup: remember that pups try to make themselves bigger when they want to communicate dominance. Standing over a pup is threatening, and the bigger you are, the more of a threat you are for a pup. If you want to lower the threat, lower your height by crouching slightly. Also, turn yourself three-quarters on to the pup, because the squarer on to a pup you are, the more threatening you appear.

HOW YOU HANDLE A PUP — SAFE AND UNSAFE AREAS

If you are going to handle a pup that doesn't know you, handle him in the chest and chin region. Handling the pup on the neck, cheek, shoulder region, the feet, the tail or the back is likely to seem more threatening, depending on the level of the dog's socialisation. As mentioned earlier, the neck, cheek and shoulder region is the dog's ritualised threat area, where dogs go in to bite another dog in threat situations, so if you handle this area you are simulating a threat.

If the pup lies down and you handle him on the tummy or close to the inguinal area, this is normally non-threatening, but most dogs won't let you access that area easily at the beginning, unless in recumbent submission.

Intonation

Your behaviour and posture are the most important signals; following them is your intonation. If you use a high-pitched intonation and a happy, soliciting voice, the dog is going to read you as less threatening. If you use low, growly, threatening tones and are telling him off, the dog will feel threatened, and there is more risk of you being counter-threatened, or of the dog showing submission or fear reactions.

Men's height, size and lower intonations mean that dogs can potentially be warier of males when they first meet them, and act more defensively or aggressively. The bigger you are, the more likely this is, so be mindful. It is for these reasons that research has shown that dogs generally see women as less threatening and more friendly. However, how a dog responds or reacts to different people will also depend on who the dog was socialised to during the formative period. This is why it is important for your pup to meet as wide a range of people as possible at that time.

Tension on the lead

Remember your pup and dog can read your emotions and state of mind through posture and pheromones — so be aware what you will also be communicating down the lead to your pup. This is particularly relevant when approaching other dogs or people with your pup on-lead. Tension on the lead and pulling away can both communicate and increase anxiety and fear. In Part C we suggest what to do with the lead in each situation to give your pup the right message. Later on in this section, under 'Role of the mentor', we discuss how you can manage your behaviour and so, indirectly, your pheromones (as much as possible). So if when training you are stressed or emotional, think about whether it is a good time for training. It might be best just to play or even rest.

THREAT-REDUCING BEHAVIOURS ARE BEST

To bring this information together: if you want to be seen as friendly and non-threatening to a dog that doesn't know you, show more threat-reducing behaviours. These include the following:

○ No direct eye contact. Instead, look just off to the side, or glance occasionally at the dog.

○ Allow the pup to approach you first, and crouch down (or remain standing, in a relaxed posture if you feel vulnerable) and turn three-quarters on.

○ If you approach the pup, approach with a three-quarter stance (shoulder presented), preferably stop a couple of metres away from the pup, and crouch down. Keep children standing, but have them turn three-quarters on.

○ Do not stand over the pup.

○ Handle the pup only in the chin and chest region at first, as this is a safer, less-threatening area. If unsure, don't handle at all.

○ Stay silent, but if you use an intonation, use a happy, high-toned voice to speak to the pup. Test one short comment first — for example 'good boy' — in a quiet, upbeat tone.

Situations in which we should try to appear as non-threatening to a dog as possible include:

○ when meeting a new dog, especially if this is on the dog's own property or in the car

○ when a dog is threatening you

○ if your dog is submissive or fearful of you

○ when entering a property, take care

○ approaching an owner when with their dog

○ when a dog is on a chain or contained.

Use your posture and intonation to communicate to your pup

Be aware that your pup or dog is reading you at all times, so use your posture and intonation (and pre-established cue words, when appropriate) to communicate the right message to your pup. If you want your pup to be relaxed, don't exhibit threatening behaviours, but remain calm and confident. If you want your pup to stop what he is doing and he knows the 'no' command, use a gruff tone of voice and

Appropriate way to greet.

Inappropriate way to greet.

stand up straight as you say 'no'. If using *fixing commands* (commands for your pup to stay put), turn towards the pup and fix eye contact in a subtle but effective manner (don't stare harshly). If you want your pup to come to you (*drawing commands*), then relax your body, turn slightly three-quarters on, smile, and use an upbeat tone — you relax your postures so you are inviting 'Come to me!'

It is important to use this body language subtly, as you are using dominance signalling at times to guide your pup. It is about the subtlety of the information you are sharing: rather than using a sledge hammer, use a refined tool. Look for effectiveness — use enough to have effect, but not so much that you scare your pup. The level required will depend on your pup's personality (whether he is bold or shy) and the stimuli or environment you are in (whether there are high levels of distraction). The important thing is to observe and recognise your pup's response, and adjust accordingly.

Don't use dominance signalling or teach a 'no' until the pup is 3 months old. (The exception is when the pup is unusually dominant or pushy, which you might see in the bull terrier breeds or bulldogs, for example.) However, it is important that these commands and signalling are established by the time the pup is 4 months old. We show how to teach the 'no' command and contrast training in Part C.

BUILDING OUR COMMON SHARED LANGUAGE — THE BASIC COMMANDS

One of the most important things we can do for our pups is equip them with a set of commands or words that enables us to keep them safe, and allows us to have a relaxed and stress-free life with them. These signals (cues) help us guide our pups, and give them clarity about what we want from them. Having them makes all other aspects of pup and dog training much easier. The basic commands include 'sit', 'down', 'Zen down', 'wait', 'stay', 'yes', 'no', 'nicely', etc. In Part C we outline how to teach your pup these basic commands and more.

Now that you know how to better understand your pup, and how your pup understands you, you can use this information to create a shared language, and with that a happy and harmonious relationship. You will be able to communicate the right messages to your pup, and understand the signals your pup is sending so that you can respond appropriately. This understanding is a very powerful part of any relationship and training with your pup, and will help you immensely in your day-to-day interactions.

Safe way to greet a pup — handling underneath the chin/neck area while the owner is focused on the pup with food reward handy.

Unsafe way — coming over the top of the head while the owner is not observing the pup's reactions.

Chapter 8

Your role as mentor

The final component to building the bond is the essential role you play as your pup's mentor. We explore what a good bond looks like, what you need to do to achieve it, and, importantly, how you need to *be* to ensure your pup trusts you and bonds with you.

THE NATURE OF A GOOD BOND

So what does a healthy mentor bond with your pup look like? When you create this mentor bond, your pup will stay close to you, look to you for direction, and study you and your behaviour. Your pup will be attuned to what you want, look at your face and eyes, knowing when you are attentive to him. Your pup will have full trust in you, as you will have been proven trustworthy in pup terms. Remember, it is fine to have more than one of the family being the mentor, in fact it is advisable so your pup doesn't grow an overly dependent bond on one person, which can lead to separation distress and ignoring the other family members.

Many behavioural issues stem from poorly established bonds between the pup and the mentor(s), so it is worth putting in the time and effort to establish and maintain a sound, loving relationship.

WHAT YOU SHOULD DO AS A MENTOR

Guidance
As discussed earlier, your role is to provide a secure base for your pup, which allows the pup to grow trust, security and love between you. You need to provide your pup with guidance, including exposing him to any stimuli he needs to understand and adjust to, give him reassurance that you have things in hand, and provide him with a sense of safety,

Your role as your pup's mentor is critical. Here is a young Puppy Zen Master click and rewarding the bond gaze. Notice the position of the lure hand.

trust and reassurance of his place in the family. You will teach him what appropriate behaviours are, so he understands the family rules, like 'don't pee on the carpet' and 'come when called'. Your pup will remain in contact with you — that is, remain reasonably close and check in with you (look at you) as he goes about his day.

Contact and love

Make plenty of time for contact with your pup, so he gets used to looking to you for guidance. Make sure that to begin with, you (as the main mentor) are the one to feed your pup and take him walking. Make time to do fun things together: just like any relationship, the more you invest in it, the better it will be. Go to the park, play a game in the backyard, go for a swim, whatever you want — spending time with your pup is key.

Give your pup lots of calm, soft physical contact — pups love to be close to you, so rest your hand or foot on your pup when you are sitting together, pat, massage and touch. (Wolves touch each other six times an hour!) Gently massaging the dorsal muscles on each side of the spine encourages a calming response. All of these things will encourage your pup to see you as his mentor and beloved companion.

Remember, however, to only offer contact for appropriate or desired behaviours, not problem ones. Contact is a reward, so don't reward inappropriate behaviour.

Play

Play has a specific role in relationship building, as it allows pups to learn and practise the family rules. Dogs and pups communicate using signals with clear meanings, such as the play bow, which says 'Come play with me!' It all seems merely fun and games, but they are actually rehearsing behaviour action patterns, such as social, fighting, hunting and even mating, and in doing so they build trust, co-ordination and cohesiveness in the pack. They can build trusting, co-operative relationships, knowing that family members know the rules of engagement and will follow them.

I like to use play to reward the successful completion of sequences of behaviour, although I do not use play to help train the actual individual behaviours. Training is done with the clicker and food rewards, as the play drive distracts from learning by stimulating sympathetic arousal,

Enrichment on clip station with toys.

which puts the pup in a very poor learning state. However, at the completion of a successful training sequence I like to use a tug-of-war rope or a ball on a rope to reward success. It is not only a great reward, but an excellent opportunity to further strengthen the bond. At the end of the overall training session, allow rest time to help your pup integrate what he has learnt.

Enrichment

You need to ensure your pup gets plenty of enrichment; that is, activities that get your pup to think, play, exercise, learn or serve a purpose. (For example, working dogs love to work, hunting dogs love to hunt, obedience dogs love to compete.) In the wild, dogs get a lot of stimulation, and to get close to that for your dog is a challenge that needs to be planned for.

I like to have a toy basket for my dogs, so they grab toys and play-chew and bring me the balls, etc., for engagement — this is enrichment. There is a wealth of DIY and modern dog enrichment toys, puzzles, brain-teasers, boredom-busters, dog-training games and feeders readily available to enrich your dog's life.

Enrichment plays a role in many other species, and is heavily incorporated in zoos worldwide, including a rescue zoo I previously owned. Be creative and use your new-found knowledge and understanding of your own dog to utilise his likes and dislikes to create opportunities that your pup will especially like.

Boundaries and contrast training

A mentor relationship isn't just providing a loving bond, although of course that is essential. It is also about providing guidance on setting boundaries and understanding consequences in this foreign human world.

During this early period in your pup's life you are shaping behaviour, so *positive reinforcement techniques* are the primary techniques that are used. However, if you start dealing with behaviour issues such as hyperactivity, fear or aggression, then *behaviour modification* becomes necessary. These require the changing or eliminating of existing behaviours as well as shaping new behaviours. To do this, we need contrast training. This involves rewarding your pup for behaviours you want him to do, and providing an apparent natural consequence for behaviours you don't want, thereby establishing boundaries. I am always protecting or enhancing the sense of safety and trust in my bond with my pups, so rarely if ever do I allow a negative experience to be associated with me or my family. I am the ally, not the enemy. This form of contrast training creates safety (you) and encourages avoidance (things the pup should be leaving alone). This is a critical part of establishing our bond and how we train, so go to Part C for more detail, both in the section on how pups learn, and the tools and techniques section.

Controlling access to resources — nothing in life is free

'Nothing in life is free' is a critical training principle that will help you establish a bond with your pup. There are two key principles to adhere to. First, you provide your pup access to what he wants (resources), and secondly, you are *always* training, as your pup always wants something (food, attention, affection, freedom).

One of the important ways to communicate to your pup that you are the mentor is to control the primary resources. You are in charge of access to the goods that your pup wants or likes: food, your attention, freedom, off-lead time in the park, play, and so on. Pups often prioritise their key relationships largely based on who controls the resources.

You can reward your pup for appropriate behaviour by giving him access to the things he wants. Importantly, though, don't give your pup free access to these things during the initial intensive training period. Your pup has to work for everything: for example, ask your pup for a 'sit' or 'wait' before he is allowed to eat or go through the door. Only reward your pup when he is doing desired behaviours or commands, not if he is misbehaving. When starting training, I recommend that for the first 2 to 3 months you ask your pup to do something simple every time before getting what he wants, to firmly establish this training. Nothing in life is free, so your pup has to work just a little bit to get what he wants. That way your pup learns that he needs to look to you for guidance before he makes his own choices.

It is important to be aware that you are always training, as often we can be rewarding behaviours without even thinking about it. For example, consider what happens if you open the car door and allow your pup to jump straight out and rush over to a tree or another dog. You are rewarding uncontrolled jumping out by giving him what he wants — freedom, trees, access to other dogs — without permission. Instead, ask for a 'sit' and 'wait', then give the 'okay' command to allow the pup to jump out. This reinforces that you are the mentor, particularly in the critical training phase. Be aware that giving freedom or pats, or even looking at the things your pup wants, are rewards, so ask for one of your cues (such as 'sit'), and then once completed reward your pup with freedom (release on the 'okay' command).

HOW YOU ARE 'BEING' AS A MENTOR

We learnt earlier that pups, like us, are 'other regarding' and have a suite of behaviours they use to regulate social interactions. Qualities like fairness, co-operation, patience and forgiveness are important to your pup, so it is important you behave similarly to help build trust and a relationship with her. Pups and dogs are highly receptive to human cues, reading our moods through pheromones, postures and intonations, so your attitude, energy and posture are important. How you are *being* matters.

Your relationship with your pup is one of love and guidance.

Remember, being your pup's mentor is not about being the dominant, authoritarian 'leader of the pack'. It is a loving relationship of guidance and support. Think of dominance as being more assertive or influential in nature, guiding rather than being overbearing, heavy-handed or authoritarian.

TRAINER'S QUALITIES

Below are some of the key qualities you need to build a strong bond with your pup and be a great trainer.

○ *Kindness, empathy and compassion*: This helps your pup feel secure and builds trust between you so she has the confidence to learn new behaviours.

○ *Setting clear, consistent and fair boundaries*: This ensures your pup knows what is appropriate and inappropriate behaviour, and that she can trust you and look to you for guidance. Pups need a sense of place and a role in their families.

○ *Being present and focused*: You are present with your pup in this moment so you see what is happening around your pup.

O *Have situational awareness*: You are aware of what is in the environment and the level of risk (other dogs and other species, cars, people) and how your pup might respond so you can identify the options you should take to manage the situation.

O *Understanding and insight*: Observing and watching your pup's behaviour and responses over time to identify patterns and insights into the pup's particular personality and behaviours. This will help you identify how your pup might respond in new situations so you can manage them proactively.

Effective training

Always remember, *effective* is the operative word when training — not too much assertiveness, not too little. This will be your challenge as the mentor: to determine what is effective for your pup. The degree of assertiveness needs to be guided by the temperament of your pup. Some pups are more sensitive than others, so soften up on those types, it won't take much. On the other hand, be more assertive with the rough-and-tumble kind of pup that is strong-willed. You are looking for whether the level of your assertiveness is having an effect. If you are frightening your pup, you are being too assertive — so soften up quickly to retain the relationship. If your pup continues to do what you don't want her to do, then you are being too soft and need to be more assertive. Remember, you are mimicking natural consequences that your pup would experience in the wild. This is explored in more depth in Part D in the section on contrast training.

What can we do to support ourselves?

Not unlike being a new parent, the mix of joy, fear and confusion can be overwhelming, and our deep wish to do right by our pups can become paralysing. Don't be embarrassed that you are feeling this level of emotion, and do not try to flick it away with a dismissive 'Oh for goodness' sake, it's only a dog'. Remember, through oxytocin and other hormones our bodies are responding in the same way and to the same level as to our babies and children, so the range of emotions is normal and understandable.

Reflect on how you normally deal with stressful and conflicting emotions, and how you might prepare yourself for your new pup. Some of the things I consider important are:

O *Preparation* is key: It is worth investing time in choosing the right breed for your lifestyle, and preparing your home for the pup's arrival. Ensure you build your knowledge so you have some resources to lean on — it's worth it! Part E will provide you with more information on this.

O Build *support*: Identify a few understanding, supportive friends and family members who are experienced in raising pups, and/or you can join our online community at www.dogzen.com

O Recognise that puppy raising is a *short but intensive period*. This formative period is short, and so devoting the two months from getting your puppy to training is very achievable.

O Understand that it is an *emotional experience* akin to raising a child, so be kind to yourself and appreciate the highs and lows of helping your wee being grow.

O Grow your *situational awareness* to build your capacity to be present with your pup, effectively growing your mindfulness so you can recognise issues early so you can intervene.

Growing a calm and mindful training state

Our behaviour and its impact on our pups is often grossly under-estimated. Many of my clients comment on the calm training demeanour of myself and my team, and how it has such an impact on our dogs and pups. It is a critical part of my ability as a behaviourist, and it is something you can practise and grow, too. Remember, we are our pup's important secure base, so if we are not calm and confident our pups can easily read this and a sense of anxiety can communicate to them.

Pups and dogs respond well to us when they know we are calm and present. Our pups and dogs can often be a mirror of our own behaviours. We easily communicate this through our posture, tension on the lead, pheromones, facial expressions and tone.

To those who are dedicated to bonding with their pups and dogs, I recommend trying some form of mindfulness training to help focus your awareness on the present moment. This will grow your ability to be present, calm and aware of your pup, in the moment. This will help enormously with your training, as you will be more aware of your pup

— what he is doing, what is going on around him, and how he is/might respond, and therefore what you need to do to support him and be the mentor he needs you to be.

EXERCISE: MINDFULNESS PRACTICE — MORITA'S CONSTRUCTIVE LIVING PROCESS

One of the key mindfulness practices I recommend is Morita's four-step process called 'constructive living'. I have trained in it and rely on it a lot in my life. (Go to the To Do Institute if you would like more details: www.todoinstitute.org.) The four steps are outlined below, and think of these in terms of your training.

O *Know your purpose.* Be clear about what you want to achieve in this training session.
   — What is my overall larger purpose? To build a strong bond.
O *Accept your feelings.* Raising a pup is an emotional experience, so accept you will have a range of emotions through this time. You can't control your feelings, but you can control your actions, so focus on actions.
   — How am I feeling? Can I accept these feelings without judgement?
   — How does this impact on my training? What needs to be done now?
O *Do what needs to be done.* Know what you need to do for your pup at this moment and do it.
   — What steps will I take in training today?
O *Do it mindfully.* Be aware of what you are doing and the quality of that doing. Am I being effective? Is my pup learning and growing, happy and connected to me?
   — Am I being kind, empathic and compassionate? What do I need to do to support these?
   — Am I setting consistent, clear boundaries, or am I rewarding inappropriate behaviours?
   — Situational awareness. What is happening in the immediate area, and how will it impact on my pup and myself? How do I need to adapt to that?
   — Being present and focused. Am I being present with my pup, or am I distracted? If I am distracted, wiggle my toes and take three deep breaths.

— Understanding and insight. What am I seeing, and how does it help me understand my pup for this training session and for future ones?

The importance of situational awareness

Situational awareness is a critical skill you need as your pup's trusted mentor. Situational awareness is your ability to read a situation, interpret what is happening, and identify how you need to respond to provide your pup with clear guidance to keep her safe. In terms of your pup, this means:

○ recognising how your pup is feeling/reacting to a situation
○ recognising what is in the environment and how your pup might respond (e.g. other dogs, species, noises, people, children, etc.)
○ understanding your pup's targeting and alerting signals so you can intervene early
○ understanding your pup's triggers and how they stack, so you can respond proactively
○ having your tools immediately available when you need them.

You are an important part of your pup's eyes and ears on the world, helping her make sense of our world, recognising and responding early to help guide her. Growing your awareness of what is in the environment, anticipating how your pup might respond, and providing appropriate guidance for your pup are critical.

We are asking our pups to look to us for direction and guidance. They need to learn that they can trust our judgement in any given situation to keep them safe. Their trust in us grows as they experience our ability to keep them safe. Having good situational awareness builds that ability. I cannot over-emphasise how critical this skill is so your pup can trust you as her loving, supportive mentor. Mindfulness is situational awareness together with being non-judgemental and acting gently and calmly.

EXERCISE: PRACTISING SITUATIONAL AWARENESS

This exercise allows you to practise situational awareness, and is a mindfulness practice in its own right.

A busy environment — be aware of what is happening, what might happen and how your pup is responding. In the pair on the right, you can see good contact, and training gear on.

First, without your pup, go to a local place you will often visit with her. Before you enter the space, take three deep breaths and feel your feet on the ground. Be aware of:

O what your training purpose is

O how you are feeling

O what steps you will take in your training.

Do it mindfully:

O What do you see? What does the environment look like, and what is in it? What trees and flowers are there? What people? What dogs? What other animals? What traffic? What other things do you see? Name them to yourself. Keep a diary or journal while learning, if you like.

O How might your pup respond to these?

O What risks might you need to consider?

O How will this influence your training today?

Practise this exercise whenever you get the chance, as it will focus your attention on the present moment and what is going on in terms of your pup. I like to teach a simple 3-breath practice to anchor you and your attention before any training. Come back to your body, your equipment and your pup. Start there. When you pick up your clicker, breathe!

When you are ready, introduce your pup to the exercise and start the exercise from the top, taking your pup through each step.

You might even want to do this exercise with a training buddy first, without your pup. Verbalise the exercise to each other, then do it with your pup. Review the golden rules of training.

Learning from our mistakes

It is our natural inclination to want to do everything perfectly, particularly if it involves something cute, vulnerable and reliant on us. Remember self-compassion is as critical as your compassion to your pup. Pups do need steadiness, consistency and love; however, they are robust beings who can tolerate some mistakes.

Our self-compassion with our own mistakes will build our compassion towards our pup's mistakes, too. Just like you, they are beings who are trying to learn and do their best, and they will make mistakes. Be patient and kind to yourself and your pup as you both grow and learn together. It is true for both of you: you actually learn through making mistakes.

EXERCISE: CHECKING FOR YOUR MENTOR BOND AND WHAT TO FOCUS ON

Next time you are on a walk, think about your current relationship with your pup. Check to see:

O how close your pup remains to you and how often your pup looks up to see where you are

O whether your pup is relaxed or stressed

O whether your pup is controlled or out of control

O whether your pup looks at you, or makes his own decisions.

If your pup is in *contact* with you, he will often check in to see where you are and what you might want him to do. If not well bonded, you will find that your pup is often away or looking away from you, and you will find yourself looking and calling for him. It might seem like it is you doing the checking in — not your pup! If you think your bond with your pup could do with more work, head to Part D and do lots of joining up.

EXERCISE: HIDE-AND-SEEK

You can also play hide-and-seek games with your pup, so your pup is looking for where you are going more often. When you are in a safe place (contained and away from traffic and other hazards):

O hide from your pup when he is distracted and not looking at you

O make a clear and simple scent path away from the pup, and make sure he can follow that path as he seeks you out

O initially create a straight line to you, then add in some twists and turns, slowly making it harder as your pup succeeds

O make some alerting sound (gently call his name or whistle).

When your pup finds you, give him lots of praise and reward — make it fun!

Continue playing this game, making it harder and harder. The game becomes self-rewarding and reinforces your pup's connection to you — seeking you out (learning to check in and keep connected) — and means lots of fun and contact (reward) when he finds you.

TO FINISH: A BOND FOR LIFE

When I talk about that ultimate bond, it is the one that most of us dog owners have had maybe once in our lives — it is very special. However, it is possible to have this with any pup and dog if you know how to create it.

It is so important that we grow our awareness and understanding of the pups that share our homes. Make sure you watch your pup, observe him and grow in understanding of him. Pups are not machines — they are loveable, unique and by no means perfect. As with all relationships, we have to understand our pups, love them and allow their idiosyncrasies.

For me it is not about training our pups to perform in a machine-like state, but supporting them to joyfully navigate and live in our very odd and complex human world. Some will be easier than others, some trickier, whether they had a difficult start or just because they are! We need to guide them, mentor them, and ensure they fit well into our lives so that we are all happy. And understand what their glorious, unique characters are, and allow and celebrate that, too. Please don't expect them to be perfect.

I hope that investing time into creating a harmonious mentoring bond with your pup will be fun and rewarding for you both, as it is the very foundation to your life with your pup.

SUMMARY

Here is a quick reminder of the key aspects of building your bond with your pup. Understanding these will provide a very sound basis for building that bond, and ultimately help you succeed in your training and life together.

O Understand the nature of the bond — the foundation to everything.
O Develop the bond
  — mimicking Nature's techniques (secure base, helper role, follower response)
  — doing that through
    • a psychological bond — joining up
    • a spatial bond — the crate/clip station
    • teaching that nothing in life is free.

— Establish the family rules (agreement on how everyone will behave).
  • Build a shared language (how we talk to each other, including basic commands).
○ Nurture your role as the mentor:
  — what does a good bond look like?
  — what do you need to do?
  — how do you need to be?

Training Foundations

These foundational principles, tools and techniques will enable you to build a harmonious, loving relationship and grow a happy, confident pup. It is also your chance to get out and start practising, so enjoy!

Puppy Zen training foundations act as the toolkit of our techniques and tools, all of which have a clear purpose and function. How pups learn our methods and the shared language we build are all described in some detail. This is also a reference section for you to come back to and clarify exactly how to do things. It shows you how to finish off and how to proof (establish) the learned behaviours out into the real world. Most of all, the bonding and socialisation techniques are demonstrated. Don't forget there are more than 30 videos on our website on what to do and how to do it, for those who are visual learners. Go to www.dogzen.com/products/

To master the training foundations, we need to build the bond and create a shared language with our puppies. To do this, we need to know:

- how pups learn
- the ways we train our pups
- the Puppy Zen toolkit
- the basic commands
- the key training techniques to create the bond, enable our pups to meet and greet other dogs and people, and cross-foster onto other species
- how to proof behaviours and fade the clicker.

Chapter 9

How pups learn

How pups learn refers to the ways in which they absorb information so they can grow new skills, knowledge and abilities. Understanding how our pups learn helps us determine how to best train our pups, and in particular understand the tools and techniques used.

THE IMPORTANCE OF THE FORMATIVE PERIOD IN LEARNING

As we noted in Part A, the formative period plays a huge part in a pup and adult dog's ability to learn. It is a period of enormous brain growth and optimal learning in the pup, and lays the critical foundations for the adult dog.

This intense learning state is in part because our pup is in a less anxious state, due to the evolution of smaller adrenals and less fight-flight reactivity. This makes them more confident and less prone to fear. When pups are fearful, they go into a non-learning state, where learning stops and development is compromised.

Pups learn in the formative period, and when trained in this period important behavioural switches and learning pathways are turned on that enable pups to retain more, be more confident, and understand their place and role in the family.

9.1   THE NATURE OF DOGS' INTELLIGENCE

An animal's intelligence and the way it understands the world is related to what its ancestors were adapted to do. Most of the dog's pre-domestication intelligence goes back to the wolf, whose intelligence was centred around hunting: navigation, co-operation and observation. Hunting large prey in very diverse environments led to the development of co-operativity, sociability and pack living. High levels of adaptability and learning ability were required to adjust to the different environments and social dynamics. We take full advantage of this learning ability in our training.

Dogs use us as intelligent tools

Often the results of cognitive tests on dogs have indicated that they are less intelligent in certain areas than the wolf. It turns out that many of the tests were misled by the fact that the dogs were in fact looking to humans for direction. More specifically, the dogs' attention was focused on where the humans' attention was, what they touched and their smells, and this interfered with the results.

Dogs were factoring us in as intelligent tools to help them solve problems. They knew that watching us or other dogs was the best short-cut to working out how to do something. Reading us, learning from us and asking us are powerful and intelligent strategies. It is this shift in focus to us that has become central to the dog's intelligence, thereby transforming it.

It is this shift to us that we utilise in our training with them. In Puppy Zen we work a lot with our pup's focus on us, cultivating and enhancing this predisposition by reinforcing the mentor bond, the bond gaze and the follower response.

DOG'S INTELLIGENCE — CAPABILITIES AND LIMITATIONS

Understanding our pups' and dogs' intelligence capabilities and limitations will ensure they can do what we are asking them to do in training. Whenever you are teaching your pup something new, review this list to see whether he is capable of learning it, saving you and your pup hours of needless frustration.

Capabilities

Pups have the ability to:

o co-operate with us
o recruit human help
o understand our communication (postural, vocal, intonation), including the 'yes' and 'no' commands

- read our moods and emotions (not always correctly)
- attend to our face, eyes, gestures and body orientation
- be aware if we are not attentive or are distracted
- potentially experience empathy and do consolation activities
- discriminate objects and classes of objects
- make inferences when solving problems, and generalise these to solve new problems
- mimic others and learn by observation
- understand simple problem solving
- remember the things that are most important to them.

Limitations

Here are some of our pups' learning and training limitations:

- Our behaviour can interfere with and influence pups, overriding their own senses at times.
- Pups can get confused by multiple words.
- Dogs don't consider a long way ahead, unless it is an issue critical to survival.
- Old memories and default behaviours can interfere with new ones.
- Dogs cannot understand the physics of their world (e.g. gravity or things moving out of sight), so therefore are not good at puzzle-type activities unless especially trained.

Dogs are not as good as wolves at navigating without landmarks.

Dogs can do some pretty smart stuff!

One study showed that Chaser, a Border Collie, could remember over 1100 objects. He was even shown to be able to put them into different piles that classified them into toys, non-toys, etc. All of this by 3 years old, which means he was still learning — that is incredible!

Teaching my amazing German Shepherd Labrador cross Reggie to fly a Cessna 172 as the world's first flying dog, in England in 2015, has to be one of the highlights of my training career. It involved Reggie learning nearly a hundred different things, including working the yoke, banking, accepting turbulence, wearing a harness and so much more.

We also taught Monty, Porter and Ginny to drive a car, the first dogs in the world to do so. Millions of people watched the YouTube

I never cease to be amazed at what we can achieve if we put our minds and hearts to it!

video, and 100 million people tweeted — clearly people are astounded by what dogs can learn. I never cease to be amazed at what we can achieve if we put our minds and hearts to it!

Ultimately, however, it is the strength of our bond, and our ability to communicate with our pups and dogs what we want to teach them, that really define how far we can take our collaboration. It is not just the dog's intelligence.

9.2   THE LEARNING STATE IN PUPS

The learning state is a psycho-physiological state that is inherent in the formative period. It is the state your pup needs to be in for him to learn, and is a foundation of Puppy Zen. It is critical that you can identify this state, switch your pup into it and maintain it while training.

The learning state is largely controlled by the autonomic nervous system, which has two sides:

O The *para-sympathetic* nervous system, which controls the *rest-and-digest* state, where a pup is calm, relaxed and not fearful. In this state your pup has the capacity to focus and learn, and is happy to eat.

O The *sympathetic* nervous system, which controls sympathetic arousal — the *fight-flight* state. In this state your pup can't eat or learn. Dogs generally can't override the 'don't eat when stressed' function, so if they stop eating it is a very powerful indicator that they are out of the learning state.

RECOGNISING THE LEARNING STATE

Your pup is in a learning state when:

O he has a calm, happy and focused disposition
O his body language and posture are relaxed
O he is attentive to you
O he eats calmly and does not snatch when presented with food (if he has normal appetite)
O he has a normal or lowered pulse rate
O his pupil size is normal — there is no dilation (expansion).

Learning state —
eating is a good sign.

Non-learning state — not
eating is a giveaway!

Unsurprisingly, the polar opposites will let you know when your pup is in a non-learning state. You pup is in a non-learning state (fight–flight) when:

- O most critically, he is *not* eating food when offered it
- O he has a stressed, anxious, aggressive or hyperactive disposition
- O his pupils are dilated, he has an increased pulse rate, and is shaking or panting
- O he is showing fear or avoidance behaviours, such as escape, submission, fear or hyperactivity
- O he displays postural indicators, such as hackles up, ears back or down, tail lowered and not wagging, posture lowered
- O he shows displacement behaviours; that is, coping behaviours that seem out of context, such as licking, squinting eyes, yawning, scratching, ground sniffing (dogs do these to avoid conflict or threat, so do these to distract themselves while simultaneously signalling avoidance and that they are not a threat)
- O acting in a predatory manner (e.g. chasing or hunting cats and birds)
- O subject to inappropriate punishment or being dominated excessively.

EXERCISE : LEARNING STATE TEST

The easiest way to test whether your pup is in a learning state is to note whether or not he is eating, or whether he is snatching food. If your pup is not taking food then he is probably not in a learning state. An important indicator that your pup is close to going into a non-learning state is if he starts to take food more aggressively, and snaps or nibbles hard to get it out of your hand. Observe and learn what situations might trigger your pup into a non-learning state so you can be prepared to prevent it.

How to switch your pup into a learning state

This is called *counter-conditioning* or *switch-conditioning*. It is a very important training technique, derived from human psychology.

The primary tools we use are the clicker and food rewards. I know it sounds contradictory that when your pup is in a non-learning state and is disinterested in food you need to use food to put him into a learning state — but if you do it the right way, it works. Food is a primary resource in Nature, so is naturally one of the strongest drivers in a dog. Food anticipation is the surest way to get a pup to switch into a learning state. I'm sure that you have seen it many times with your own pup or dog: you bring out food and suddenly your pup/dog becomes very focused and attentive; it dampens fight-flight.

By conditioning your pup to anticipate food, you can switch him into a focused learning state. I do this using a clicker. Once your pup learns about the clicker and its association with food, you can use it to switch your pup into a learning state. After a few days of training with food rewards and the clicker, your pup will start to switch quickly, start to work for you and look to you for direction. Soon the mere presence of the tools (the clicker and a training pouch with food) becomes a switch. Test this yourself after a few days of training with the tools. Watch closely the next time you bring out the clicker and pouch, and see how quickly your pup starts throwing a 'Zen sit', and focusing attentively on you.

Basic commands (learned cues, like 'sit', 'down' or 'stay') can also be used to switch pups into a learning state. Once taught, they act as a signal to pups to pay attention as something is being asked of them. When your pup responds to a command, he is working from the pre-frontal cortex (the thinking brain), which dampens any fight-flight or emotional responses, helping switch your pup into a learning state. That's why we almost always begin training sessions by running through some basic commands that are well known or understood, such as 'sit' and 'down', using the clicker, to help activate the learning state.

'Zen down' in particular is a powerful learning state, as the position stimulates the vagus nerve by relaxing the dorsal muscles and activating the 'gut brain'. This dampens anxiety or fear reactions, allowing focus on the source of the food, which enhances learning and calms your pup, encouraging the learning state (rest and digest).

If your pup is highly anxious or aggressive, it can be more difficult to switch into a learning state, because he is in a high level of sympathetic arousal. In this situation, take away as many stressors as possible (loud noises, traffic, etc.), so your pup isn't overwhelmed and distracted by these stimuli, particularly during the early learning phase.

EXERCISE: HOW TO SWITCH YOUR DOG INTO A LEARNING STATE

Once you have learnt the basic commands and use of the clicker (covered later in this section), you can try this exercise to see just how effective the clicker is in switching on the learning state.

O Make sure you have your tools present (through sight and smell):
— use food (it is a primary resource in Nature)
— prepare the clicker (have it paired/associated with food).
O Remove stressors from the learning environment by simplifying it (close curtains and doors, turn off the radio).
O Do 'sit', 'down', 'wait' — these cues (commands) become switches by moving your pup into their pre-frontal cortex and out of emotion.
O Pop your pup into 'Zen down' (this activates the 'gut brain' to calm the body). See page 180.

How to maintain a learning state

Lots of things can switch your pup out of a learning state, many of which are fear-related, so it is important you have a healthy bond and your pup feels safe (the secure base effect). Establishing a trusting relationship is critical: the safer your pups feels, the more his nervous system will remain calm and relaxed, allowing him to remain focused and in a learning state. Joining up and contact act as switches, too, and even just calling your pup's name (if you have a good bond) activates oxytocin and creates that calming effect.

The elements that help keep your dog in a learning state include:
O a trusting, happy bond with you
O the presence of food
O managing access to food, so that day food is for training and is high-value, while less palatable food is given at night in your pup's meal
O a safe and simple environment
O you being focused, calm, alert and non-threatening
O clarity and consistency in your communication
O teaching your dog clear boundaries — what he can and cannot do
O when appropriate, the presence of another friendly, confident dog that can provide social facilitation.

Keep your pup happy and 'up', and don't bore him with too long a session. Don't use any corrections (harsh or abrupt intonation); instead, use a 'wrong' marker said in a neutral tone if needed. (See more about the 'wrong' command in the section on basic commands.)

9.3   THE WAYS PUPS LEARN

The key ways pups learn that relate to Puppy Zen are outlined below. Now you might say, 'But why are you telling me this stuff? It's a bit heavy!' Well, primarily it is so you understand more deeply why we use the most important tools and techniques in Puppy Zen: so, trust me, it's worth it! Note that the use of classical learning psychology and terminology still underpins modern learning psychology (e.g. reinforcers and punishers). However, when you see terminology like 'punishers', understand them in the modern context of setting boundaries, providing consequences and contrast so pups can learn better.

Dogs learn in a number of different ways. The key ones for Puppy Zen training are associative learning, reinforcement and punishment (correction), learning by contrast, desensitisation and counter-conditioning. If you are interested in a more detailed explanation of the ways dogs learn, then head to my book *Dog Zen*.

Associative learning

Associative learning is one of the most fundamental forms of learning that all species use. All mammalian species, including us, learn by association between an event and an associated positive stimuli (do more of) or negative stimuli (avoid). Pups from 4 weeks old already have associative learning capacities.

A natural example of a positive association is a pup finding food in a rubbish bin. After a few rewarding experiences/associations (finding food when searching in rubbish bins), this will increase the frequency of the behaviour of searching through bins. The fact the pup gets rewarded now and again (intermittent schedule of reward) maintains the behaviour, just like the gambler on his one-armed bandit ('just one more!').

Conversely, dogs also learn by negative associations, such as getting pricked by a hedgehog and learning to avoid spiny creatures. Therefore, investigating hedgehog behaviours correspondingly decreases in frequency. These associations can also be called 'punishers', in this case, a natural consequence.

Reinforcement and punishment (correction)

Reinforcement and punishment (correction) are the two forms of associative learning. These terms are defined by their effect on behaviour; both can be either positive or negative. Reinforcement increases the frequency of a behaviour, whereas punishment decreases the frequency of a behaviour. We also have the extinction of a behaviour through no reinforcement.

Reinforcement and correction are learning methods that occur in Nature. We mimic these learning methods in our training, allowing us to distinguish what is appropriate and inappropriate behaviour (set direction and boundaries). What is important in Puppy Zen is the humane and intelligent use of them, mimicking Nature as best as possible. Where the reinforcement or correction comes from, from the pup's point of view, is critical, ensuring our relationship is protected.

Reinforcement

I am going to go into some depth in this section as *positive reinforcement* is the main principle behind the clicker — the primary tool used in Puppy Zen. A clicker is an amazing tool: if you don't use one you can't say you are doing Puppy Zen, because without this tool you won't achieve 90 per cent of what I recommend. So please get one and use it — there's nothing like it! You can use a 'Yes!' marker, too.

Reinforcement must follow immediately on completion of a behaviour, so the behaviour seems to cause the reinforcement.

In training terms, a positive reinforcer is the offering of something your pup likes. If a pup does something like a successful sit (the behaviour), then you follow immediately with a pat or food reward (the positive reinforcer). The association of the behaviour and the reinforcer increases the likelihood of that behaviour occurring again in the future. So you must make sure that the timing of the reinforcer is immediate.

A negative reinforcer is the removal of something your pup dislikes, such as being let inside (removing separation from you). The removal of the thing he dislikes also increases the frequency of a behaviour.

In training terms, a positive reinforcer is offering something your pup likes.

For example, if he is quiet you let him inside, so you are removing his separation from you (negative reinforcer) and increasing the frequency of the behaviour (being quiet). Your seat-belt beep does the same for you. When you click your belt (behaviour), you take away the thing you don't like, which is the loud beeping (negative reinforcer).

A conditioned secondary reinforcer (also known as a marker) is a stimulus that is originally meaningless (like a click or a whistle) but becomes associated (conditioned) with a primary positive reinforcer (the true reward like food, a pat, praise or something else your pup likes). A marker is any stimulus that can identify the right behaviour easily, and is immediate, discrete and difficult to confuse with other things. It is best if the marker doesn't have any confusing emotional overtones or features, the way speech can have.

THE CLICKER

Clicker training is a form of conditioned secondary reinforcement, and is the most effective training tool I have come across in my 40 years of training. The clicker is the conditioned secondary reinforcer, and the food (or whatever reward you choose) is the primary positive reinforcer. The click sound is a promise of a food reward, and must always be followed by a food reward. As outlined earlier, another lesser known but extremely important purpose of the clicker is as a switch conditioner: the click and food anticipation help switch your pup into a learning state.

I like to think of the clicker like a camera: you click immediately when you see the behaviour you want. You can imagine that you are trying to take a photo to show the exact moment your pup demonstrates the behaviour you want to train, and make the *click* the moment that happens. This immediacy is why the clicker is one of the most effective training tools — it is more precise at marking the behaviour, as the *click* is instant (voice and food rewards are slower, and often mixed with confusing emotional messages due to tone and posture). Remember, your pup doesn't know what you want him to learn, but the clicker makes this exacting and clear.

Once your pup understands how the clicker works (and that it is always followed by a yummy treat), he will learn faster each time you use it to train a new behaviour. Now that's encouraging! The size of the reinforcer (if food) should be as small as possible, so you can do more repetitions and keep drive high. Every now and then when your pup does exceptionally well (e.g. comes back to you on command in a crowded dog park), you can jackpot the reward (give 3–5 times more than normal) to reinforce exceptional performance.

Schedule of reinforcement

The number of times and when we click and reward is called the schedule of reinforcement. To start, we click each time we get the desired behaviour: this is called a continuous schedule of reward, and is what creates the initial, important association of the requested behaviour with the click and food reward. We do this when we are establishing behaviour.

Once the behaviour is established (approximately 90 per cent consistent), we move to an intermittent or random schedule of reinforcement. That is, we start to click and reward on every third or so successful attempt. Think of it operating like the gambler's 'one-armed bandit': what keeps the pup trying is he does not know which effort will result in a reward. Remember it is the number of clicks that you are reducing — each time you do click, you reward with food.

In summary, use continuous reinforcement to establish a behaviour, and an intermittent schedule to maintain the behaviour long term. The clicker is only a temporary tool, and so we later reduce the frequency of the click and reward until you completely fade both for the behaviour you are training. However, when you begin to train a new behaviour, you start with a continuous schedule of reward again. Depending on the complexity of the behaviour, you will fade the clicker over a number of months as you proof (establish it) in increasingly complex environments.

Punishment (correction or consequence)

A punisher is the opposite of a reinforcer, in that it decreases the likelihood of a behaviour occurring. Positive punishment is when the behaviour decreases in frequency due to the delivery of something undesirable, such as a check (a snappy collar pull from the lead), a growly tone or the pup being put outside. A negative punishment is the removal of a reward (or resource) in response to inappropriate behaviour with the goal of decreasing the behaviour in the future. For example, if your pup is hyper-excitable inside your home, you might put your pup outside away from you (removing contact). This is essentially how time-out works.

Consequences or corrections (punishment) occur in Nature to enable pups to learn how to behave appropriately and stay safe. For example, in the wild a dog would growl at or lip raise (signal) before reprimanding a pup if he bit too hard in play. In Puppy Zen, the consequence (correction) mimics natural consequences.

The primary correction we use in Puppy Zen is the effective check (this is a snappy collar check). Puppy Zen then enhances this by ideally following it with a contrasting positive reinforcer as the pup does an acceptable alternative behaviour (often a click and reward). This contrast is critical in Puppy Zen (see the section on contrast training, below).

Learning by contrast — bringing reinforcement and correction together

All animals learn by contrast — we need to understand hot in order to understand cold (and vice versa). Your pup needs the contrast between reward (clicking and rewarding the behaviour you want, e.g. playing with a good toy) and apparent natural consequences (correction if your pup chews your favourite cushion). Contrast offers choice, and choice allows animals to make decisions and learn by them. If there isn't enough contrast between behaviours, your pup can't learn because it is the contrast that facilitates the decision and therefore the learning. It is the combination that creates the contrast, a powerful learning context that is much faster than either reinforcement or correction alone, and maintains the behaviour long term.

Safety and avoidance

Primarily in Puppy Zen we use contrast training to teach safety and avoidance. We teach and reinforce that safety is with us (through positive reinforcement like the clicker) and that our pups should avoid the things we want them to avoid (cats, chickens, our favourite shoes) through remote correction.

The most important thing in terms of correction is where your pup sees the correction to be coming from. We aim for the correction to be remote from you (not associated with you), essentially teaching your pup that the item he is acting inappropriately towards (e.g. the other dog or plant or chicken) appears to be delivering the correction. I call this *apparent natural consequences*, and it is often achieved using a long-line. We use this for avoidance training, teaching our pup to avoid inappropriate items like chickens or our favourite cushion.

There are two reasons why it is important that the item is offering the correction and not you. Firstly, your pup associates the correction with the item, so if it sees a similar item again he will have learnt to avoid or relate to it properly, with or without you being present (avoidance). Secondly, he will not associate the correction with you, which will preserve your all-important bond (safety). This is an important effect that reinforces your positive status, because you appear not to be delivering the correction, and instead are helping protect your pup from the world (being his ally). Your goal is to build, not weaken, your bond with your pup while ensuring that safe boundaries (e.g. not

Adult dog providing consequence to moderate pup behaviour.

killing the chickens) are established, so our training is enriching not inhibiting.

Conditioned aversive signal (the 'no' command)

Once the avoidance behaviour has been firmly established, and importantly not associated with you, then you can introduce a *conditioned aversive signal*, and in Puppy Zen we generally use the 'no' command. The conditioned aversive signal ('no') says that something negative (a consequence) will happen unless the pup stops what he is doing. This signal (cue) warns (not threatens) your pup that a consequence for his behaviour is about to happen. It gives your pup an opportunity to make a choice to stop their inappropriate behaviour and avoid correction (and so succeed).

This is a more effective way to learn than threats, as your pup has a chance to avoid the consequence (make a decision). The opportunity to succeed increases the chances he will avoid the correction and stop the behaviour. Go to the basic commands 'No' section to see how and when you teach this cue.

Sequence of training

The sequence of how we teach these is essential. Firstly, you create avoidance of an item by using apparent natural consequence, using a correction remote from yourself (a snappy collar check on a long-line). This ensures your pup associates the correction with the item, and therefore avoids it while maintaining your bond (you as safety), as you are not associated with the correction.

Secondly, once this avoidance behaviour is firmly established, then (and only then) can you apply your conditioned aversive signal ('no') to provide your pup a warning so he can make a decision and avoid the consequence (reinforcing your role as their ally and mentor).

Habituation, desensitisation and counter-conditioning

We use the learning processes of habituation, desensitisation and counter-conditioning to help our pups adapt to social and environmental stimuli.

Habituation is a natural process of merely exposing your pup to stimuli at the right time; you don't have to actively organise the order of stimuli or switch your pup into a learning state. It just happens through natural exposure as it is happening at the right time in a pup's development. This is the common way pups learn in their critical periods.

If you haven't exposed your pup to stimuli at the right time of his development, then you will need to use desensitisation and counter-conditioning methods, as your pup has now potentially developed aversive responses to the stimuli he hasn't been exposed to. We also can use desensitisation even in appropriate critical periods to speed up learning and ensure things go well.

Desensitisation is when you expose your pup to stimuli he finds frightening in an ordered, systematic way, which you then generalise into everyday situations. To do this you order the stimuli your pup finds frightening from least fearful to most, and expose your pup in this carefully ordered manner while counter-conditioning (switching into the learning state) and rewarding for appropriate responses. We will use desensitisation and counter-conditioning a lot in Part D.

This is also a very important technique when treating behaviour issues in dogs, particularly fear-related behaviour and phobias. The technique was field-tested on humans, then extended into dog training — some might say it is even more effective on dogs than humans!

HOW PUPS LEARN AS IT APPLIES TO PUPPY ZEN

O Pups learn by associative learning (learning by association between an event and an associated stimuli) through both positive and negative associations.

O We use positive reinforcement to teach our pups what we want them to do (e.g. click and reward will increase the frequency of desired behaviour).

O We use punishment (correction or consequence) to teach pups what we don't want them to do through mimicking natural consequences (e.g. an effective check).

O Pups learn by contrast: this is what I want; this is what I don't want.

O In Puppy Zen we use contrast training to teach safety (us as our pup's mentor) and avoidance (things we want our pup to avoid).

O We establish safety through positive reinforcement (click and reward) and avoidance through correction (remote effective check).

O We do the effective check remotely to ensure that the correction is not associated with us, thereby reinforcing our bond and our role as ally (safety).

O Once avoidance behaviour is firmly established we can introduce the conditioned aversive signal (the 'no' command) to help our pup avoid the correction and make a decision.

O Habituation, desensitisation and counter-conditioning are ways we expose our pups to social and environmental stimuli.

O Habituation is through exposure to stimuli at the right time in our pup's development.

O Desensitisation and counter-conditioning are needed once we are outside the critical period for learning. We expose our pup to an increasing hierarchy of these stimuli (desensitisation) while using a clicker to reward calm, appropriate responses (switching our pups into the learning state — called counter-conditioning).

You will soon see how we use these principles of learning throughout our training techniques.

Chapter 10

Ways to train pups

There are two overarching training processes we use when we train our pups and dogs: we are either creating (shaping) new appropriate behaviours or modifying (changing) old inappropriate behaviours.

10.1   SHAPING AND MODIFYING BEHAVIOUR

Shaping is the creation of new behaviours in a pup or dog, rather than modifying old behaviours. It is much easier to achieve than changing established behaviour patterns in older dogs. This is particularly fundamental in puppy training in the formative period, where you have a blank slate and are teaching all new behaviours. Because you are teaching new behaviours, most of the training is focused on positive reinforcement, as we don't need to remove inappropriate behaviours as much (particularly up to 3 months of age). I usually use the clicker and food rewards as my preferred shaping tool. Some contrast training is needed by 3 months of age, as pups learn inappropriate behaviours and start pushing boundaries as their confidence grows.

Shaping is done by breaking a behaviour into small pieces or steps, in order to teach it in stages and build it back into a sequence. However, some of the simpler behaviours, like a 'sit' or a 'down', can be taught in a single step, so you won't have to shape it in increments.

The core principles of shaping are:
O Use shaping to establish any new behaviour.
O Break behaviours into small increments or steps and outline the steps required to achieve the behaviour.
O Induce the behaviour largely through luring (drawing the pup into a desired behaviour through food or touch).
O Starting with the first step, click and reward behaviour that is close

enough to the desired behaviour. Click and reward this for a few times to consolidate.

O Then start successively rewarding behaviour that is getting closer and closer to the desired behaviour (this is called successive approximation).

O You can use the 'wrong' command with older pups to help guide them. With younger pups in the early stages of training this has the potential to distract them or shut them down, so it is best to concentrate on small increments towards the end goal.

Behaviour modification

It doesn't always go as we hope, so we also focus on modifying behaviour problems where necessary. This requires the changing of old habits (inappropriate behaviours) and replacing them with the new behaviours we want. Behaviour modification becomes important in older pups that have developed inappropriate behaviour. For example, with an aggressive older pup that has poor meet-and-greet skills, we will first stop them rushing up and barking (modifying old behaviour), then replace that behaviour with appropriate social greets (shaping new behaviour). The main techniques we use here are contrast training, counter-conditioning and desensitisation.

10.2   THE ESSENTIAL RULES OF TRAINING

How you set up your training sessions can make or break your success, so it is worth following these guidelines to support yourself and your pup as best as you can.

Keep the environment simple

O Keep the environment as distraction-free as possible when training new behaviours, so be aware of olfactory, visual and auditory factors that might distract your pup.

O Make sure you are the most interesting thing in the area — your pup should be focused on you and what you are asking.

O Exercise your pup moderately beforehand, to blow off steam first and keep her calm.

Set up each training session and keep tasks simple

O Make sure your pup is in a learning state.

With pups we are most often shaping behaviour, rather than modifying it.

- Set up your training objective — know what you are training before you get started and stick to it.
- Train one thing at a time so your pup doesn't get confused.
- Train simple tasks — break bigger tasks into small steps, and then teach each step (shaping).
- Keep your training sessions short (approximately 5-10 minutes), particularly when you are training new behaviours.
- Finish on a good note: make sure the first and last thing your pup does is the right thing, as that is what she will remember best.
- Finish a training session with play (like a tug toy) and/or a calm walk, then clip her up on her clip station or kennel/crate for 15 minutes, so her brain gets an opportunity to consolidate.

Your role is important
- Be patient, consistent, dependable and predictable.
- Don't rush: sometimes repetition is necessary.
- Be aware of your posture, voice intonations and mood.
- If you feel impatient or frustrated, either calm yourself or

Keep the training environment simple to start off with.

finish the session.

- Take care to have the same trainer during the training phase of each command, so your pup has consistency.

Have effective commands

- When you are teaching a new command, start by visual signals (ideally using a food lure that becomes a hand signal).
- When your pup is performing consistently with the hand signal, introduce the spoken command on top of the hand signal.
- Word commands should be simple: one word/single syllable, don't change them, and don't mix meanings.
- Check your timing: are you using the commands and the clicker at the right time?
- Make sure you release your pup from the command: if you ask your pup to wait, make sure you let him know when it's okay to come out of 'wait' (e.g. say 'Okay' to signal release).

Your pup's name is not a command

O Only use your pup's name to orient your pup to you. (Let your pup know you are talking to her, not her mate!)

O Keep names short — ideally one syllable (or use a nickname).

O Don't use your pup's name as a command; for example, yelling 'Spot, Spot, Spot!' when you want Spot to come to you. Instead, say: 'Spot. Come!'

O Using her name just tells your pup who you are talking to, and to pay attention (especially if you have other dogs); the command then tells your pup what you want her to do.

Make training fun

O Keep training positive but calm.

O Praise regularly, but don't overstimulate and take your pup out of a learning state.

O Accept that neither you nor the pup is perfect, and that mistakes are part of learning.

O Remember pups learn by trial and error.

O Reward your pup with play and/or a calm walk after a successful training session, then rest.

Rewards hierarchy

O Start with a continuous schedule of reinforcement: click and reward every time your pup does the correct behaviour to help establish it.

O Move to an intermittent reward (rewarding every now and then) once behaviour is 90 per cent established.

O Fade the use of the clicker once you are confident that the behaviour is established in complex environments (e.g. high-arousal places like a dog park). This is called proofing.

O Know your pup's preferred food treats and the order of preference. Use high-value food rewards for training unless your pup is hyper food-motivated, in which case you might need to use low-value food so she doesn't get too distracted by the food.

Your body language is important

For *drawing commands*, when you are asking your pup to come towards you or be with you (e.g. 'come' or 'heel'), you are being friendly and encouraging.

○ Your body language should be inviting and non-threatening.
○ Use happy 'up' tones when speaking.
○ Your body should not be in a square-on posture; instead, turn slightly three-quarters on to your dog.
○ Bending or squatting down to lower your body can help you seem less assertive.
○ No staring — smile and be encouraging.

For *fixed commands*, when you want your pup to stay in one place (e.g. 'sit', 'down', 'wait', 'stay'), you are asking your pup to stay put, maybe away from you).
○ Use a slightly firmer tone of voice.
○ Have your body square-on, and make eye contact that is a little more assertive.
○ Increase this as you get firmer, and deepen your intonation slightly, but start out lightly.
○ As your pup succeeds, ease the pressure. Again you are offering contrast for your pup to learn. Remember: be responsive to your pup's temperament, and use only enough pressure to be effective.

Applying how pups learn to training

Now that we have covered how pups learn and the ways we train them, let's apply that to our training tools and techniques. In the next section we will first introduce you to all of the key tools we use in Puppy Zen, then show you how to teach your pup the basic commands using those tools. Once we have both the foundation tools and the basic commands in place, we bring them together so you can learn the key training techniques we use. Finally, we outline how to fade the clicker and proof these techniques and behaviours into everyday situations. That is, we ensure that our techniques are effective in more challenging everyday situations, as opposed to contained training environments. Remember, for training to be successful your pup must be in a learning state. Not being in a learning state is one of the biggest barriers to learning. Master identifying, switching and maintaining a learning state in your pup and you are well on track towards mastering your training.

Chapter 11

The Puppy Zen toolkit

Here I will take you through all of the tools and techniques you will need to successfully complete my puppy training programme. We will look at the purposes of the tools, what role they play in mimicking Nature, and how they come together to effectively build your relationship and train your pup.

The primary purpose of our tools is to shape our shared language and communicate to our pups exactly what we want them to do. Our methods are based primarily on positive reinforcement and the use of natural or apparently natural consequences to shape boundaries and consequences, and to build strong relationships. Our tools are designed to give as much information to our pups as possible, in order to make their decisions easy.

11.1   THE CLICKER — HOW TO USE IT

Earlier we looked at what a clicker is and its basic premise. This section is focused on how to use it effectively. Do not underestimate how powerful the clicker is. It is well worth the time you invest in learning to use it.

Remember the clicker, when timed well, is a conditioned secondary reinforcement tool. It *marks* the right behaviour with the *click* sound, and is paired with a *primary positive reinforcer* (a food reward) that reinforces the behaviour we are training. It is like a camera, as it highlights to the pup exactly what we want.

All about the clicker
- The clicker is a small hand-held tool with some form of button or metal strip that makes a distinctive *click* sound when pressed.
- The *click* acts as a *marker* (indicator) that tells your pup exactly what you want him to do (what is being reinforced).
- It is also a *switch conditioner* that gets your pup into a learning state.

O The click is a promise to your pup that he will get a treat, so when you click the clicker, you must *always* reward your pup with a small piece of high-value food.

O It is more effective than just praise or verbal markers, because it has none of the confusing emotional messages that your voice may contain. However, verbal markers are better than no marker at all.

O *Timing is everything*: you must click exactly when your pup does the behaviour you want. Timing is critical. For example, for 'sit' you click as soon as your pup's bottom hits the ground.

O Click and reward every time at first, and then once it is going well move to an intermittent schedule of click and reward to retain the behaviour. Never fade the food from the clicker; you are reducing the *click* and food together.

O It is temporary: you fade it once the behaviour is well established (see the section on proofing in Part D). However, bring it back at intervals, especially if you feel that your pup is relapsing or you want to start training a new behaviour.

Learning to use a clicker

Equipment required

O Clicker

O Pouch filled with high-value food (small pieces of cooked chicken, cheese or dog roll)

O Hand-held lead

O Retractable lead or long-line

O Tennis ball

EXERCISE: MASTERING TIMING OF THE CLICKER

O Make sure your pup is not within hearing distance.

O With your clicker ready, take a tennis ball in your right hand and drop it from waist-height.

O The second the ball touches the ground, click.

O Practise this a few times, and once you are confident with your timing, start working with your pup.

O Remember that your pup will complicate things quickly, so make sure you are ready and confident.

The clicker — the most powerful training tool.

Getting your pup started on the clicker

Preparation

- Start in a quiet, inside space with minimum distractions — a corner works well for highly distractible pups.
- Tie a wristband to the loop end of the clicker, so that it stays available at all times.
- Secure the clicker to the wrist of your non-dominant hand (your left hand if you are right-handed, and vice versa). The length of the wrist band should allow the clicker to sit in your hand. If possible, use your left hand for holding the lead and clicker, so that your dog is on the preferred left side of you.
- Have a pouch that has a wide, open mouth, with high-value food inside, tied to your waist, and accessible to your free hand.
- Cut the food into very small pieces so you can do lots of repetition: repetition is more important than the amount of food given each time. (Ensure that training food gets taken out of your pup's overall diet.)

Introducing your pup to the clicker

O First you need to teach your pup to associate the clicker with food (the reward).

O Some pups initially will be wary of the sound of the clicker, particularly if they are sensitive to noise. This will change quite quickly. However, it is important to not frighten your pup with the clicker, so test it carefully.

O I recommend using a very soft-sounding puppy clicker so your pup doesn't create negative associations to the clicker.

O As an additional precaution, start using your puppy clicker behind your back, to reduce the noise.

O Throw the food reward on the floor, and click as your puppy eats it.

O You are trying to get your pup focused on the food, not so much the clicker at this stage, so, to ensure your pup is not too intensely focused on the clicker, start by throwing the food away from you so your pup moves away from you, too. This helps desensitise the pup to the clicker, creating a positive association (this is called 'loading the clicker').

O Watch your pup's reaction. If he is focused on the food and isn't reactive to the *click* sound, then all good, continue on with your clicker in front of you as normal. However, make sure you keep the clicker away from your pup's head and ears to start with.

O If your pup is at all reactive with the clicker noise when the clicker is behind your back, wrap it in a piece of material to muffle the sound. Making sure the clicker is not too near your pup's head or ears, work the clicker from the opposite side of your body to where your pup is.

O For very sensitive pups the muffling material needs to be thicker, and be very careful — maybe try working it from within your pocket. Don't let the pup get a fright from the clicker, so be conservative.

O For a moderately sensitive pup, 10–20 repetitions should be enough to get the food association kicking in. Watch for your pup relaxing through this time.

O Once your pup works out the food association with the clicker, he will love it!

Take care with sound-sensitive pups. Test carefully and use a puppy clicker, which has a lighter sound.

EXERCISE: USING THE CLICKER TO TEACH COMMANDS

Go to basic commands 'Sit' section (page 177) to practise using the clicker to teach a command.

Removing the click and food lure: it's just a training tool

○ Once your pup is performing the command consistently, start removing the click and the food (that is, click and reward intermittently — not every time), so that the behaviour becomes reliant on the hand and verbal signals alone.

○ Clicking and rewarding intermittently will make the behaviour more resistant to falling away (extinction).

○ Click and reward less and less frequently, until you eventually fade the clicker completely. Remember, you are fading the click *and* the reward: never remove the food from the clicker. Once a behaviour is fully trained, it is okay to occasionally use food only.

Teaching the 'sit'.

○ Once you get to intermittent reinforcement, you can also move to teaching the next behaviour (e.g. 'down'). With confident pups you can start 'down' soon after the pup has got the 'sit'.

○ See the section on proofing and fading the clicker at the end of Part D to learn how to proof (establish) this behaviour in more complex environments.

TROUBLE-SHOOTING

Having trouble establishing the required behaviour? Check these things out.

○ Is the environment quiet? Try an even quieter environment. Keep simplifying the environment until your pup is focused on you and training.

○ Ensure you have toileted and exercised your pup moderately beforehand.

○ Is your pup overly tired? Is the session too long?

○ Are you touching your pup too much?

○ How is your own energy level? Stay relaxed and confident.

○ Is your pup particularly highly aroused or distracted?

○ Is your pup too distracted by the food reward? Use high-value food if it motivates but does not distract, and lower-value if your pup is too aroused.

○ Does your pup have a low food drive? If so, either cut back on his breakfast or increase the value of the training food (e.g. cheese, dog roll).

○ Are you putting your hand in the rewards pouch before the behaviour is completed?

○ Make sure your pup isn't frightened or anxious and out of the learning state.

○ Check your timing is right: are you rewarding the right behaviour?

○ Have you removed the click and food lure too quickly? Try going back a few steps and adding back the click and food lure.

○ Does your pup seem flat and slow? Keep your pup in a happy, upbeat state. Does your pup like toys or balls? If so, bring out their favourite item after a couple of clicks to get him excited at the ball, then click and throw the ball rather than offer food.

○ Does your pup seem like he is not interested in food?

— For picky eaters, control all food and do not put down food freely for them.

— Control your pup's food during the day. Start with low-value, palatable food for breakfast, high-value food during training all day, and finally any leftover food (to make up their required dietary amount) for dinner. Remember, training food is counted in your pup's overall diet, so make sure you include it in the pup's daily intake so you don't overfeed.

— When training, use the clicker and a high-value food reward (like cooked chicken, cheese, ham) and test what your pup will eat. As soon as your pup is eating, pair the clicker with that food.

— After a period of time, throw a piece of food away from you, and click as your pup eats it.

— Once you get the pairing with the clicker, you will begin each meal with clicker training, trying to pair the low-value reward with the clicker as well, and alternating the food types in the routine.

— Ideally get your pup to sit, then click and reward. Remember that activating the pre-frontal cortex, the decision-making brain, dampens any sympathetic arousal (marked by fear and not eating) and switches on appetite.

— If you continue to have problems with your pup's appetite, check with your vet, especially if your pup is underweight. There are appetite stimulants available.

11.2   COLLARS

I use lighter leads and training collars on pups: a flat collar from 4 to 8 weeks of age, a half-slip (limited-slip) from 8 to 12 weeks, then a slip collar after that. However, this can depend on the confidence of your pup. If you have a more fearful pup, use a half-slip for a longer period of time. If you have a strong, dominant pup, you might move to a full slip earlier. Look for effectiveness.

Flat collars

These are the standard dog collars we are all familiar with. They are an important everyday management tool — we can put our contact details and dog registration on them. They are *not* useful training tools, as they don't provide the subtle contrast (information) of the half- or full-slip collars (see below). However, we start our young pups off on these collars, and ideally breeders should be carefully introducing pups to them from 4 weeks of age.

If your breeder hasn't done so already, you may need to introduce your pup to a collar, in which case follow the instructions below. Be careful as you do this, as you don't want your young pup to get a fright and develop any collar aversions.

Introducing your pup to a collar

Start with a flat collar or a half-slip and put it on your pup gently. Try to distract her initially by doing some click-and-reward work. For example, throw some food on the floor and click and reward retrieval, or maybe practise some sits if you have started that training (or now might be a good time to start). Reward her for calm, accepting responses. After a period, let your pup rest from the training. She is likely to start scratching a bit at her new collar for a while, then she should ignore it. This is okay: let her work it out for herself unless she is seriously panicking, which isn't likely if introduced calmly in this approach.

Don't put any resistance on the collar by introducing the lead at this stage, as it is too much to start with, and your pup might start pulling on it.

If your pup is hyper-sensitive to the collar, keep using the clicker and rewards, and repeat until you de-sensitise her. Don't let this behaviour develop into a problem, as it is important for many reasons that pups can tolerate their collars.

Safety slip collar

○ This is a nylon collar fitted with an 'O' ring at each end, like a nylon check collar. To use, make a bend in the nylon rope, and push it through one of the O rings. Pull the loop until you have made a 'P' shape.

○ It is designed to provide information to your pup in association with a lead, tightening as your pup pulls away, and loosening when your pup stays close to you (this is called 'pressure on' and 'pressure off', and is an important part of contrast training).

○ With your pup on your left side, place your pup's head through the loop, with the tail of the P hanging under your pup's neck and closest to your left leg so that the slip is loosened when the lead is relaxed.

○ Your lead is clipped to the O ring at the end of the P-shape's tail.

○ Try the safety slip collar on your arm first to test the impact it has on your pup: it isn't a major pressure, but it is enough to let your pup avoid the discomfort and change behaviour.

○ Get the right-sized safety slip collar: the minimal size should be the measure of the widest point of your pup's head (just in front of its ears), then add about a centimetre. It is too long if it can slip too easily over their head and delays the information being delivered. It should be snug so it can't come back easily. You will need a couple of different sizes as your pup grows.

○ For more advanced or highly sensitive pups you can use a half-slip as below.

Half-slip collar (limited-slip)

As the name suggests, this collar doesn't fully contract, as it has only a limited range to tighten: it still provides the contrast explained above, but not to such a degree. This type of collar is good for young pups and very sensitive, submissive pups. Correct sizing is important: when you pull the collar tight the two ends should meet with about 2 centimetres yet to tighten (this allows for some check effect to take place). It is used with the same principles as the safety slip above.

11.3   LEADS

In this section we cover a number of leads and their different uses, including hand-held, umbilical and retractable leads and the long-line (drag-line). The lead is a tool that, when used with the clicker and the safety slip collar or half-slip, helps create a psychological bond between you and your pup — the lead is an extension of you. In Nature, the wolf has this bond imprinted through pheromones, vocalisations and the primal drive to stay close with the mother wolf or the pack, all of which create the following response. As we don't have these natural bonding agents, we help stimulate the follower response through the use of the lead, slip collar and clicker. I use lighter leads on pups when they are young.

Introducing your pup to a lead

It is tempting to think you just pop your pup on a lead and off you go, but don't be fooled! This will possibly be your pup's first experience of resistance (constraint from the lead), so it is important that it is done slowly and carefully so your pup doesn't develop an aversion to resistance and leads.

I sometimes use a long-line for the first time, as it allows pups more freedom and less resistance to start with. I then gradually and gently start shortening the lead so that it slowly increases the pup's sense of resistance. Click and reward your pup for calm, accepting behaviour. Ensuring there is little resistance on the lead at first ensures you are slowly desensitising your pup to the pressure from the collar — you will gradually increase the pressure by shortening the lead.

As you gently increase the pressure, click and reward when your pup comes to you — this is the beginning of her understanding the contrast of the pressure on the lead and collar (as she pulls away) and the pressure off the lead and collar (as she moves towards you).

Ideal way to hold the lead and clicker

I hold the lead in my left hand. The part of the lead attached to your pup should be coming out of the back of the hand (by your pinky finger) as this makes use of the strongest part of your arm (which becomes important as your pup grows). The other end of the lead is looped around three fingers (from the pinky to the middle finger) on my left hand, with the end of the lead looped over my pinky finger. This also leaves the forefinger and thumb free to hold the clicker in place, which is attached to the wrist by a lanyard or an elastic band.

This keeps the right hand free to get food rewards from your pouch to give to your pup throughout training, and also means your clicker is ready to be used as needed. This is very important as you need to mark the *exact moment* your pup does the behaviour you want.

The lead and slip collar, combined with the clicker, and later a check if necessary, offer all the information you need to shape joining up and create the bond. You will see how this lead is used in the section on joining up, below.

Hand-held lead

This well-known type of lead acts as a physical connection between

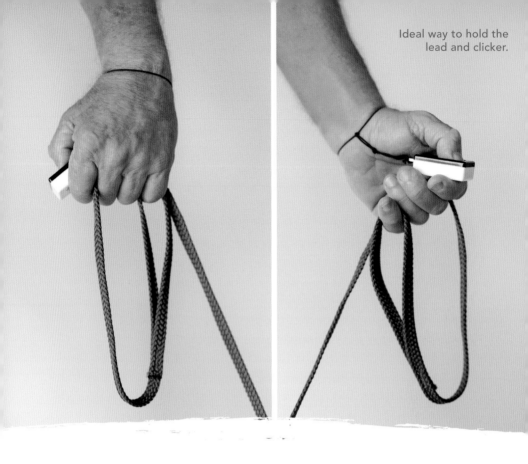

you and your dog, which stimulates a bond when used in the joining up and umbilical training, and provides control and boundaries. You are communicating at all times down the lead: each subtle movement gives your pup information about what you want or expect from her. It is up to us to teach our pups what those subtle messages and pressures mean.

A hand-held lead paired with a safety (half-) slip collar serves as a kinaesthetic tool that communicates different messages to your pup, and hence should evoke different responses. For example:

O *Pressure off*: When the lead and slip collar are loose, it tells your pup, 'Good, stay in the safe zone', which is the space near you. Click and reward to tell your pup, 'Great, that's what I want.'

O *Pressure on*: When your pup pulls on the lead, thereby tightening the (half-) slip collar, it tells your pup, 'Don't move away from safety' (that is, from beside you).

O Together these two activities offer *contrast*: a loose lead and click and reward is 'Yes, that is what I want', whereas a tightening of the slip collar is 'No, that isn't what I want'.

○ From 3 months of age you can then add a *conditioned aversive signal*: 'no', followed by a 'no' with a check to the pulling on the lead. This says 'No, not that way'. (You will learn the technique later on in this section.) However, unless your puppy is especially strong or overly confident, it is preferable not to introduce a conditioned aversive signal (like 'no') until after 3 months of age. For young pups, initially try just using the clicker to shape the right response, rather than adding the 'no' command.

Umbilical lead

This should only be trained from 3 months of age onwards, and only when your pup already understands contrast and pressure on/pressure off, otherwise your pup will panic from the constraint. Make sure you have progressed with the on-lead joining up first before you graduate to this stage, as you don't want to drag your pup around.

The umbilical lead is when you tie your hand-held lead to your belt to be hands-free. (You can get specially made belts with leads attached as well.) This allows you to go about your day-to-day activities with your pup beside you and moving with you, further cultivating the following response.

Using an umbilical lead encourages your pup to stay in your safe zone and move in relation to you while you go about your day, encouraging her to look to you for guidance and follow you, rather than ignore you or lead you. This practice will translate into any aspect of life; for example, when you are out on a walk and don't want your pup to pull away from you on the lead.

○ With your pup tied to your umbilical lead, go about your everyday life in your home.

○ Practise 'sit' anytime you stop moving, and the 'down' and 'Zen down' when stopping for longer periods. This keeps your pup in a calm, non-reactive learning state when around you.

○ Care needs to be taken so bigger and hyperactive pups don't throw you off balance. If you are not steady on your feet, this is probably not a good exercise for you.

Pressure on — collar tightens (signals 'wrong way' to your pup).

Try it on your own arm to get a sense of what is effective (not too much, not too little).

Reinforce the click with a reward, and keep moving.

Pressure off — collar loosens (signals 'yes'/ 'safety' to your pup).

Long-line and retractable leads

Long-line and retractable leads allow you to train your pup from a distance. Working and reinforcing commands from a few metres away begins to simulate the off-lead relationship. It also allows you to deliver a remote correction (one that is away from you) if needed. They are great for practising recall and other commands in the proofing stage (see the section on proofing in Part D). These leads are great for delivering an effective check from a distance — we use this with our conditioned aversive signal (our 'no' command). You will learn more about this in the contrast training section. They also allow pups to move at their more natural speed, and smell and enjoy when they are off-command, without the continued sense of pulling or pressure on the lead.

Long-line lead

Commonly these leads are around 5 to 10 metres long, and can drag behind the pup during training so you can stand on it and grab it if your pup is not responding or coming when called.

The size and weight of the long-line should be in relation to your pup, and as lightweight as possible, so your puppy is not dragging around a heavy lead, which would put constant pressure on her. Ensure the length is manageable for you, and not too long.

Retractable lead

The retractable lead is a lead that can extend up to several metres and has a hand-held braking system. There are many sizes of retractable leads, so make sure your equipment matches the size and strength of your pup. As long as you know how to use a retractable lead, you can start with them early. (Note that the lead itself comes in either a ribbon or a cord form. Some people prefer the ribbon, as the cord can cause nasty cuts if it gets caught up and under pressure. However, the ribbon makes more of a humming noise in the wind, so may be a less suitable option for a noise-sensitive pup.)

You need to learn how to use the retractable lead properly for it to be effective, and this takes practice. Here are some tips:

O Don't grab the line: as it can retract and extend very fast, it can burn your hand.

O Never tie your pup up on a retractable lead, as pups can chew through them.

The long-line is useful to teach recall.

○ Take care not to get tangled, particularly when the lead is extended. Never have so much line out that you or your pup get tangled.

○ Practise how to use hand-brake effectively, both on lock and release, before you use it on your pup.

○ If your pup gets tangled or wrapped in the line (body or legs, etc.), release more line to allow your puppy to calmly walk out of the tangle.

An effective check

The lead (long-line, retractable or hand-held) associated with a slip collar is used to create an effective check (used to apply a consequence in contrast training).

To apply an effective check when your pup acts inappropriately, quickly snap the lead in a firm and swift upwards or sideways motion to momentarily tighten the collar around your pup's neck, then release. (Important: this is a snap movement, not a pull or a drag.)

This is used when you want your pup to avoid something or to tell

Teaching discrimination using the retractable lead.

your pup 'no'. This is done remotely where possible, and a warning signal ('no') is later introduced to give your pup an opportunity to avoid a correction where appropriate. Your pup mustn't associate the check with you, so ensure your pup is looking away from you when you apply it.

A check is only effective if it stops your pup's behaviour but doesn't frighten him, so if you find you are delivering a check and it is having no effect, you need to be firmer. If you are frightening your pup, immediately adapt what you are doing to be more gentle. (This will ensure your pup gets back into a learning state.) Strong pups will need a much firmer check than weaker and smaller pups.

Practise this until you know what 'effective' is for your pup. It is worth putting the nylon slip collar or limited slip on your wrist so you can feel the effect. It is only a minor discomfort as it is about disrupting behaviour through a snappy check. Remember it is offered in *contrast* to the positive reinforcer (click and reward), which is what makes it more effective as well, and reinforces you positively as the ally.

11.4   GOING BACK TO THE DEN

The clip station and the crate (described below) are the physical representations of taking our pups back to the den: they are secure, contained spaces that allow our pups to be calm. These spaces will be associated with the mentor and inherit their safe influence, reinforcing the secure base effect. They re-create the trust of having a mentor (and their environment) around, which gives the pup the confidence to learn and do new things.

11.4.1   The crate

We introduced the significance of the crate in Part B (page 74), so go back and review that section if you need reminding. It is a critical tool in establishing your pup's sense of a secure base, and is useful for house training and teaching separation.

Set-up

- As a rough guide, the most basic crate needs to be at least 30 per cent longer and 20 per cent higher than your pup, but not more than 50 per cent more, otherwise the nest-site soiling inhibition loses its effect. Note that for larger breeds a larger crate might be required at a later date once the puppy is fully grown.
- I like to have a house-training and initial crate set up in the pen area, and that is normally a fold-up crate in steel mesh like the puppy pen material. I cover it with something initially.
- I also have a travel crate, which is for taking in the car and travelling to friends' places (often a plastic carry-crate). I use this around the house before the clip station comes into play.
- In your main home crate, your pup should be able to stand up and turn around comfortably inside the crate, and it should have a bed inside, plus water and food bowls — that's about all the space you need. Pups won't want any more room than that, as they like it to be snug, enclosed and 'den-like', at least when they are 4 to 10 weeks old. See the crate photo on page 75.
- Make sure the crate is secure, so your pup can't pull it apart or drag it around.
- The bottom should have a tray or some kind of waterproof base — just in case the pup spills the water or toilets there if left too long.
- When pups are young (2-3 months old), it is nice to have the crate

largely covered to make it extra-snug, like a natural den would be.
○ Decide on where you want to put it in your home: pups love to be near us, so in a living area is a good choice, and/or by a dog-door out to a fenced yard.

Introducing your pup to a crate

○ Hopefully, the breeder starts the pup in a small travel crate, which can be as soon as 4 weeks of age, for very short periods, as they start the clicker training. However, the process below is similar for introducing an older pup. Ideally, you would want to start this before a pup is 8 weeks. Whatever age, get it started as soon as you get your pup or dog, as it is an important aid for many behaviours.
○ Pop a comfy bed in the crate (ideally within a puppy pen) and feed your pup in the crate. Click and reward your pup as it enters, scatter food around the crate so he hunts it out, or just in front of his feet.
○ Briefly close the door — click and reward. Open it, and click and reward. Do this a few times, slowly lengthening the time you keep the door closed.
○ Near the end of the session, leave the door open and let your pup go in and out of it while he plays. Click and reward any voluntary entry.
○ Gradually leave a longer-lasting food source (e.g. a packed mini Kong or a puppy bone) in there, and close the door for a short time. Before your pup gets upset or vocal, click and reward your pup going in and out a few times, and finish that session.
○ Repeat this a couple of times a day, until your pup falls asleep in there by himself. Leave him in the crate for longer and longer periods until he accepts it.
○ For very young pups, you may start with a litter mate in with him (social facilitation), then work to leaving him just by himself.
○ Particularly when he is young (from 4 weeks), use the crate for all of your pup's naps and when you go out for an hour or so. Having access outside or into a puppy pen with an appropriate substrate is even better. (See the section on house training.) At 4 weeks when the breeder starts him in a starting crate, I often use the smaller travel crate, as it is only for short timeframes.
○ Keep a positive association with the crate by clicking and rewarding, and feeding your puppy in there regularly.

○ If your pup vocalises in the crate (seeking attention), take care not to reward that behaviour by paying attention to him, making soothing noises or taking him out. After 8 weeks and in his new home, you may want to hook a long-line to the crate and give it a gentle (though effective) tug (remote correction) to quieten the pup. Watch the effect of this, so you don't frighten the pup but just interrupt him and stop the vocalisation.

11.4.2   The clip station

Note: For a pup, start this from 3 months of age.

We introduced the significance of the clip station in Part B (page 76), so go back and review that section if you need reminding. The clip station is a critical tool in establishing your pup's sense of a secure base, and is useful for house training and teaching separation.

How do you build it?

○ Choose a location. It is good to have 2 or 3 clip stations around your home, all in social places as your pup loves to be close to you. Also place one just outside the back door.
○ Secure a clip into the wall's baseplate, or onto heavy furniture. Ensure the clip is anchored and secure.
○ Attach a length of light chain or a lead (if your dog doesn't chew) to the wall clip with a safety swivel, and a dog clip at the other end. The chain or lead should be the length of your pup — 0.5-1 metre long, no more.
○ Place a comfortable mat or bed down beside the clip station — you want it to be an appealing place. Leave a dog toy there (such as a toy packed with food, like a Kong) and make it a desirable space with something to do.
○ Make sure your pup hasn't got access to inappropriate things to chew, like furniture.

Introducing your pup to a clip station

○ Start this training from 3 months of age (or earlier if your pup is very confident).
○ Care must be taken when introducing pups to a clip station, as we don't want them to get a fright and form bad associations with this safe place.

○ Initially run a long-line through the wall hook where the chain travels. Clip your pup to the long-line, which will provide you with control while allowing your pup more sense of freedom to start with. Slowly encourage your pup onto the mat (drop food onto it), clicking and rewarding him for going on his mat. Slowly shorten the long-line until your pup is contained on the mat. Be patient, and time this according to your pup. Don't let him get panicked by the restraint.

○ Run your pup through his basic commands, being mindful to keep him in a learning state and thinking. Graduate towards a 'Zen down' position to assist in a positive and relaxed association with the clip station. (See the basic commands section, in Chapter 12.)

○ Your clip station will become an invaluable tool for training sessions and day-to-day routine. Over time and once a positive association has been established, you can have your pup remain content on his clip station from 5 minutes to 3 hours. This is also the beginning of separation training.

11.5   CONTRAST TRAINING

Before we get down to training our basic commands, it is important to re-visit a fundamental technique in Puppy Zen, contrast training. (We introduced the theory earlier in the section on how pups learn.) Understanding and applying this technique is fundamental to effectively implementing Puppy Zen. It is often misunderstood or inappropriately applied, so take your time to really understand and apply this. For puppies, start contrast training at 3 months at the earliest (unless you have an exceptionally confident, dominant or pushy pup, in which case you can start earlier).

Pups learn best from contrast, and in Puppy Zen we use the principles of safety and avoidance to achieve contrast. Here we teach our pups that we represent safety (they look to us, their mentor, for guidance) and to avoid consequences from inappropriate actions or objects. In Nature, we have seen that wild dogs and wolves are provided positive reinforcement for good behaviour through social contact and access to resources, such as food. Equally, they are given corrections for undesirable behaviour from other wolves/dogs and other things in their environment, so they learn what is appropriate.

In Puppy Zen we reinforce safety through positive reinforcement (such

The clip station.

as the clicker and food rewards, praise or a pat) and shape avoidance through apparent natural consequences (primarily through corrections, such as an effective check). Your pup learns that you represent safety and comfort, while 'something out there' represents discomfort and consequences that should be avoided. In this way, you are the guide or ally your pup should look to when deciding how to respond in a situation.

Communicating consequences to your pup is provided initially through pressure on the collar (as in joining up, which can start happening from 4 weeks of age onwards) and later an effective check done remotely (not associated with you; from 12 weeks of age onward). Later on, a conditioned aversive signal (the 'no') can be added.

Establishing contrast training through safety and avoidance

There are three key steps (in order) to establishing contrast training.
○ Introduce contrast training through joining up on-lead.
  — Teach safety through pressure off (click and reward).
  — Teach avoidance (in its simplest form) through pressure on.
○ Extend avoidance training to avoid inappropriate objects through apparent natural consequences (the effective remote check).
○ Introduce the conditioned aversive signal (the 'no' command).

Introduce contrast training through joining up on-lead

Joining up is an important first step in establishing contrast training. Using a nylon safety slip (or half- or limited-slip) collar and lead provides the contrast of *pressure off* paired with a click and reward, to provide comfort and a reward when your pup looks at you and follows your lead (safety), and *pressure on*, which creates mild discomfort and discourages your pup from straining away from you (avoidance). See later in this section on how to do joining up.

Extend avoidance training to avoid inappropriate objects

Avoidance training is when we want to teach our pups not to touch/do something, without the negative reaction being associated with us. This is achieved through apparent natural consequences and the effective remote check. We correct remotely so that the check is associated with the thing we are trying to get our pups to avoid, and also so that it does not build a negative association with us.

The technique
For example, say you don't want your pup to eat food off the table.

o Leave food on the table and put your pup on a long-line.

o Hide (so your pup doesn't associate you with the correction), still holding the long-line.

o When your pup touches the food, you provide a remote correction (a snappy collar check) for the wrong behaviour. This correction should appear to come from the food or the table if applied correctly. (The pup is looking at the item and away from you, and you don't use a command.)

o Repeat until your pup understands not to touch food.

The same goes for shoes or chickens: for example, we want our pups to associate the correction with the shoes, so they don't chew the shoe whether we are around or not, hence no command.

Introduce the conditioned aversive signal (the 'no' command)

Once this avoidance behaviour is firmly established, then (and only then) can you apply your conditioned aversive signal ('no' command) to provide your pup with a warning, so he can make a decision and succeed and avoid the consequence. This reinforces your role as the pup's ally and mentor. The good news is the effect of the check is learned and associated with the external enemy, not you, but you get the benefit by cueing it, which is what a conditioned aversive signal is.

Importantly, the conditioned aversive signal ('no') should be taught first, out of context of what you are teaching your pup to avoid. I normally teach the 'no' command through teaching recall.

The technique
Let's now look at how to teach the 'no' command through recall training.

o Fit your pup with a safety (half-) slip collar attached to a long-line or retractable lead.

o When your pup is some distance from you and you want him to come back to you (recall), try your 'come' command. Click and reward if he comes back.

o If your pup doesn't come back, after you say the second 'come', say 'no', and on a second 'no' (and at the same time) apply an effective check on the long-line. Because you have previously established the check as being given by an external object (e.g. by the food in the example before) your pup already understands what a check means. What he doesn't understand is what 'no' means. The first 'no' he won't understand (as he hasn't learnt it). The second 'no' has a check applied: as he understands the check, he will start associating the first 'no' as a warning.

O Importantly, ensure that your pup doesn't associate the check with you (so you remain associated with safety). For example, make sure your pup is looking away from you when you give the check. The subtler you can be on the delivery of the check the better.

O Remember it is a snappy check, do not continue pulling on the lead and tightening the collar. You are not trying to harm the pup, just trying to create a quick sense of discomfort to interrupt the undesirable behaviour so that it stops.

O We want the pup to think this correction is coming from the external enemy — from 'out there'. We are the pup's ally, and help him anticipate and avoid the enemy (avoidance). Again, this mimics the natural consequences of something 'out there' providing a consequence, and, because you have not been associated with the check, your pup will come back to you for safety. Clicking as your pup looks to you, and rewarding when he comes back, reinforce this sense of safety.

O As you progress, you can appear to be the one saying 'no', which will reinforce your elder status. For more dominant pups, this may be necessary sooner.

Ultimately the aim of this training is to fade the clicker and remote check, so you can rely on your commands (e.g. 'sit', 'down', 'wait') and your 'no'.

Chapter 12

Basic commands — the foundation of our shared language

One of the most important things we can do for our pups is equip them with a set of commands or words that enables us to keep them safe, and allows us to have a relaxed and stress-free life with them. These signals (cues) help us guide our pups, and give them clarity about what we want from them.

It is best to start basic command training from 4 weeks of age, in particular the 'sit' and joining up if the breeder is really committed, otherwise at 8 weeks old when you get the pup. The exception is the 'no' command, which we introduce from 3 months of age unless you have a significantly dominant or pushy pup, particularly one with no bite inhibition.

Once established, going back to training these commands regularly ensures your pup stays strong on the basics. It is also a great way to spend time with your pup, building your bond and keeping your pup motivated to learn and have fun. Clicker training ensures the pup enjoys it and makes for rapid learning.

Here is how to teach the 10 crucial basic commands — the basis of our shared language. I think these are the essentials for a happy, stress-free life with our pups. Remember to review the essential rules for training sessions, and get your clicker, food and pouch ready.

12.1 'SIT' AND 'ZEN SIT'

Hand signal: Move your hand like you are turning a key in a lock.

In Puppy Zen, the 'sit' is the first behaviour in the sequence we call joining up, which engages the ancient follower response and the bond gaze, both of which reinforce the lifelong bond.

We begin with the normal 'sit' command, which then transitions into the 'Zen sit', which is when your pup sits voluntarily, without being asked to. This is a sign of your pup fostering his reciprocal language: he is experiencing asking us for something (food and attention) by sitting and looking at us, and our responding to his sit (rather than us always asking).

The 'Zen sit' with the bond gaze together activate oxytocin and dopamine, and so switch the pup into a learning state. With the body calm and switched into the decision-making part of the brain, which dampens fear, the pup is better able to learn.

'Zen sit' ideally starts as soon as 4 weeks old, but most will start at 8 weeks when you get your pup. This should become your pup's go-to behaviour, replacing jumping up, pawing and soliciting behaviours. A human being present should induce this default behaviour.

The technique

○ Set up a simple, distraction-free environment. Train your pup on a lead, but work in a corner. For very young pups (4 to 8 weeks) train without a lead.

○ Start with clicking and rewarding all four feet on the ground, ensuring no jumping up.

○ If your pup throws (does voluntarily) a 'Zen sit', click and reward.

○ Get your pup to focus on the lure in your hand: you can do this by bringing the food lure (in your closed fist) close to your pup's nose to give her a sniff of it. (Make sure she doesn't eat it.)

○ Move your hand with the food lure in it up over your pup's head and she will sit. Click and reward. Use a signal (like turning a key), which should shape her going into a sit, and click and reward as her bottom hits the ground. Repeat until established.

○ Timing is critical: try to make the click *exactly* as your pup's bottom hits the ground, then follow with the food reward as soon as possible (0–3 seconds).

○ Don't put your hand in your pouch before you click, only *after* the required behaviour. This is very important: if you put your hand in the pouch before the sit, your pup will likely chase your lure hand and get distracted from the actual learning. (She's just thinking about chasing the food!)

O Repeat, clicking and rewarding success. (Approximately 10-20 repetitions should be sufficient for most pups.)

O In your second or third training session (once the behaviour is consistent), you can start introducing the verbal command: 'sit'.

O When teaching a new behaviour, do a couple of 5–10-minute training sessions most days while on-lead for 4 weeks; then 2-3 sessions per day on the long-line, then off-lead for 2 months. However, each pup is different, and some will learn and respond more quickly than others. For pups aged 4 to 8 weeks, only 2-5-minute sessions; and for all pups, rest for 15-30 minutes after each session.

O Slowly withdraw the lure so the pup starts to voluntarily throw the sit: it is this decision to do the sit voluntarily that takes this from a normal 'sit' to a 'Zen sit'. It is the decision that counts, so slowly delay clicking and rewarding (on an intermittent schedule of reward) until you don't need it and your pup is doing it all the time when engaging with you or others. It is then her turn to ask, through soliciting behaviour.

12.2   'DOWN' (LIE DOWN)

Hand signal: A downward movement of your hand with a downward pointed finger. (You can use other words and signals, but be consistent.)

The technique

O Start with your pup in a sit position.

O After making the 'down' hand signal, with a food lure run your hand in a motion down your pup's chest line (about 5 centimetres out from your pup's chest) then along the floor in front of her at a right angle. Don't move the food any further than the distance your pup's legs will go when she is lying down: if it is too far, your pup will stand up; if it is too short, your pup won't go into a down.

O Do this slowly so that, as your pup follows the food lure closely with her nose, she goes into a lying-down position. As she does, say 'down'.

- If your pup does not follow the food lure, put a little pressure between her shoulder blades. Push gently as you move the lure into the exact down position: one pup length plus 5 centimetres. Encourage her down: not too much pressure and not too little. When she is down, release your pressure immediately. Avoid doing this too much, as touching the pup's body can inhibit training, so only do it if you need to.
- As soon as your pup's chest hits the ground, click and reward. Throw the food reward between your pup's front legs so that she does not have to stand back up to get it from you.
- I like them to hold the 'down' for some time before allowing the pup to stand back up. Initially, the pup won't stay down long, which is okay; train the 'down' behaviour first.
- Once your pup is reliably going into a 'down', start extending the time she is down for, by extending the time you wait until you reward her — expect and reward longer and longer time spent down. This will take place over a series of training sessions.

12.3   'ZEN DOWN'

Hand signal: Use the normal 'down' vertically, then finish with the bottom of an L-shaped gesture in the direction you want his legs to go.

The 'Zen down' is an advanced lying-down position in which the pup rolls onto his hip and into a relaxed, calm position. It is more curled than the traditional 'down' position. In this position, both of your pup's hind legs will be on the same side of his body.

The purpose of 'Zen down' is to induce the learning state. It relaxes the dorsal muscles (the ones down the middle of the pup's back) and activates the vagal nervous system, which enhances learning and induces a state of calm in the pup. This is known as *embodied cognition* in humans, where your body posture communicates your state to your brain, which in turn affects your attitude. This means you are basically changing the chemistry in your pup's brain and his emotions with his body posture.

Once your pup has been trained to go into a 'Zen down', you may find he does it automatically whenever you ask for a 'down' — which is fantastic and the exact outcome you want! This mimics the relaxed down position wolves adopt in Nature when relaxed.

The technique

O Start your pup in a 'down' position.

O With a food lure in your hand, work your hand from in front of your pup's nose to his side, so that as your pup's nose follows the lure, his head curls over his front legs, and he flips over slightly onto his hip. If your pup doesn't seem to get it, use a finger to gently push the lower part of his side to encourage his back legs to flip over so that he is lying semi-sideways. (His lower legs are lying on their side, but his upper legs may still be lying straight.) Take care, as some pups are touch-sensitive and push back — don't force them.

O Click and reward as soon as your pup rolls onto his hip, dropping the food reward between his front legs to encourage him to remain down and relaxed.

O Continue to click and reward your pup while he remains in 'Zen down'. Encourage the duration of this position by clicking and rewarding your pup with food thrown between his paws at regular intervals.

Teaching 'Zen down'.

O Delivering food to the ground like this encourages your pup to stay down longer because it doesn't release your pup from the command. You can also smear bits of food onto the ground, so that it takes longer for your pup to eat and keeps him in the position longer. Delay clicking to extend the duration.

O Move to only rewarding intermittently, and later fading the clicker.

EXERCISE: IMPACT OF 'ZEN DOWN' — OBSERVING YOUR PUP'S EMOTIONAL STATE

Before you start this exercise, notice your pup's emotional state. Is it hyperactive, fearful, too low-key, destructive? Try a few 'Zen down' exercises. Notice the postural change in your pup's emotional state of calm: it is reflected directly in the posture. Do you see the power of the position and how it keeps pups calm and in a learning state?

12.4   'WAIT' AND 'STAY'

'Wait' hand signal: Move your hand with a pointed finger in front of your pup's face from left to right, like you are drawing an invisible horizontal line in the air. 'Stay' hand signal: Show your pup your flat hand (like a stop signal).

Training 'wait' and 'stay' is very similar, so I have combined them here. Both mean 'wait in that spot until I release you'. The difference is that in the 'wait' you can release them from a distance, whereas with a 'stay' we must go back to our pup to release them. It is best to train the 'wait' first. Both of these are *fixing commands*, so our body language is more upright, with slightly stronger eye contact and stronger tones to keep our pup in place. (However, you don't need to be overly strong with most pups, so take care.) I like to virtually bomb-proof the 'stay' command, so that when I ask for it the pup stays there no matter what.

The technique

O With your pup on a lead, start with a 'sit', 'down', then a 'Zen down'.

O Position yourself square-on to your pup, standing tall and giving some eye contact.

O From the 'down' or 'Zen down' position, make the 'wait' hand signal, then take a step backwards (still facing your pup).

O Return straightaway, then click and reward your pup for staying in the 'down' position. Reward your pup when you are really close to her, and put the treat between her legs to prevent her from wanting to stand or sit up to take the treat from you.

O If your pup continues to get up, reduce your distance and come back faster — give her a chance to understand the process. (If you find that it is still not working, then get a retractable lead or a long-line and use the backline set-up, as described below; but use it with care with young pups.)

O Gradually extend the distance, moving further and further away, until you can get that 'wait' or 'stay' from a long distance and for a long time.

O At first, always walk backwards, still facing your pup as you move away. You can repeat the command and hand signal as you walk backwards.

O Later, try turning around and walking away, not facing the pup.

O If your pup makes signs of getting up to move when you have asked for a 'stay', say 'wrong' in a neutral tone. Later, once the behaviour is trained, you can say 'no' if your pup breaks the 'stay' (after 3 months of age).

O When you do a 'wait' command, initially you can release it by walking back to your pup. Later, once the command is established, release it by calling your pup to you from a distance using your 'come' command.

O Remember with a 'stay' you must go back to your pup to release her. I usually clap my hands and say 'okay' with an up intonation.

O Once well-established, try these commands in more distracting outdoor situations (proofing the behaviour).

Backline set-up

O If you are having difficulties getting your pup in the 'wait', try the backline set-up. This is when you have your pup on a retractable lead or long-line that goes through a loop in the wall before being attached to the collar, like a pulley system. This allows you to hold your pup in place from a short distance away.

O Go through the process above, and if your pup moves say 'wrong'. Click and reward if she waits. Try this about half a

Teaching 'wait' and 'stay'.

dozen times. If your pup still is moving, say 'no'. Click and reward if she waits. After one go if she is still moving, say 'no' with an effective check on the lead. Click and reward a 'wait'. Continue practising this.

○ If you are trying to proof this behaviour outside you can use an environmental anchor, such as a tree or a fence to establish the backline.

○ Be careful not to scare your pup with the backline or the check.

12.5 'WRONG' (NON-REWARD MARKER)

'Wrong' is a signal meaning 'don't carry on down that track' ('Give up — there is no reinforcer following', e.g. click and food). It is said in a neutral tone, which is more helpful for training because it is not aversive. It is a signal we can use before we step up and use the 'no' command. (A 'no' is more associated with a correction, although it is still a conditioned aversive signal — a chance to avoid correction.)

The technique

O Start teaching the 'wrong' command by saying 'wrong' when your pup is focused on you but doing the wrong behaviour — do not click and reward. Continue this until your pup does the behaviour or something close to it (*systematic approximation*), then click and reward.

12.6 'NO!'

Note: Start teaching this command from 10 to 12 weeks of age, unless you have a particularly dominant or pushy pup, in which case you can teach it earlier. You must, however, teach it before 4 months of age if possible.

The 'no' command is a *conditioned aversive signal* taught remotely. You'll remember this is taught by using an effective check in conjunction with a 'no' command when your pup is doing something you don't want him to do. This quickly shows the pup that 'no' means 'stop immediately' otherwise a negative consequence is coming. See the section on contrast training on page 171 for a description of establishing the 'no' command after teaching the 'come' command.

12.7 'LEAVE IT'

Note: Start teaching this command from 3 months of age unless you have a particularly dominant or pushy pup, in which case you can start teaching it earlier. You must teach it before 4 months of age if possible.

The 'leave it' command is taught by teaching our pups discrimination, so they know that they can do what we allow them to do, but must leave alone what we tell them to leave alone. This is incredibly important. For example, imagine a situation in which you see your pup about to eat something dangerous or poisonous and you can command 'leave it'.

First set your pup up on her safety (half-) slip collar with a retractable or long-line lead attached. Using these types of lead for this training enables you to apply a remote correction (see the earlier section on contrast training), so the correction appears to be coming from whatever you have told your pup to leave alone. This means that when you tell your pup to 'leave it', your pup quickly learns that if she doesn't leave it, there is likely to be a negative consequence that appears as if it has come from the item. This imitates natural consequences in the wild, which is why I call it an apparent natural consequence.

When you are ready, mentally divide the room into 2 halves, with one half of the room for 'good treats' and the other half for 'bad treats'. (The 'bad treat' is the same food treat and value as the 'good treat', but the pup just isn't allowed them.) Your pup is allowed the good treats, but not allowed the bad treats. Don't use high-value treats initially, as that will make the contrast too marked for your pup.

The technique

○ Throw a treat into the left side of the room and tell your pup to 'get it'. Click and reward your pup when he gets it.

○ After about 5 repetitions, throw a treat into the right side of the room, and tell your pup to 'leave it'. If your pup leaves it, click and reward. If your pup doesn't immediately respond to 'leave it' by leaving the treat alone and returning to you, give her an effective check (a snappy check) from a distance (so it appears the check is coming from the food item itself). Don't use a verbal 'no' command; again, this is so that the correction appears to be coming from the item, not you. Click and reward as your pup comes back (contrast).

○ In the next session, if your pup persists after the first check, say 'no' firmly at the same time as giving a second check, to reinforce the 'no' command and to teach the pup that there is a negative consequence if she doesn't listen. You and your 'no' are warning her about a likely consequence, so you are acting as her ally.

○ When your pup leaves the treat and turns back to you, make a click and then reward with a treat from your hand.

○ Continue to practise, throwing treats at random either to the left (good treats) side or the right (bad treats) side, using the same series of commands and rewards as outlined above.

○ Only do it as long as the pup isn't getting scared. For the first session, 3 or 4 repetitions are often enough. For sensitive pups, delay training this until they are a bit older.

This teaches the 'leave it' and reinforces the 'no' command. If you have got your pup performing consistently while in a distraction-free room, test your training in a different space with different items (such as shoes or cushions, but not toys) to proof your pup for other circumstances. The 'leave it' command is very handy if taught in this way, as you can steer your pup away from something dangerous while outdoors together (plants, other dogs, cats).

12.8   'OFF' (PEOPLE OR THINGS)

Hand signal: Flat open-fingered hand, faced at your dog.

Start this training at 10 weeks of age.

When your pup approaches you as if to jump up, put out an open-fingered flat hand (signal) and say 'off'. If he doesn't jump up and has four feet on the ground, click and reward with food on the ground. Repeat several times as necessary, until your pup has calmed down. Once calm, ask for a 'sit', and click and reward. Then handle (pat) your pup around his head: now you are providing a physical reward (patting/handling) for 'off' behaviours and four feet on the ground. For small pups, if patting around the head is difficult because they are too short, then just keep delivering a food reward dropped on the ground. Introduce a 'no' command if your older pup persistently jumps up, and you may pinch between his toes if he persists or hold his feet firmly as an aversive signal to stay off. Click and reward when all of his feet are on the ground.

Note we use an 'off' command, not 'down', as the 'down' command has a different meaning, as discussed above.

12.9   'ON YOUR MAT'

Hand signal: Point to the mat.

This is a command to send pups to their clip stations or other mats or beds. You want your pup to associate this command with her clip station, so each time you take her to the clip station, give her the 'on your mat' command and throw a food reward onto the mat. The second her feet hit the mat, click, and she will retrieve the food from the mat. Once on the mat, ask her for a 'down', click and reward, then clip her up. At the beginning, deliver a jackpot (a larger amount of food than normal) so you are reinforcing positive associations with the clip station. Slowly fade the click-and-reward as this behaviour is established.

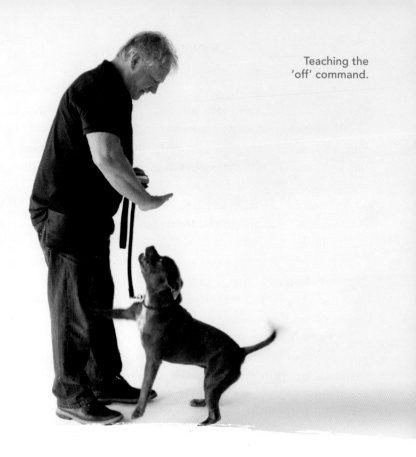

Teaching the 'off' command.

12.10   'HEEL'

A 'heel' is when your pup is walking beside you and looking up to you at intervals. The conventional 'heel' position is having your pup on your left side and so his right shoulder is beside your left leg.

You can start teaching this at 4 weeks old, as just the follower response. Click and reward the pup following on the left-hand side, without a lead on, when very young. This leads to the start of the joining-up sequence and later leads to the 'heel' below.

The technique

O While on a lead, walk around a room in circles or squares, asking your pup to 'heel', and clicking and rewarding your pup when his right shoulder comes into line with your left leg. You should start walking slowly.

O Use the principles of *pressure on* and *pressure off* (from contrast training) to keep your pup focused on and following you.

O Proof in lots of different situations, then try the same technique off-lead (see the section on proofing in Part D).

12.11 'COME' (RECALL)

This is one of the most important commands: it is the one that will save your pup from getting run over, help you remove your pup from a sticky situation, and prevent your pup from upsetting others who may not be so dog-friendly.

Remember this is a *drawing command*, so you need inviting, friendly body language and tone. Stay three-quarters on to your pup, relax, smile and use an 'up' tone.

The technique

- Young pups from 5 weeks on can be encouraged to come, using the food call and clicking and rewarding when they are close to you, with no lead needed at this stage.
- At 8 weeks on, put your pup on a short lead and a (half-) safety slip collar to begin with.
- Toss a bit of food away from you so that your pup moves away from you. Once away, give the 'come' command, then click and reward your pup when she comes back to you (even just a turn towards you to start with).
- When you are achieving this consistently, move to a retractable or long-line lead and repeat the technique, this time throwing the food further away, so your pup is further away from you and has a bigger distance to cover to return to you when you ask for a 'come'.
- Repeat this for several days without any correction for not coming, just luring back (holding out food).
- Later if your pup ignores you and doesn't come immediately when asked, give her a 'no' command, and click and reward if she then returns. If she doesn't return, say a second 'no' and give an effective check. Click and reward, when she comes back to you.
- Keep working with this technique when dragging a long-line or on a retractable lead.
- Click and reward every time your pup comes back to you.
- Keep up your recall work, doing it often and in most places, until almost perfect.
- Once you have faded the clicker and food reward, continue to give praise and a pat when your pup comes back to you.
- Proof the behaviour in lots of different situations. Proofing is about systematically making it more and more difficult for your dog to

Reinforcing recall ('come') on the long-line. Here, we are starting to proof the behaviour with a little distraction.

obey — adding distractions or a decreasing amount of fencing, for example. (See the proofing and fading the clicker section in Part D.)

○ Certain breeds are more inclined to be less responsive to recall than others, so start training early and do lots of practice.

○ Make sure you have a strong bond, so your pup is used to looking for you for direction — do lots of joining-up practice.

12.12   'NICELY'

Later in the meet-and-greet section I will walk you through positive greeting routines for you to practise with your pup. For now, I will teach you the all-important 'nicely' command. This is the command to use when your pup is greeting people or other dogs. It tells your pup that you are in control of this meeting situation, have noticed the new dog or person and have judged them as okay, so your pup does not have to react; everything is okay. It tells the pup to be nice, and not jump up or act aggressively. See the section on meet and greet in Part D for more details around how this command is used in meeting both dogs and people.

The technique for greeting another dog

O When learning this command, start with friendly dogs you know, or at the least judge to be friendly.

O When your pup is about to meet the other dog and is close by to it, ask for a 'sit', then say 'nicely' and click and reward your pup for sitting nicely and calmly.

O Move closer and closer to the other pup, then allow them to sniff each other's inguinal (groin) areas and click and reward both dogs for doing this nicely. (Importantly, reward only once the meeting is complete.)

O Click and reward both dogs throughout the interaction for having all four paws on the ground, not resource guarding and not vocalising, but having wagging tails and behaving sociably.

O Praise both dogs at the end of the meeting.

O You are always trying to teach 'nicely' through positive reinforcement: click and reward appropriate behaviour. If your pup makes a threatening or inappropriate gesture (growling, staring, lips up), use a check as if it is coming from the other pup or dog. That means that you do not use the 'no' command initially, although after weeks of training you can introduce the 'no'.

As with any training, remember that putting in the time and practising consistently will be what ensures you master each of these commands. Just try one at a time, only moving on to a new command when you have mastered the command you have been working on. Enjoy learning these commands with your pup, as they are the basis of your shared language and will allow you to effectively communicate with one another. And, hopefully, they will reduce those frustrating head-scratching moments, when you're wondering why your pup won't listen to you!

Puppy Zen Training Techniques

In the previous Part we laid down the critical foundations for our shared language and our training — our key tools and basic commands. Here, we pull all of these together and start applying them to the foundational techniques we will use extensively in Part F: What to do, when.

Chapter 13

The techniques

Do take the time to first practise your tools and basic commands, and ensure you have that solid foundation before you head into this section. It is important that you understand the purpose of your tools, have good timing and are effective. Also ensure that you and your pup understand each other well through your basic commands. You need these to be successful, so take the time to establish them well.

13.1   CONTRAST TRAINING

Although this is strictly a training technique, it was covered at the end of the Puppy Zen toolkit section as an essential technique that underpins teaching basic commands, so head there if you need a refresher.

13.2   JOINING UP

We have talked a lot about joining up and the mentor bond, but it is so important that it is worth covering again before going into specific practice. Joining up is the natural process of bonding and cultivating the following and look-to responses (bond gaze) that mum and the helpers inherit in the wild world, and that you need to create.

Joining up is a training technique that I developed after years of working with dogs, as it helps you establish the fundamental relationship you need with your dog. It cements you as your pup's mentor — the person he looks up to for direction and guidance in all situations. If he is looking to you for guidance, it is far less likely that he is going to make inappropriate decisions. It harnesses all of the innate bonding behaviours that wolves and dogs have evolved over 50 million years, and cultivates them in a beautiful inter-species collaboration that brings us together into one family, where we can act as one for the good of each other.

Teaching discrimination — a check is about to be given for touching the wrong object. The shoe will appear to bite back — don't use a command.

How to do joining up

Before you get started, you will need to familiarise yourself with the use of the essential tools. Once you feel comfortable with these tools and have got yourself set up with them, let's start.

I recommend you do this practice with 4–8-week pups off-lead for 2–5 minutes at a time, ideally 3 or more times per day for about 3 to 6 weeks. It is fundamental. Once established and the bond is sound, I recommend you go back and practise it at regular intervals, even when just on walks, so that you keep the behaviours and your bond strong.

There are four stages to establishing joining up:
- *Stage one: the hand-held lead*: This psychological joining up creates the secure base effect. It mimics and encourages the following response and looking to you. (It is this stage that we generally call 'joining up' through the rest of the book.)
- *Stage two: the clip station*: This is site-specific joining up, to further create the secure base effect.
- *Stage three: the umbilical lead*: This is the beginning of proofing joining up by extending it to hands-free in daily life.
- *Stage four: off-lead*: This is ultimate proofing to achieve controlled freedom in daily life and, finally, off-lead.

Stage one: The hand-held lead (psychological joining up)

This technique develops the bond between you and your pup: it encourages your pup to want to be in your personal space, and teaches him that being close to you means safety, protection and an enjoyable experience, whereas pulling away from you is undesirable and uncomfortable.

Remember the bond and the follower response in the wild are facilitated by the dog's or wolf's pheromones, vocalisations, touch, etc.; you are simulating these. We use a lead and contrast training to encourage the *follower response*, teaching your pup who is in control of the resources, and where and what safety is. However, a lead and an umbilical lead are of little use if they do not offer contrast to finding safety. The other important thing is that you are doing it at the right time, and, as in any imprinting process, experience is necessary, not just genes, as together they allow the dog to adapt to numerous different situations and relationships.

This training is done using a safety slip collar or half-slip (limited-slip) collar and a lead. When the lead is pulling tightly on the collar, your pup feels pressure on his neck; when the lead is slack, the pressure comes off. The *pressure on* is not harmful to the dog, but it does feel a bit uncomfortable. This basic contrast and discomfort of *pressure on* versus the comfort of *pressure off* is what forms the basis of how you use this contrast training technique to guide your dog to the right behaviour.

However, here's the bonus: using the clicker and food rewards with pressure off switches your pup into the learning state, and reinforces and enhances the contrast to the positive. This enables your pup to understand that you hold the resources, and that proximity to you is the safe place. Dopamine and other reward neurochemicals increase, and oxytocin is stimulated. Bonding is strengthened, and the learning state is maintained. Dopamine and related neurochemicals also activate the wiring of the brain and the sheathing (myelin) of the fibres to hard-wire the behaviours in.

The technique

Set up in a quiet, distraction-free room, with your pup in a (half-) safety slip collar attached to a hand-held lead. Review and teach the 'sit', 'Zen sit', 'down' and 'Zen down' commands, as these are also reinforced in joining up. You can start joining up without them initially if you like, but it is best to have them so the joining up becomes your go-to ritual when you are generally out and about.

- Start gently, using plenty of positive reinforcement. Click and reward your pup for good behaviour, such as looking at you or turning his head towards you.
- Everything you do is communicating to your pup, so you need to be very relaxed, with no tension on the lead if possible.
- Walk slowly in circles or squares around the room, keeping a food reward in your hand and initially positioned just in front of your pup to lure him ahead and beside you: your pup's right shoulder to your left leg approximately.
- At intervals, move up the hand with the food lure in it so that it is positioned between the pup and your eyes, to encourage your pup to keep looking past your hand to you (contact). Wiggle your lure finger to attract his looking up, and click.

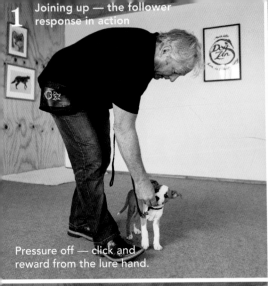

1 Joining up — the follower response in action

Pressure off — click and reward from the lure hand.

2

Pressure on — no click, a bit uncomfortable.

3

Pressure off — click straight away and keep walking. Deliver the reward.

4

Luring the follower response, later to become the 'heel'.

5

Luring the 'sit' — the pup is allowed to smell (but not take) the food held in the lure hand.

6

Click and reward 'sit' as the pup's bottom hits the ground.

7

Luring the 'down'.

8

Following the lure.

9

If necessary, apply a little pressure on the shoulder.

10

Bring the lure to the end of the paws so the pup doesn't stand up but lies down.

11

Move the lure to the side to lead to a 'Zen down'.

12

Continue to move the lure around at shoulder level and place on the floor between the front and back legs.

O Stay non-verbal initially, as it is less confusing for your pup.

O When your pup makes eye contact, looks up at you, or is walking on the lead with no pressure on the line, click and reward (pressure off). This is the follower response happening, activating an ancient bonding response.

O When your pup pulls and looks away from you, there is pressure on the lead — the lead is tight (pressure on — discomfort is the consequence).

O As soon as your pup turns back towards you (safety) and gets in line with your walking, the pressure comes off the lead and you can click and reward your pup (pressure off).

O This teaches your pup that pulling away results in discomfort (pressure on), while turning towards you and walking nicely with you results in no discomfort *and* a click and a treat (pressure off). This is how dogs learn best — by contrast. The pressure is a mild discomfort, so your pup understands the difference between being with you and being away from you: being away is not comfortable.

O You can click and reward your pup whenever he is walking beside you nicely and intermittently looking at you for guidance with the pressure off.

O Using corners offers more contrast as you turn 90 degrees. A circle is gradual so the pup might not notice it, whereas a square creates more distance between you as you go around the corner, so the pup feels the contrast.

O A more advanced example is using a 180-degree about-turn: walk in a straight line, then turn straight around and head back in the same direction. This provides a strong contrast as you change direction — so your pup has to keep alert and think — he will notice the contrast and will learn clearly.

O If your pup continues to pull away, look away or is not focused on you, apply more pressure until he looks back at you. If your pup tries to jump up or paw at you, give an 'off' cue with an open-fingered flat-hand signal. Reward your pup when four feet touch the ground, and again when he returns his focus back to you and the pressure is off the lead.

O Early on, stick to positive reinforcement only: click and reward pressure off.

O After a few sessions, if your pup is still pulling, and is over

3 months old, introduce a 'no' command, and click and reward pressure off. If this doesn't work, then on your second 'no' add an effective check. However, use this only if you have been unsuccessful over a number of previous sessions.

O Remember it is the contrast you are after, not dominance. You are shaping the follower response seen in the ancient helper role. Dogs thrive on a clear sense of role and place in the family, with clear knowledge of who to look to, especially when confused.

O This method teaches your pup to move when you move, and to stop when you stop, always keeping in your space and looking up to you for direction at intervals.

O Each time you stop, practise 'sit', 'down' and 'Zen down'. Use the 'sit' hand signal, and click and reward him for obeying; if he sits naturally without the signal ('Zen sit'), also reward.

O Deliver food from your hand when rewarding a 'sit' or 'Zen sit', and throw the food on the floor between your pup's front feet for rewarding a 'down' or 'Zen down'.

O Eventually you want your pup to automatically go into a 'Zen sit' for a short stop and into a 'Zen down' for longer waits, whenever you stop moving. He is then staying in the learning state.

Stage two: The clip station (site-specific joining up)
This training is to be started from 3 months of age.

We use the clip station regularly when training pups, because it keeps them contained and focused on what we are teaching. With regular use, it also simulates a den-like space for pups, which helps them settle and relax, or even act as time-out.

The technique
O Establish a comfortable clip station, and place your pup on it until she is calm.

O Don't look at your pup very much: wait for her to settle of her own accord; be patient. You can put your pup in a 'down' to begin the process, though.

O Stay non-verbal; don't say anything to your pup.

O Subtly watch your pup (remember staring is a threat and counter-productive), and click and reward her for calm behaviour. (Throw the food on the floor between her feet.)

○ Once she is settled, it is likely she has moved into a learning state.
○ Use hand signals (staying non-verbal) to ask your pup for a 'sit' and then a 'down'. Click and reward your pup each time she does a 'sit' or a 'down'. Keep practising these commands throughout the session.
○ Aim to get the 'Zen down', as this activates the vagus nervous system to further stimulate the rest-and-digest or learning state.
○ Leave your pup in a 'Zen down' after a while, with only an intermittent click and reward.
○ Move on to the next stage when your pup is relaxed and settled.

Stage three: The umbilical lead (beginning to proof joining up)
Start this training from 3 months of age.

Umbilical training involves having your pup on a safety (half-) slip collar and a lead that is clipped to your waist, moving with you as you go about your daily activities. Your lead should be just long enough to allow your pup room to lie down. It extends the joined-up behaviour you have cultivated on the lead, and brings it into your everyday life, hands-free, enabling your pup to get used to following you with less direct intervention than on the hand-held lead. This is the beginning of proofing joining up.

Make sure you have progressed with the on-lead joining up before you graduate to this stage, as you don't want to drag your pup around or stand on your pup. You are ready to move to the umbilical lead when your pup is starting to do joining up on a hand-held lead with limited amounts of pressure on.

Bigger or more hyperactive pups may require more work on the hand-held lead before they are ready for the umbilical lead. Be aware of any physical limitations you might have (particularly if you have a big, strong breed as well). Ensure your equipment is appropriate to the size and strength of your pup. Be careful your pup doesn't pull you around or over. If in doubt, do more hand-held joining up first. You need to make a call as to whether you are safe doing this.

The technique

○ Clip your pup's lead to your belt, with your pup wearing his safety (half-) slip collar.
○ Go about everyday tasks as per usual with your pup attached to

you by the lead. Start slowly inside your house, having him tag along with you, and observe how he mimics your movement and relates to you and your space.

O Click and reward good following behaviour — pressure off (when your pup is moving with you happily, and not resisting or pulling away from you).

O Give your pup a check if he is slow on the uptake of commands. (See the section on contrast training for details on how to deliver an effective check.)

O Continue to uphold the principles of pressure on versus pressure off. Later, cue a 'heel' command for better and better walking beside you.

O Whenever you stop, ask for a 'sit', and reward your pup for stopping when you stop. If you stay in one place for any amount of time, go through your 'sit', 'down' and 'Zen down' commands, particularly rewarding a 'Zen down' as it enhances an alert learning state.

O When you move on, your pup's awareness of you should be such that he comes with you — it becomes second nature, and a beautiful synergy develops. As you both get accustomed to this, you should be able to go about your daily activities with limited pressure on the lead. You are training your pup to move with you throughout your day.

O Once released from training, your pup can relax and run free, but he should still be in contact with you (checking in with you) by staying in proximity; an approximately 20-metre vicinity is ideal. We call this the *check-in boundary*. I use a 'close' command for this. Say 'close', and if he turns towards you, click and reward by tossing food towards him at intervals.

Stage four: Off-lead (proofing joining up)
Now we want to proof the joining-up training in real-world situations. Go through this series of steps to ensure that the bond you are building carries over into real life. Pups started as early as 4 weeks off-lead should be very good at this and may need little of the other lead techniques; even so, do some.

The technique

O Start with low-arousal environments (e.g. on-lead, inside the house or in your backyard). Click and reward your pup for moving with you.

O Once you have that established, start work on the long-line or retractable lead in more stimulating environments.

O Remember to apply pressure on for behaviours you don't want, and click and reward pressure off when your pup is near you and looking at you.

O Once your pup is consistently staying near you and exhibiting pressure-off behaviour, then start taking your pup off the lead for periods of time: first in low-arousal environments, then increasing the stimulation (e.g. by moving to a dog park). To help with this, see the proofing and fading section.

O Positively reinforce the sense of closeness and safety by clicking and rewarding your pup when he stays close. You want your pup to be aware and looking for you, and to follow if you leave the area.

O Play hide-and-seek to make it fun. In safe environments, duck behind trees or bushes to have your pup actively get used to looking for you, and click and reward your pup for finding you.

By practising these training techniques regularly, you will be able to build a close bond with your pup. Once these behaviours are well established, I would consider your dog or pup is well joined-up: your pup is relaxed, but is aware of you and stays close to you, and looks to you for direction. You will have become your pup's mentor, which will enable you to complete the rest of the training programme successfully, happily and easily.

The pup can relax when released, but once given a command should join up and hang with you. You don't want your dog working all the time.

13.3   MEET AND GREET

As discussed earlier, when pups meet new dogs or people, they need a formal greeting, just like we do. The nature of first introductions can set the tone for future relationships. Review the section on shared language in Part B. Here, we will focus on teaching how we do the meet and greet.

Meet and greet the wrong way — the pup lunging up at the adult dog's face could get him into trouble. Reggie, the adult dog, is turning eye off but is not happy. These are signs of an emerging issue you need to address.

Meeting new dogs

Dogs have a greeting routine to tell other dogs that they are friendly. They do this by checking and sniffing other dogs in the groin and rear-end area. Coming head-to-head is more threatening for a dog, so we can often unwittingly set dogs up for negative interactions while we are out walking. Because both dogs are likely to be on leads and walking beside their owners, they are often likely to meet face-to-face, which can be perceived as threatening. It is important that you give any new dogs approaching your pup the opportunity to first sniff your pup's rear end before they approach your pup's face, so it is good to formally teach your pup a formal meet and greet routine.

Pups tend to want to go to the face more than adult dogs, but it is important to teach them the dog handshake so they are greeted in a friendly manner. Adult dogs don't normally like puppies jumping up and licking their face, even if this is natural, so you may need to moderate this with a long-line and check, as if it is coming from the other dog. It will save your pup learning the hard way. This moderation technique is also explained in bite inhibition, later in this chapter.

Dog meet-and-greet the right way.

Preparation

O When you are first practising this routine, start with friendly dogs that you know have confident owners, so you can limit the risk of anything negative happening. If any offensive aggressive behaviour occurs, remove your pup from it as calmly and quickly as possible.

O Establish the 'nicely' command (see basic commands), which tells your pup that 'Yes, I have seen this other dog or person, too, and have judged them as safe and friendly'.

O Teach your pup the rear-present technique beforehand. Do this by gently pulling your pup's head towards the front of your body so she is standing side-on in front of you (rather than face-forward beside you). Also practise stopping and move your pup around, holding her under her loin so that her rear end is facing the approaching dog: 'rear present'. Get your pup used to these interactions before you need them. Click and reward your pup for letting you hold her like that out of context (not meeting dogs) so she is happy you are doing it before you really need it. Very few dogs would attack from behind, except fighting dogs and mal-socialised dogs.

The technique

O When you first see a new dog, use your 'nicely' command to let your pup know that you have seen this new dog and have judged them as friendly. Use an upbeat tone.

O Approach the other dog calmly. The inexperienced pup is the one that should make the approach, so ask the other dog's owner to hold their dog in place (quietly on the lead) if they have control, to present their dog's back end for your pup to greet (rear-present). You also should be able to rear-present your pup to defuse any reactivity.

O Try to approach from the side if you can, as this is less threatening than a direct face-on approach. Normally three-quarters on is best, as it allows sniffing of the groin. Watch the posture of both dogs (refer to the earlier section on reading postural signs), to make sure they are relaxed.

O Set up the interaction so that it is natural for your pup to go straight into an inguinal sniff of the other dog.

End of a good meet-and-greet
sequence — here I click and reward a
head-to-head greet once the inguinal
is complete.

○ After sniffing is complete, click and reward your pup's appropriate, friendly responses. (You reward after the sniffing is complete as you don't want to disrupt this naturally occurring response as this area has natural appeasing hormones.)

○ It is also a good idea to get permission from the other pup or dog owner to click and reward their dog for this encounter, to further reduce the risk of an aggressive response.

○ Sometimes you have to lure the dogs into the engagement with a piece of food in your hand and draw them towards the other dog's groin.

○ If possible, get both dogs sitting beside each other while you click and reward both, with their heads near each other and not being aggressive.

○ Finish walking them side by side until you can allow them to play if possible.

Trouble-shooting

If you are finding your pup isn't responding to your meet-and-greet techniques, check the list below to see where your technique might need improving:

○ Is your pup in a learning state? If not, he won't be retaining the learning.

○ Check the timing of your clicker and any checks: ensure you are rewarding appropriate, sociable behaviours. If your timing is off, you are rewarding or correcting the wrong behaviour.

○ Are you using enough contrast if things are failing? (Make sure you are using an effective check for inappropriate behaviour, and clicking and rewarding appropriate behaviour.) The check should appear to be coming from the other dog.

○ Are you reading your pup's response correctly, and have you given him enough guidance early? (Re-visit the orient, alert, target sequence in the shared language section in Part B.) Use the 'nicely' cue at the start.

○ Are you reading the other dog/pup correctly? If your pup has had some bad experiences or you haven't allowed your pup to have enough experiences (due to your own lack of confidence), go to the section in Part B on shared language.

○ Make sure you are doing enough repetition.

If your pup seems to be developing aggressive tendencies and/or has experienced some sort of trauma in terms of another pup or dog, you might need to elevate your training to our online programme, which has more resources on how to address emerging behaviour issues. If you think you have a problem, go to www.dogzen.com/puppyzen.

Meeting people

When it comes to meeting people, the routine has the same principles but looks a little different. It is good to have in place a routine for meeting people, so that your pup knows how to act when meeting someone new.

Some pups will be naturally friendly or very well socialised already, in which case the routine will just serve to control hyperactivity. If started young with the 'Zen sit', the pup will do a Zen sit by default in front of people, and wait for a pat and attention or just relax. Other pups will need a more formal greet, as below. You can also do a 'hand touch target' to enhance the efficacy, as described in the following technique section.

The technique

○ Practise first with known, confident people.
○ When you first see the person you will be meeting, use your 'nicely' command to let your pup know that you have seen the person and have judged them as friendly.
○ Ask the person you are meeting to stand still, then you can approach them with your pup so she can sniff them. Remember a pup feels more comfortable approaching others than being approached, as a direct approach can seem threatening.
○ It is important when your pup is first learning how to greet people appropriately that the people she is meeting don't unwittingly demonstrate threatening behaviour, such as staring, standing over the pup, or handling the head, cheek or shoulder area of the pup. This is particularly important with bigger men.
○ If your pup is a bit wary or timid, have the person turn slightly side-on and lower their gaze, so they are not staring at your pup as she approaches them. Alternatively, you could ask the person to crouch down or sit on a chair for the meeting, to further reduce the threat level.

Human meet and greet done the right way. Have pup approach new person.

Offer food to new person to give to pup (creates good associations).

First have your hand in front of the other person's hand.

All going well? Then new

- Click and reward your pup for positive, social responses, including a wagging tail, sniffing the person's hand, and having all four paws on the ground and not jumping up. Throwing a 'Zen sit' in front of them is ideal.
- You can also train and use a hand target with your pup. Teach your pup to touch your hand with her nose, and click and reward her. Once established with you, you can then get visitors to do it as well, and click and reward your pup for touching the visitor's hand with their nose, creating positive interaction and desensitising your pup to someone reaching out and having a good meet and greet.
- Encourage the new person to feed your pup treats as you click and reward your pup for her sociable response. First, put your hand and the new person's hand together with the treat: click and reward. Once the pup is comfortable, have the person give your dog a treat on their own — click and reward for sociable responses.
- When your pup has greeted the person, ask for a 'sit', 'down' and 'Zen down'. This is what I encourage my dogs to do while I am chatting to people after they have met, so I click and reward them for Zen sitting or Zen down while I am talking. They can then survey the situation while calm and relaxed.
- If you see any sign of your pup being uncomfortable (submission or fear) or showing aggressive behaviour (growling, snarling, snapping), remove your pup from the situation and go to the trouble-shooting section below or to the online resources.
- Ensure you practise this greeting routine with many different types of people — age, gender, race — wearing a range of clothing. Particularly, introduce your pups to babies, toddlers and children during the formative period, so the pup doesn't develop child-oriented aggression as an adult dog.

Trouble-shooting

If you are finding your pup isn't responding to your meet-and-greet techniques check the list below to see where your technique might need improving:

- Your pup wasn't in a learning state and so did not retain the learning.
- You were reinforcing the wrong stage in the meet-and-greet

sequence, thereby reinforcing the wrong behaviour.

O You did not cue the meet and greet with the 'nicely' command (which helps switch the pup to a learning state, and asks the pup to look to you and be nice).

O You did not time the clicker correctly, ensuring you are rewarding appropriate, sociable behaviours.

O You were not reading your pup's responses correctly.

O You were not reading the other person's posture correctly, and how your pup might interpret it.

O You did not do enough repetition (practise) or proof well enough (take the training out into everyday situations).

O In cases of threat or low-level aggression, you did not use enough contrast if things are failing: ensuring the use of an effective check for inappropriate behaviour (threat) and saying 'no' at the same time. Ensure you teach your pup 'no' out of this context beforehand (such as while teaching recall or 'leave it'). On the 'no' and check, your pup should stop doing it, at which point she should withdraw slightly — click and reward this non-threatening behaviour. Move away, and only try again if you think she understands what is required.

O Stop further away the second time, and try the hand present and sniff (if you have taught this; again, out of this context). If your pup sniffs and doesn't growl, click and reward the positive response. Next ask the visitor to deliver the food reward after clicking. Only continue the routine if your pup is now responding sociably. Continue clicking and rewarding for appropriate behaviour. If effective, you need to do lots of this now.

O Make sure the visitor is sitting down not staring, and is calm and relaxed, and not threatening. (See the section on shared language in Part B.)

If your pup seems to be developing aggressive tendencies to people or dogs, and/or has experienced some sort of trauma in terms of another pup, dog or person, you might need to elevate your training to my book *Dog Zen* and/or our online programme www.dogzen.com/puppyzen, which has more resources on how to address emerging behaviour issues.

13.4   CROSS-FOSTERING WITH OTHER SPECIES

Predatory behaviour in adult dogs (chasing and/or killing cats, sheep, birds, etc.) is a major cause of euthanasia and a major source of stress in owners. Over 50 per cent of dogs have a natural inclination to be predatory, so cross-fostering (socialising them with other species) during the formative period is by far the best and only really effective way of addressing predatory behaviour. It is best to do this with as many species as possible, but at a minimum with the ones you know they will be exposed to as an adult dog. Doing this brings the other species into the family or pack, and protects them from predatory behaviour.

If you leave introducing your pup to other species until after the formative period, the pup's predatory arousal will likely increase, and they may start attacking these animals or birds. This is significantly breed-dependent, so if you have hunting breeds, like terriers, Spitz and sight hounds, it is imperative you cross-foster them broadly during the formative period.

Ideally, you need to expose your pup to multiple species multiple times (at least 5 times) by the time they are 12 weeks old. Certainly it must be done before they are 16 weeks and out of the formative period. The younger they are, the more positive and gentle the techniques used. Aversion therapies become the only therapy later in life, and this takes knowledge, experience and the right tools to correct once the predatory drive has developed. Remember their ancestors are predators, so this is a natural if undesirable behaviour.

This training can be started carefully from 5 to 6 weeks of age (so breeders can start this). 'Carefully' means ensuring that the pup does not get a serious fright or be attacked by the other species. A minor correction is okay, but ideally you want your pup to initially have positive or neutral associations with the other species, so that he includes them in his social group. You want your pup to be in a calm, learning state and be relaxed around the other animals, and most importantly not chasing them!

The technique

O You are slowly introducing your pup to an increasing level of stimulus (hierarchy of desensitisation), ensuring he maintains a relaxed, calm, non-aggressive disposition and stays in the learning state. Click and reward for friendly, calm responses.

Pups must be introduced
to multiple species during
the formative period.

○ The hierarchy is normally the same for each species: firstly, expose your pup to a crated animal, then to an animal that is not contained but is still and quiet, then to an animal starting to move/flap wings and make noises, and finally to a moving animal. This is increasing the arousal stimulus for the pup.

○ For example, introducing your pup to a friendly cat or a calm chicken. Desensitising with chickens is sometimes easier to do in a garage or pen, and in a room for a cat.

— Pop your pup on a long-line and limited-slip collar, or a full slip if very aroused. Do some joining-up exercises so that your pup is well connected to you.

— Crate a friendly cat, so that it is contained but the pup can see and smell it. Do all of this in an enclosed room.

— On the long-line or retractable lead allow your pup to go up to the crate and sniff and investigate. Click and reward for calm, friendly responses. Throw food on the ground near the crate. Some pups will be wary, some aroused: click and reward anything but aggressive or over-aroused behaviour.

— Repeat until your pup settles and is sniffing and happy, or at least neutral.

— Next take the cat out of the crate, and hold it still (maybe with the help of a friend). It is preferable for the cat to wear a harness if possible. Be careful that the cat doesn't panic or attack your pup.

— Again, on the long-line allow your pup to go up to the cat and sniff and investigate. Click and reward for calm, friendly responses. Be mindful of the cat's responses, so that it doesn't give your pup a serious fright or injury (mind your pup's eyes). Also take care of yourself: if the cat is frightened, it can bite and scratch you, too. See the videos on my online programme.

— Next, allow the cat to start moving and meowing (if you can). Again, on the long-line allow your pup to go up to the cat and sniff and investigate. Click and reward for calm, friendly responses. Continue this a few times.

— The above sequence might take place over a day or many days, depending on your pup's reaction. If your pup is showing high levels of arousal, then slow the process down so that you maintain your pup in a learning state and don't over-arouse

him. If your pup shows little interest, then you can go faster.
— Some days later: the final test. Let the cat run off, and again on the long-line allow your pup to cruise away from you if he is doing what you want. Click and reward for calm, friendly responses.
— If at any stage your pup (if he is over 3 months, or is a confident, robust younger pup) shows overt interest and starts lunging at the cat, you will have to provide your pup with an effective check remotely. Ensure the check is effective: strong enough that your pup turns away from the cat and avoids it, but not so much that it gives your pup a big fright. Note that if you have a young pup exhibiting this behaviour already at 8–10 weeks, then it is likely you have a pretty strong-willed, robust individual, so you can introduce the effective check technique early, and he will probably need a reasonably strong level of correction. Watch for your pup's reaction, and stage your level of increasing responses slowly if needed.
— So, check when your pup is rushing at the cat, and click and reward when he is moving away or towards you, throwing food on the ground.
— Remember to run your pup through this exposure technique at least 5 times (per species) before they are 16 weeks old, and start before they are 12 weeks and as early as 4 weeks. The earlier the better — particularly with the breeds predisposed to predatory behaviour.

○ This is the best place to start your remote check without commands. It allows your pup to get a check and think the cat is to blame — perfect! Click and reward away from the cat or chicken, so that you are confirmed as the ally, and your pup should hang close to you.

○ For larger, more dangerous species to your pup (like horses, sheep, cows), using friendly animals that ideally know pups and dogs is a must, so that you know their behaviour is predictable and friendly and the pup isn't in danger. Otherwise undertake the introduction behind a safe barrier. The technique is similar. Start around the horse on a halter, and move around desensitising your pup while someone controls the horse. Teach your pup with a check to keep away from the legs, and to keep a bit of distance between himself and the horse. The same applies with other big stock species: more avoidance is better than none.

This technique must be effective at this age, otherwise you are heading down the predatory route, which isn't easy to fix in adult dogs without professional clinical intervention. It is serious and life-threatening behaviour, and most councils will euthanise a dog proven to have killed another animal.

Trouble-shooting

The following are some reasons why your pup might be exhibiting emerging predatory behaviour, even if you have tried the cross-fostering techniques described above:

- Your pup didn't get enough socialisation with a wide enough variety of other species (breeds, size) in the critical 4–16 weeks period, at least 5 times per species.
- The behaviour was not proofed (by training in different contexts) or the exposure was not generalised (covering a wide variety of species).
- You were not effective in your meet-and-greet routines because:
  - your pup wasn't in a learning state and so did not retain the learning
  - you were reinforcing the wrong stage in sequence, thereby rewarding or correcting the wrong behaviour
  - you did not time the clicker correctly, ensuring you were rewarding appropriate, sociable behaviours
  - you were not using enough contrast if things were failing: ensuring the use of an effective check (firm) for inappropriate behaviour, and clicking and rewarding for appropriate avoidance behaviour
  - you were not reading your pup's response correctly
  - you did not do enough repetition
  - you were going through the hierarchy too fast, and getting your pup hyper-aroused.
- You have a particularly challenging pup, possibly breed-related, that needs more effective use of tools and techniques to sort the issue.

Summary of meet and greets

I hope this section will help you to establish good meet-and-greet routines with your pup. They are so important in helping your pup understand that you are looking out for him, and that you are analysing situations involving new dogs, people and other species to ensure he is safe. This also adds to your pup's trust in you, and thereby strengthens your bond.

You are shaping the most important extension to your family bond: the acceptance of visitors and friends, other dogs and other species. Discrimination of who is a threat and who is not can be useful. Pups that are well socialised have good discrimination, because their first choice is to be friendly, but they are also good at reading signals that are a bit 'off'. You may choose to allow a couple of barks when a stranger enters the property, for example.

However, mal-socialised dogs treat everything as a threat, and that will make for a very reactive dog that causes you a lot of issues, and can and does lead to aggression. Ensure you prevent that by socialising widely in your pup's formative period. You want a broad multi-species family.

13.5   DISCRIMINATION TRAINING

To prevent destructive behaviour (such as chewing inappropriate objects, such as your shoes or furniture), we use a similar technique to cross-fostering. It is a form of avoidance or aversion training.

The technique

O Start with joining up, so your pup is focused on you.

O Have your pup on a slip or limited-slip collar and a long-line or retractable lead.

O Gather items you don't want your pup to chew and items your pup can play with (especially tug toys).

O Start with playing with the toys, throwing them around the room and having fun. Click and reward some of this play, so your pup knows it is fun.

O Place a couple of inappropriate items (cushion or shoe) in a separate area to one side of the room. (This is to help your pup discriminate between the items to start with.)

O If your pup goes to grab the inappropriate item, check effectively. Do not give a command — stay silent. As with the cross-fostering technique, here the item appears to bite back: a remote apparent natural consequence.

- As your pup starts moving away from the item, click and throw a food reward on the ground away from the item.
- Get your pup playing with the toy again, and distract him from the item that gave the 'correction'. Relax your pup again by calling him over, and click and reward.
- Set your pup up with the same inappropriate item again. (Throw it or bait it with food secretly.) If your pup heads back to the inappropriate item, use a check again, and click and reward as your pup moves away (contrast).
- Again, get your pup back playing with another toy.
- Repeat as needed. Three to 6 repetitions should be enough, although more robust pups might need more. You don't mind your pup getting a little fearful of inappropriate objects, but you don't want your pup getting generally fearful of the whole situation. With very anxious pups take it very slowly, and consider whether this is okay for that pup. Repeat sessions once every 2 days for 5 to 8 repetitions per day. He should become wary of the inappropriate items by the first or second day.
- Work with anything he has a predisposition to chew that he shouldn't.

13.6   HOUSE TRAINING

Understanding toileting behaviour

To understand your pup's toileting behaviour and how to train it, we can look directly back to the ancestral wolf. In spring, wolf packs create a den for the mother wolf to birth her puppies and reside in this den with the new puppies for 6 to 8 weeks after they are born. Initially, the infant puppies' mother will lick up the urine and faeces off the pups directly, and so keep the den clean.

As the puppies approach 3–8 weeks old, their instinctual desire to not soil the den kicks in, and they will naturally want to go away from the nest area of the den to toilet. This is called 'nest-site soiling inhibition'. Puppies learn the difference between their den and the outside world through texture discrimination: the floor of their den feels different under their paws to the ground outside. This ability to discriminate texture is the primary tool we use for house training.

Starting house training when your puppy is 3–8 weeks old means

You can teach your
pup the difference
between toys and
household items!

you teach your pup the behaviour at the same stage as they would have learnt this in the wild. The training should ideally start with the breeder offering the pups a chance to toilet in a litter box from 3 weeks old.

Using this natural learning process, you can teach your puppy to discriminate between surfaces that are inappropriate for toileting on (such as carpet, tiles, lino or wood) and surfaces that are appropriate (newspaper, grass or garden). By using textures and substrates to teach our pups the difference between indoors and outdoors, we essentially teach our pups that inside the house is an extension of the den. Once the whole house is established as the den, your pup will not want to toilet inside. In fact, most pups, if they get the chance early, will try to toilet away from the house as far as possible.

How to house-train your puppy

I think the most effective way to house-train your puppy is to use a combination of crate, puppy pen, and a dog door opening onto a safe fenced outside area with grass or garden available to toilet on. At the end of this section, I will also mention the crate-only technique as well. If you don't have a dog door, leaving a door partly open is helpful; otherwise she can just soil on the newspaper.

Set up

Ideally the breeder has started both nest-site inhibition and toileting using a litter box or paper, and started crate training. That's a big advantage. Check in with your breeder to see what has been done, and replicate as much as you can for familiarity, then extend as follows.

- Create a contained nest (den) for your pup in her crate: an area just big enough to include a nice, soft bed, and food and water bowls.
- Surrounding the crate, set up a puppy pen for full containment. Ideally, this should be adjacent to a dog door to a safe, fully-fenced area with grass or garden for toileting on, so your puppy can learn to let herself out. At the least, position the crate by an external door, opening onto a fenced garden. Many people find a laundry works well, as it is a restricted space which often has an external door.
- The closer to your social areas, the better, as your pup will feel connected and won't be trying to get your attention or feel too isolated. The crate and pen should not be on carpet, or the carpet should be covered with heavy plastic or lino, so your pup gets the substrate differentiation. Pups prefer to be in or as close to your sleeping area as possible (wolves sleep together). Those who have their pup in their room will find that they adapt there more easily, and the room will be safe from soiling very quickly. However, start as you mean to go on, and set your pup up where you want her to be long-term, as it will be hard to change.
- The entire floor of the pen must be covered by newspaper or another non-household substrate.

Technique: Using crate, pen and paper

- Ensure you (or your breeder) have safely introduced your pup to her crate. (See how to do that in the toolkit section in Part C.)
- Pop your pup in her crate at nap time, for blocks of time during the day and overnight, to help her learn not to toilet in her nest, and to learn to hold on as long as she can. Initially, leave her in the crate

for approximately 15 minutes, then gradually lengthen the time.

○ At night and in the first few days to weeks after you have taken your pup home, your pup will be able to hold for about 4-5 maybe 6 hours, so you will need to let her out right before you go to bed, possibly once during the night (delaying this time by a further half-hour each night), and then again first thing in the morning. Try to get her to last all night as quickly as you can. Take her water bowl out at night, and no food 3 hours beforehand.

○ Very quickly she will naturally want to hold off going to the toilet until you let her out. Leave the crate open so she can soil on the newspaper if she can't hold.

○ During the day when you are not supervising her, leave your pup in the pen area (ideally with free access to a safe, fenced area outside through a dog door). Remember the puppy pen floor is covered in newspaper or other non-household substrate. She will avoid toileting in the crate (den) and choose to go on the newspaper or outside. Take care initially if there are stairs or obstacles to getting outside.

○ Because your pup doesn't want to toilet on her bed, and newspaper or outside (if you have a dog door) are the only options, your pup will learn that newspaper or grass are the surfaces she toilets on, and will continue to toilet only on these.

○ Gradually shrink the area of newspaper inside the puppy pen over a couple of weeks, moving the newspaper square until it is in the furthest corner of the pen, closest to the external door, then eventually right outside.

○ Initially, it is best if the substrate under the newspaper is lino or another waterproof, cleanable surface. As you move the newspaper away from the crate, instead add a small piece of mat under the door end of the crate to further encourage your pup to move away from the crate to soil on the newspaper or outside. This is discrimination training: providing a contrast between the surfaces she won't soil on (carpet, lino) and those on which she will (newspaper or outside).

○ After this, with free access outside, start to move the newspaper outside of the house, starting with it by the door, then gradually moving it further into the garden and onto the grass. Give your puppy free access outside to toilet as much as possible.

○ If you are around, pop your pup outside after all of the appropriate times, like feeding, exercise and sleeping. Use the 'be quick' cue before she starts toileting, and then click and reward afterwards, and praise. Ensure you click and reward afterwards — you don't want to interrupt her business!

○ Once your pup is going outside on her own, systematically open the house to your pup, one room at a time, making sure she doesn't start toileting inside the newly opened rooms.

○ You are generalising the idea of the house being the den. She has established it in one part of the house where her crate is, and now you are trying to extend that to the rest of the house. The secret is to be systematic and go slowly. Don't open up too many rooms to your pup all at once, as the training might not have consolidated.

○ First let her free in the room her crate is set up in (ideally not on carpet) until she proves she can be there successfully without toileting, then extend access to adjoining rooms, one at a time. That way you are gradually increasing your puppy's concept of her den across your entire house, so the whole home becomes her nest or den, and she will choose not to toilet inside.

○ You may wish to start with rooms that aren't carpeted, and are therefore easier to clean up if your pup has a small accident. If you do catch her in the act of toileting inside, immediately and calmly pick her up and pop her on the grass until she has finished her business. Don't make a big deal out of it. I say 'wrong' (in a *neutral* tone) as I pick pups up if I catch them in the act, but that's all: no punishment.

○ If you do have some accidents to clean up, use 1 part white vinegar to 3 parts water as a cleaner to remove the smell. Vinegar is a good neutraliser of urine smell. It is important to remove the smell (apart from it not being pleasant), because if the smell remains it will remind her that this is where she toilets, and will establish a habit for her.

○ Use a clip station once introduced (see Part C), to allow your pup to be unsupervised anywhere in the house where you have put her on a clip station. She won't soil on the clip station (which is another den site to her) unless she is absolutely desperate.

Technique: Using the crate only

Although having a dog door outside is ideal, or at least the pup being near an external door, this is not always possible, so here is how to house-train using just a crate. You are using the same principles as above; you will just need to take your pup outside much more often to toilet.

This method suits people who are at home with their pup most of the time, so the pup doesn't need to be in the crate for more than 2-3 hours.

O If just using a crate, I would recommend that it is slightly bigger than normal. Half of the space in the crate should be a nice, soft bed, and the remainder should be covered with a non-household substrate like newspaper.

O You need to have an area the pup can go out into to play and toilet regularly, of course.

O Keep your puppy in her crate for a period of between 1 and 2 hours when unsupervised (except at night, when it can be longer).

O Take her outside to give her an opportunity to toilet on the grass as often as possible. Use the 'be quick' cue beforehand, and click and reward after she finishes.

O Also take your puppy out for intervals of playtime, but always return her to the crate for sleeping and eating. Remember, we want to retain the nest-site attachment and the secure base.

O Ideally, you are taking her out often enough that she doesn't need to toilet in the crate, and is learning her substrate discrimination between her crate and the garden.

O However, if she needs to toilet while in the crate, she will do so on the newspaper, as she will not want to toilet on her bed.

O When successful, you can start to extend the time between toilet breaks.

For both methods, ideally take your pup outside as often as possible after feeding, drinking, playing, exercising or sleeping, so you are directly encouraging toileting outside. Make sure you create an outdoor toilet space as out of the way as possible, as soon as possible. Whenever you can, take your pup there to toilet, say 'be quick' as a cue, and click and reward after your pup has toileted. Make sure it is on a substrate like grass or garden bark, and avoid substrates like decking and concrete. You are cueing her toileting behaviour on command, which can be handy on those cold, wet nights when you want to get back inside, or encouraging her where and when to go to the toilet when you are on a walk.

Crate and puppy pen set up for housetraining.

Remember

O Always give your pup the chance to go to the toilet outside. If she *has* to go inside, she will do so, so don't blame her for that.

O Never growl at your pup or rub her face in her urine or faeces. This will only confuse and scare her. If you catch her midway through toileting inside, say 'wrong' (in a neutral tone, not as a punishment), and just pick her up and pop her outside calmly, and encourage her to continue on the grass. Click and reward after the act (praise, or click and give food), and cue the toileting with a 'be quick' command.

O Soiling is largely involuntary, so punishment has little or no effect. In fact, because pups urinate to indicate submission, if you, as the pack leader, tell them off for urinating, they will want to signal 'I give up!' and may urinate more — setting off a vicious circle that just gets worse, and is the opposite effect of what you want. (See the section on excessive submission on page 245.)

O Don't even use the 'wrong' command with submissive pups — just pick them up and pop them outside.

O Use a 'be quick' command, and click and reward your pup after she goes to the toilet in the right place. Your pup will quickly learn the command, and it is useful to let her know to toilet when you use the 'be quick' command. Wait until your pup has finished her business before clicking and rewarding — you wouldn't like to be interrupted either!

Trouble-shooting

So what are the possible causes why housetraining isn't working, and how do we resolve it?

O How you set up your house-training system for your pup can influence whether your pup can succeed, so check your set-up to ensure you are setting your pup up for success.
  — Make sure there is clear surface delineation between what should be your pup's bed and what should be her toilet area.
  — Make sure there is sufficient room for your pup's bed and the toilet space to be clearly separate.

O Potentially, you have introduced your pup from her den (crate/pen) into your broader house too quickly, or without a systematic approach, so she hasn't generalised the idea of her den into the whole house. If so, go back to basics and reintroduce your pup to your house room by room — go slowly, ensuring she is well established in each room first before moving on.

O If your pup is older, you can use the clip station rather than the crate to do this generalisation work. Your pup won't soil on her clip station unless desperate.

O For very tough cases, you might need to move the clip station around *within* each room, so the pup gets a clear idea that the whole room is not a toilet, before you extend into another room.

O Ensure you disassociate any areas your pup has toileted inside as not being a toilet area, most importantly by removing the smell. Use a mix of 1 part white vinegar to 3 parts water on the spot. Once dry, pop a clip station on top of that area and clip your pup up there at intervals. After a few stays on the clip station, she will start associating that space with her den.

O Don't allow free access around the house for some time (weeks). This treatment does need patience.

O Help your pup succeed. Make sure you are regularly toileting her outside in the appropriate place (using your 'be quick' command), and on the appropriate surface — grass and garden. Take your pup out after eating, play, exercise and sleep.

13.7   SEPARATION (LEARNING TO BE BY THEMSELVES)

The importance of teaching separation

Usually at around 7-9 weeks old, wolf puppies move away from their mother and go out to meet the rest of their pack. At this stage (called their 'secondary socialisation period') the puppies form a bond with their mentors and wider family. This naturally occurring critical period for separation happens over a short period of time. This is the time puppies naturally learn separation, so if done at this time it is simple and easy to achieve. They lose this association quickly, however, so separation needs to be established in this key 7-10 weeks of age period. Hopefully the breeder has started some early separation in a crate, too.

When the development of the mentor bond is not managed carefully, and the puppy doesn't develop the ability to be alone, anxiety and fear of separation develops (separation distress). This is a very common problem I see in my clinic, and can be one of the more difficult behavioural issues for an owner to address, so getting this right at this time is critical.

A common mistake that loving, caring owners make is going out of their way to ensure that their beloved new puppy is with them all or most of the time — tending to his every whimper or cry, always keeping him happy and entertained. Although this comes from a place of love, in reality the puppy is learning to become over-dependent and attention seeking. These attention-seeking behaviours are often inadvertently rewarded by the owner, causing them to intensify: for example, a young pup whines when he wants to be patted, and the owner pats him, thereby rewarding the whining. Even just attending to your pup, or just looking at him when he shows anxiety, can effectively reward this anxious state and resultant behaviours, and increase the frequency of it.

Right from the start, give your puppy plenty of time with you *and* away from you during the day and at night. Start using the crate first, then the clip station when older. Also ensure that you separate your pup from his playmates for periods of time, so he doesn't get overly dependent on other dogs either.

A good amount of structure and routine is good for a young pup, including lots of sleep.

Preparation and set-up

Ideally the breeder will have started some separation for short periods from 4 weeks old. Some separate crate experience early would be a real bonus, otherwise separation training starts soon after you get your pup, as it may be the first time he has been removed from his mum and siblings. He will be aware of their absence. He may get distressed and give distress vocalisations, so you need to ensure you are prepared to manage this so it goes well.

Before you get your pup home, make sure you set up a crate or a puppy pen area so you can start to teach separation. Remember, these areas are representations of the den, which is a natural place of comfort and safety for your pup, and which is why pups like holes, kennels, being under tables, etc., as these places simulate their natural dens.

Your pup will be experiencing a lot of firsts during this period, so be mindful that your pup is supported so these firsts go well. Remember that if you are getting your pup at 8 weeks of age, it is during a fear-imprint period, so be particularly mindful as you achieve separation and do it in a more graduated way. You may choose to keep your crated pup close to you in this week, and systematically move him to the house-training crate and pen area at gradually increasing distances as you increase separation. Hopefully smells have been introduced (like lavender or a blanket from mum) that you can use in his crate to help settle your pup.

Set up the environment to minimise distress. If there is another pup, toys or anything you can put in the pen or crate that he can cuddle up to, that will help a lot with the separation, distracting him as you leave him alone for periods of time. If there is no other pup, put in a surrogate soft toy and/or something that smells of his dam or litter mates, or anything that is warm and soft. A hot-water bottle wrapped in a towel is good, as pups love warmth. (Do this just for the first few days while your pup is getting used to the new environment.)

The technique

Here are the key steps in this training:

- O Understand your role: you can be part of the problem — don't be!
- O Create a psychologically secure base through joining up, so your pup feels fundamentally secure.
- O Create a physical secure base in your pup's crate (the den is associated with mum).
- O Switch your pup into a learning state using the clicker and food rewards, and put him in 'Zen down' for longer and longer periods.
- O Do desensitisation through graduated departure (see next page), to learn to separate.

Teaching separation using the crate

Pop your pup into his crate with a puppy Kong/food, toys, etc., as above, and move away out of sight but stay within earshot. Monitor how your pup responds. You can expect some whining and vocalisation, so don't be concerned, and most importantly don't respond. If you return to your pup while he is vocalising, you are rewarding the vocal behaviour with your attention, and so are teaching him that he will get what he wants through noisy behaviour — setting up a cycle of behaviour you do not want. Allow your pup to get through it. Reward quiet behaviours with your attention and presence and letting him out. This can take some time, so be prepared. A little bit of tough love might be needed at this stage. It is the best time to train this behaviour now, as the pup is in the right stage to learn, so commit to it and establish it.

When you go back to the crate, take your clicker and a food reward with you. Your pup will start vocalising when you return, so wait for a period of quiet (even just a couple of seconds of silence), then click and reward your pup's non-vocal behaviour (tossing the food into the crate). Continue to click and reward quiet behaviour, extending the quiet period out until you get 20-30 seconds of quiet, then you can release the pup from the crate. The reward is freedom for quiet, non-vocal behaviour.

Start with periods of separation for an hour or so, and extend out from there.

The clip station is an important
tool for teaching separation.

Trouble-shooting

If your pup is a bit more difficult and not settling, then you need to
formalise the way you separate him. We use a method called *graduated
departure*, which can be done in the crate or later on a clip station. This
is systematically removing yourself from your pup in slow increments.
Because your pup is having difficulty with this, we have to break your
departure into smaller steps.

Pop your pup into his crate, and click and reward quiet behaviour.
Timing is really critical to this: ensure your click is rewarding *quiet*
behaviour!

○ If your puppy vocalises, wait until he stops. Then click and reward
   (throwing food into the crate).

○ Move a few metres away, but where your pup can see you, and look
   away from your pup. Click and reward quiet behaviour.

○ Move away and out of sight. Wait for quiet behaviour, then return
   and click and reward. Only go back when your pup is non-vocal, so
   you don't reward vocal behaviour.

O Continue until you can leave without a fuss for 15-minute periods, then slowly extend the time.

O Gradually extend the time to 2 or 3 hours, leaving a stuffed Kong and toys.

O For particularly anxious pups, you can use a homeopathic option like Rescue Remedy. I wouldn't use other drug therapies at this young age.

O Once your pup is old enough for a clip station (10–12 weeks onwards), you can leave him on different clip stations around the house and outside while you go about your daily activities without him shadowing you. You need to train him to the clip station. (See the Puppy Zen toolkit section in Part C.)

O Keep extending separation into other areas, and for longer and longer periods.

Remember how important the ability to be alone is in your pup, and later your dog. Dogs that suffer separation distress as a phobia can't stay non-anxious when separated. They don't find home, their clip station or crate comforting, and so suffer anxiety for long periods of time, making life miserable for them and you. I have had clients whose lives are determined solely by their dogs' needs, and it can be very painful for all. Don't be one of these statistics.

13.8   BITE INHIBITION

With puppies between 2 and 5 months old, mouthing is natural, because they use their mouths like we use our hands. Puppies also use nipping and biting as part of their play and dominance tools. This is naturally seen when pups play with each other in the wild: they are basically learning how to play and establish dominance order by play-fighting with each other. The adults in the pack teach the pups what is appropriate and what isn't, by gesturing: snarls, growling and then pinning them on the muzzle. This is largely ritualised, and is them being assertive to the pups when they bite too hard. This is how the pup naturally learns bite inhibition: natural consequence or correction. After 4 months of age, pups are getting their second teeth, which can set off more biting.

For young pups, this behaviour is unlikely to be aggression-driven, but is mainly rough play. However, it is essential to teach your puppy that mouthing and biting people are not acceptable. As your puppy gets bigger and stronger, this behaviour is no longer cute or fun, it becomes dangerous, so from the start it is important not to allow painful biting.

There are a number of techniques to address bite inhibition in an escalating order of necessity (in case your pup isn't responding). They are grouped into:

O proactive training (shaping non-biting behaviour before biting starts)
O addressing inappropriate behaviour (emerging issues)
O trouble-shooting for persistent issues.

It is a very important behaviour to address early, so make sure you work on this training.

Proactively shaping appropriate behaviour

These techniques are actively trying to shape appropriate non-biting behaviour before it gets started by teaching a soft mouth and docility.

Desensitising your pup to body handling

The first thing is to desensitise your pup to body handling, so she is less reactive to handling.

O Gently squeeze your pup's paw, jaw, mouth, ears, neck, feet, tail and body.
O Systematically start with one part, and work through all of the body parts.
O Click and reward calm responses. (Because your hands are busy handling your pup, it can be helpful to initially do this with a friend helping. Keep the food reward close by.)
O This is also helpful for when a vet will handle her.
O Ideally, the breeder will have started this gently from 2 weeks of age, but make sure you are doing it as soon as you get the pup.

Joining-up practice

O Continue to develop the follower response (through joining up), clicking and rewarding your pup for following you and not nipping or jumping, but keeping four paws down on the ground as she walks beside you.
O This can start at 4 weeks old or as soon as you get the pup.

'Gentle' command

O The best approach is to be proactive and teach your pup the 'gentle' command as part of early training, so you don't have to correct biting later.

O Start very young, from 4 to 8 weeks.

O Carefully put your hand in your pup's mouth and say 'gentle'. When she is gentle, click and reward her gentle behaviour.

O This can be part of the handling desensitisation, too.

O Repeat this often.

Redirecting to appropriate toys (discriminating what to bite)

O Get a rope tug toy, maybe with a ball on the end.

O Play actively with the toy and your pup, moving the toy from side to side, stimulating her chase response.

O Once your pup grabs the toy put on some resistance, and encourage her to tug back.

O Do this regularly with your pup.

O Whenever your pup gets into biting or nipping behaviours, bring out the toy and redirect her on to it.

O Your pup is learning discrimination: that she can pull and bite and have fun with her toy, but not with your hands.

O This type of play can also be used as a reward at the end of a training session: finishing with her running around and playing with the toy herself.

O Some people worry that this will increase aggression, however research shows that this is quite the opposite. (And it's fun!)

Resource-guarding desensitisation

O You need to teach your pup not to guard resources. This can be a difficult and scary behaviour to change if established in adult dogs, so work on this training.

O Puppies often bite when protecting a resource because, to dogs, possession is nine-tenths of the law.

O The best way to prevent this is to teach them to trade you for something better: remember, as the mentor you need to control the resources. (Review Your role as mentor in Part B.)

O Ideally, start this young (around 4 weeks) or at the very least by 12 weeks.

○ At this young age, use a puppy bone or a Kong packed with food, and give it to your pup and let her chew it for a while.

○ Take it away, and click and reward with a really high-value food treat.

○ While your pup is this young her threat is minor, so you can take away something and trade it for a higher-value treat — she'll catch on quick.

○ Repeat until your pup is relaxed and understands that you are trading and that you control the goods.

○ Once that is established, approach your pup's food bowl and add something better, clicking as you do it. Once you are confident of your pup's response, move your hand around in the bowl, too.

○ Your pup will start anticipating you coming with gifts, and will look to you in a friendly way.

○ Keep doing this regularly to prevent resource-guarding behaviour early.

○ Continue to increase your trading game, and make sure your pup is looking expectantly at you as you approach the bowl and the bone.

○ Use a similar method as soon as you notice your pup guarding other things, like the mentor (lap protection), toys, a couch or a bed. Proactively walk towards your pup, toss high-value food beside her, and click and reward as she eats. Then proceed to handling her, and click and reward. Do lots of practice. Your pup will see you as coming with gifts.

○ Make sure all family members do this work, so your pup thinks of you all as her mentors and controlling the resources.

○ You are also reinforcing you and your family's bond, and preventing resource guarding and dominance aggression (aggression towards family members) raising its ugly head.

Teach children how to play with a pup

○ Children's movement can stimulate your pup's natural play behaviour to grab and scruff. (Imagine two pups together!)

○ Before you allow too much play with your pup, make sure you have already introduced the tug toy and taught your pup how to discriminate and redirect onto it when she nips or bites you.

○ Tell children that if your pup starts to bite or nip when they are playing, they should slow down, be quiet, and slowly get her tug toy and help her redirect onto it.

O Let the children know that they are an important part of teaching your pup to play gently with children, and we don't want to teach him bad habits!

O Get children to rehearse the 'gentle' command, too, and you click and reward.

Addressing inappropriate behaviours

'Ouch' signal

O This signal is used to interrupt and alert your pup that you are not happy with her behaviour.

O If your pup starts to nip or bite, then say a loud 'Ouch!' so she knows it hurts and is alerted to that.

O Using an alarmed tone is important, so make sure the 'ouch' is meaningful and acts as a disruptor.

O If this is not effective (over 2–3 occasions), then move on to the 'gentle' or 'leave it' commands.

O Reflect on your pup's temperament: this technique is most likely to be effective with more gentle, sensitive pups; move active, robust pups will need the other commands.

Point teeth away technique and time-out

O If your pup is biting, pick her up under the chest and hold her in such a way that you have control of her, pointing her head (and teeth) away from you.

O Use soothing words and handling to settle her.

O If she persists, pop her in her crate for time-out (or on the clip station, if introduced) to settle down.

O Remember, don't use the crate or clip station as time-out until your pup has been well introduced to them and has established positive associations (after about a month from starting).

'Leave it', 'gentle' and 'no'

O If you find these previous techniques aren't working, you might have to introduce the 'leave it' command (from 10 weeks of age). Review this in the section on basic commands in Part C, using a tug toy as the item you want to teach your pup to leave.

O Ultimately, you want to have your pup respond to play and then leave it on request, so you know that you have control of her play drive so she doesn't get overly aroused in play.

O Once 'gentle' and 'leave it' are trained, alternate the 'gentle' command while the pup is in low arousal and not biting (and not pulling). Pop your hand in the pup's mouth and say 'gentle', then click and reward, and repeat often. You can then also use 'leave it' if the pup gets rough with your hand, and click and reward when she leaves it. Keep this up until your pup has it clearly learnt.

O Once taught, you can introduce the conditioned aversive signal (the 'no' command) as well. The retrieve game is similar, too.

Moderating a pup nipping children in play (using a slip collar and lead)

This technique can also be used to moderate excessively rough play and biting other pups.

O Initially, the children should stop playing and be still if the pup nips, which may resolve the behaviour by itself (see the earlier advice).

O If that doesn't work, then you need a moderating technique to manage the issue.

O Children, especially if young, won't have the confidence to do what is needed, so you need to orchestrate some training situations for your pup around children.

O Set your pup on a long-line and a slip or half-slip collar (from 8 weeks on) and let a child play with her.

O If your pup starts to nip, provide a check; don't use a command.

O As soon as the pup withdraws, click and reward, throwing food on the ground away from the child, or getting the child to throw the food if they are confident. This allows your pup to lower her level of arousal and regain the learning state, then re-engage with the child in a less aroused state.

O Graduate your check's firmness until you find what is effective.

O Encourage your pup to move on to a tug-of-war game or to chase a ball, thereby reinforcing what are appropriate mouthing objects (redirection and discrimination).

O You don't want the pup to avoid the child, so up the play

component if the pup seems to avoid the child excessively after the check. It is a balance: you want to empower the child, but not develop avoidance of the child by your pup.

O If at all possible, get the child to do some clicking and rewarding, or at least make it look like that.

O Do this carefully and under strict supervision: the child can play tug, too, but take care your pup stays on the toy. Use a check if the pup redirects to the child.

Moderating jowl-licking adult dogs

O Pups often excessively jowl-lick adult dogs, and sometimes can get pinned or hurt. You can use this same moderating technique in that situation and, because it often occurs earlier, you can practise the technique on dogs first and master it.

Trouble-shooting

This section is for the more resistant and aggressive pups that may even be a little older. If your pup persists, then the next level of techniques includes the jaw pinch or the lip roll (see photos on page 240). These two techniques are used to stop the more dominant puppies from biting in the formative period. Both replicate the way pups would learn in the wild (the muzzle pin). Please note that this is only suitable for puppies aged 2–6 months old. I also don't recommend children use the jaw pinch or lip roll techniques.

This behaviour is an exception to most Puppy Zen techniques, in that *you* are delivering the correction (like the wolf dam does to its pup by pinning). However, like all of our Puppy Zen approaches there is a rationale for this. Instead of using a standard correction, you use a conditioned aversive signal ('no') to warn your pup, so she can choose to stop the behaviour and avoid the correction. These techniques need to be applied effectively and properly, and they need a little confidence, but when done correctly they are effective.

The jaw pinch technique

Let the pup approach to mouth or bite you, and, when she does, press your thumb on top of the puppy's tongue into the 'V' at the bottom of her mouth and pinch down against your forefinger on the underside of the jaw. Do this until she starts to pull away, then hold for a couple of beats, saying 'No!' The pup will pull back in discomfort, and as she pulls away either divert her attention onto a tug toy or ball, or click and reward any other non-aggressive behaviour, even the pulling away. Note that more reactive or dominant pups may come right back at you. Pop those dogs on the clip station or lead, and make sure you can get control. I try to move into the 'gentle' routine if possible, allowing the pup to mouth me gently, and clicking and rewarding while saying 'gentle'.

The lip roll technique

When your pup approaches to mouth, bite or nip, you simply let your hand be enclosed by her jaw, then roll her lip onto her teeth and press down slightly as she bites. Do this until she starts to pull away, then hold for a few beats, saying 'no', before releasing and trying to divert her attention onto a tug toy or ball. Use the same approach as in jaw pinch method, with clicking and treating, or teaching the 'gentle' command if possible. Don't let it escalate, and put her away in time-out if it does.

Summary

Nipping, mouthing and biting are natural, and pups just need to learn to be gentle as the most positive way of handling it. However, persistent and dominant pups may need more. For young pups we have a number of preventative techniques that all use positive reinforcement techniques. For the more difficult cases (often older pups) we move to contrast training techniques. If it persists beyond these techniques, go to my online resource and videos: dogzen.com/puppyresources.

13.9 FEAR AND PHOBIA PREVENTION (HABITUATION AND DESENSITISATION)

What are we doing and why are we doing it?

With puppies, as a general rule, we use habituation to adapt them to novel stimuli, and what could be or become frightening stimuli. Habituation is just exposing them so they learn to adjust to novel things, and this happens best when they are very young. If fear is involved, then they can't learn just by habituation and a process of desensitisation is needed. Novelty and change generally should be

The jaw pinch.

The lip roll.

introduced early: go to Part F to find out when to start this.

It is safer to habituate using a desensitisation hierarchy: graduating the stimulus in incremental stages of intensity (e.g. increasing noise volume, or light intensity with a camera flash). In many cases this graduated approach will desensitise your pup if she is not over-sensitive. If needed, you can add in counter-conditioning (switching into a learning state) with the clicker and food rewards. The food anticipation and clicker pairing will switch more anxious pups into a learning state, and then the graduated exposure hierarchy will allow the pup to desensitise to the stimulus and adapt to it. I find it is often better to be proactive and use the clicker and address each issue early.

The critical period for accepting loud noises like gunshots and firecrackers is 6–10 weeks, so get started and do it early, using the clicker. Starting with joining up reinforces the secure base effect and the bond, too, which gives your pup confidence that you are his ally, which will help his confidence and facilitate learning.

Key steps

Identify
Identify and make a list of the things, items, environments and other stimuli that your pup will likely be exposed to as an adult, for example:

- loud noises — thunder, fireworks, gunshots
- vehicles — cars, truck and traffic noises, back-firing
- noisy, moving things — skateboards, rollerblades, bikes, motor bikes, lawn mowers, chainsaws
- household noises and items — vacuum cleaners, kitchen whizzes, washing machines, brooms
- unusual clothing — hats, glasses, hi-vis vests, hoodies
- strange objects, big colourful or flapping items (flags), fire.

The technique
- During the critical period for habituation (4–10 weeks of age), exposing your pup to potentially frightening stimuli through general habituation can be enough to prevent fear or phobia developing. That is, you just have the various stimuli in the background as your pup goes about his daily life, which exposes him to them, without him having to actively engage with them.

Desensitise to noise by gradually increasing volume while clicking and rewarding.

Pups can develop phobias to household items.

I show you what to expose your pup to in Part F.

O For example, for noise, play audio of scary sounds in the background to habituate your pup, slowly increasing the volume over time.

O I also activate the 'startle and recovery response' by exposing the pup to banging pots, etc., when he is in the least fearful stage of his life and can grow startle-recovery resilience at this formative time.

O However, if your pup is fearful, we switch to desensitisation and counter-conditioning to be safe. This is particularly important after 10 weeks of age as the critical period closes.

O At each stage when you increase the volume, pay attention to how your pup reacts, to see whether he has any sensitivities or fears.

O Be aware during the fear-imprint periods, and wind back the challenges (i.e. at 5 weeks, 8 weeks, 12 weeks and 16 weeks).

O If you observe any signs of sensitivity (see the section on shared language to help you read your pup's body language), do the following immediately:

— Do some joining up and basic commands to start the session, which will ensure your pup is connected to you, and feels safe (you are his secure base) and is making decisions.

— Use a desensitisation hierarchy: write down in order from low to high what your pup is reacting to.

— Use the clicker and food rewards (counter-conditioning) to switch your pup into, and maintain, a learning state. If he stops accepting the food rewards, slow down the steps.

— Reinforce (click and reward) non-reactive calm behaviour as you gradually expose your pup to the stimuli in increasing increments (e.g. if noise, it is getting louder).

EXAMPLE: DESENSITISING TO NOISE

Start this aspect of the training by sourcing a recording of different sounds. Search for 'sounds scary' on YouTube or iTunes.

With your pup on a lead next to you, play these sounds at a very low volume. Click and reward your pup for calm responses as you play the sounds. Don't go overboard: keep it very soft and low in volume to begin with. If your pup stops eating, you need to reduce the volume.

Encourage your pup to go into 'sit', 'down' and 'Zen down' as you play the sounds. As you continue the training, very slowly start increasing the volume of the sounds in increments, systematically clicking and rewarding your pup's calm responses.

Keep in mind

Go carefully and take it in stages. Remember to observe how your pup is coping — the more sensitive your pup, the more careful you should be and the smaller the steps you should take. Don't make the training context fearful: this is an exposure technique, so you need lots of repetition, not big leaps.

Any stimulus that your pup is looking wary or fearful of should go through desensitisation, using the clicker and food rewards.

Prevention is definitely better than cure. As your puppy's brain is being wired in the formative period, he is much more able to habituate or adapt to sounds, flashes, flapping and other novel stimuli, so start this early (see Part F for timing). If your pup is wary, use desensitisation and counter-conditioning to help him avoid developing fears or phobias. See my online trouble-shooting if the problems are more serious, or go to www.dogzen.com.

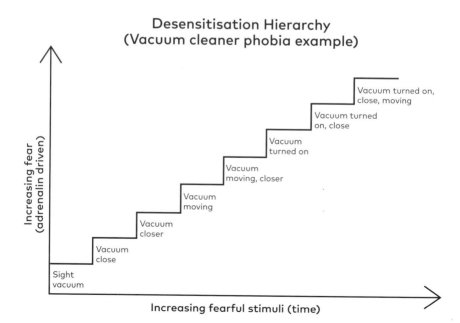

Desensitisation Hierarchy
(Vacuum cleaner phobia example)

Trouble-shooting

Below are some reasons why your pup might be exhibiting emerging phobic issues even if you have tried the techniques above:

o Your pup did not get enough exposure during the formative period.
o Your behaviour wasn't proofed (trained in different contexts) or the exposure generalised (containing a wide variety).
o You were not effective in your techniques, because:
   — your pup wasn't in a learning state, and so did not retain the learning
   — you were reinforcing the wrong stage in the sequence
   — you did not time the clicker correctly, thereby ensuring you reward appropriate, calm behaviours
   — you were not reading your pup's response correctly, and so pushed him too hard, creating early issues — so go back and increase the number of steps (increase graduation)
   — you did not do enough repetition.
o You have a particularly fearful pup, possibly breed-related, that needs a slower, more careful approach.

13.10   EXCESSIVE SUBMISSION

What is submission?

Submission is an important part of dog communication, where a pup or dog communicates she gives up or acquiesces to the dominant dog. (See the section on shared language in Part B.) Excessive submission often occurs when you are not aware that your pup is signalling submission and your behaviour is signalling dominance.

For example, your pup might see your approach as threatening (remember your appropriate body language), so shows submission postures, like lowering her body down or rolling over. You misread this as your pup being happy to see you, and so (understandably) continue to approach your pup to say 'hello'. Your approach continues to signal dominance to your pup, so she escalates her submissive posturing. This cycle can escalate until a more fearful pup urinates and some might bite.

This very common catch-22 situation comes about from a simple misunderstanding between human and pup communication. This is particularly likely if you have a more sensitive or fearful pup, and is more common with female pups.

Preparation

Before you get started:

O establish clicker training

O teach a 'sit' and 'wait' — pups taught the 'sit' early usually won't have this issue . . .

O *do not* teach or practise a 'down' yet, as it is similar to the lowering behaviours of excessive submission.

The technique

The following are the key steps:

O Use appropriate body language that doesn't express dominance (see the section on shared language in Part B).

O Create a calm, confident greeting routine, and reward upright behaviours.

O Practise joining up after building the greeting routine.

Establishing a calm and confident greeting routine

O Appear as least-dominant as possible. Use a positive, upbeat tone of voice only, and don't get too excitable or hype up your pup.

O Initially call your pup to you. Do not approach your pup, as this might seem like dominance behaviour for a timid pup. Click and reward your pup for approaching you.

O If your pup is very timid and hesitates to come to you, drop food in front of your pup, between the two of you.

O Deliver food on the floor rather than directly from your hand, at first. This will mean you are not leaning over your pup.

O Once your pup has come to you, ask your pup to 'sit' with an upbeat tone.

O As soon as your pup sits, click and reward, again delivering the food on the floor.

O If your pup rolls over, ask her for a 'sit', luring her back upright with a treat, or throw the treat away from you again to decrease any threat.

O Gradually move to delivering the food from your hand. It will help if you hold the food below your pup's head rather than above it, as having your hand above your pup's head can be intimidating. Then, gradually and systematically, deliver the food higher and higher.

You can inadvertently signal dominance to your pup and cause excessive submission. Don't handle like this on the head or back.

○ As your pup's confidence grows, gradually handle her under the chin/chest area. This is the best area, and the least intimidating. Click and reward your pup for staying upright.

○ Only handle or pet her when she is upright. Do not reward your pup if she rolls over or pat her belly, as this will only reinforce such submissive gestures.

○ Your sensitive pup will likely be anxious about looking at your eyes, so desensitise her to your eye contact by placing food in a line between your eyes and her eyes. Click and reward when you get confident eye contact and posture. Ensure you do not stare at your pup, though.

○ When your pup is ready, move from only patting your pup on the chin/chest area to patting her on the head and around the neck. Click and reward your pup constantly as you do so, to teach her to accept it.

○ Start to approach your pup rather than always calling your pup to approach you. Only do this once your pup is consistently approaching you with confidence.

O Similarly, start to remain upright when approaching your pup (rather than lowering your body every time). Again, only do this after your pup has proven confidence with you in a lowered position. Continue to click and reward positive, upright behaviours as you do this.

O Continue with this training for around 5 to 15 minutes each day (you can split this up into a couple of sessions). After 2-3 weeks you should be seeing a great improvement in your pup's confidence, after which you can progress to the next stage of the technique.

The returning home routine

O When pups are prone to excessive submission, a major trigger can be the owner's return home at the end of the day. For this reason, it is important to be ready to practise at this time.

O Keep your pouch full of treats and the clicker in the car, in your bag, or up high and near your front door (or wherever the greet will happen).

O When you arrive home, proceed through your greeting routine (as outlined above) immediately upon entry. As it is the first greeting after you get home, it can be the most anxiety-inducing for your submissive pup.

O Teach your friends and family members the best way to approach your submissive pup, too.

Joining up — building the relationship

O Now that your pup has more confidence with you, you can progress to building and strengthening your relationship with joining up.

O We reserve this training until after you have begun treating the problem of excessive submission, because initially a highly submissive pup may find it stressful or intimidating to be on the clip lead and be doing pressure on/pressure off work.

O Click and reward calm, upright behaviour by only practising the 'sit' command to begin with.

O Once your pup seems confident and relaxed, practise the 'down' command, and then graduate into 'Zen down'.

O Notice how the effects of this position are different to excessive submission — how quickly your pup can calm down and learn, focusing on you; how her demeanour and confidence grow, and her overall learning speed increases dramatically now there is no longer excessive submission at play.

13.11 CALMING BEHAVIOURS — ADDRESSING HYPERACTIVITY

Hyperactivity results from a pup's natural play and soliciting behaviours, which evolved in the ancestral wolf as the desire to interact physically with the pack and solicit food through regurgitation. When these behaviours are excessive, it is not tolerated by older dogs, who moderate with muzzle pinning, snarling, growling and standing over the pups. However, our love for pups can result in us unintentionally rewarding them for their over-excitable tendencies, and therefore exacerbate them.

At the start of the formative period (2–10 weeks), puppies sleep a lot, are less active and so are ripe for learning. This period is definitely the time to capture calm behaviour and wire it in before the over-excitable responses develop. By the time puppies get to 12 weeks of age they are typically highly active and excitable. This is particularly once they have bonded and feel confident with their new pack or family. Therefore, the earlier you start this training (from 3 to 9 weeks) the better.

Hyperactive behaviour is often inadvertently rewarded by:

O talking to or handling your pup when he behaves hyperactively
O over-stimulating your pup with your own excitement when you come home
O giving your pup the outcome he desires when he is hyperactive, such as letting him out the door
O turning hyperactive tendencies into a game.

Hyperactive tendencies can be exacerbated by an excessively stimulating environment. For example, highly active and playful children can increase a pup's level of hyperactivity. Some breeds of dogs are more genetically predisposed to hyperactivity, due to being selected by humans for high-arousal activities such as hunting and herding.

The treatment
The steps to addressing this are:
- exercising and stimulating
- switching to a learning state
- setting good boundaries
- teaching four feet on the ground
- teaching that nothing in life is free
- joining up
- establishing discrimination — 'leave it'
- establishing good meet and greets.

Exercising and stimulating
- Make sure your pup is getting an appropriate level of exercise, play and mental stimulation.
- Exercising your pup before training will help burn off some of his energy before you ask him to become focused and attentive.
- Structure your pup's day and training well, and rest your pup often. Giving time for controlled rest and sleep actually decreases hyperactivity.
- There is a fine line between excitable play and hyperactivity. You need to be in control of any play activity, and be able to turn it off when desired. Have clear start and finish signals, like 'get it' to start and 'okay' or 'that'll do' to finish.
- Make sure you finish when you say you are finishing!

Switching to a learning state
The main issue with hyperactive behaviour is that your pup is in a non-learning state, so, to calm a hyperactive pup, first get him into a learning state.
- Get your pup on the clicker and teach the basics: 'sit', 'down', 'Zen down'. Practise lots of joining up. Focus on the calming postures.
- Deliver food to the ground initially so your pup stays on the ground. As your pup gets more consistent, you can start delivering the food reward from your hand so your pup can learn to bring his attention to you while at the same time having four feet on the ground. (Your pup is learning that he doesn't need to jump up to get your attention.)
- If you find rewarding from your hand has started your pup

jumping up again, go back to delivering rewards on the ground until the behaviour is better established.

O When delivering a food reward from the hand to a hyperactive pup, close your hand over the food and slowly open up your hand as the pup nibbles it gently, so he doesn't snap at your hand. (Hyperactive pups have a tendency to snap.)

O When trained also use the clip station (see Part C).

O Never reward pawing, jumping up and vocalising — remember a reward includes any eye contact, touching or speaking to him, as well as traditional pats and food treats.

O If you cannot get your pup to settle at the clip station, you may find it easier to start with a moving on-lead joining up for your busy wee pup.

O Once your pup is focusing on the food lures and responding to the clicker, he will quickly go into a learning state. (Watch for the signs: pupils shrinking, calm demeanour, and taking food treats more calmly.)

O Do this 3 times a day.

Setting good boundaries

Hyperactivity in pups is inherently extreme affiliative behaviour, which often results in inappropriate behaviour (as defined by us), such as jumping up and snapping up at faces. Hyperactive pups also tend to have poor boundaries, as they are often out of the learning state and don't retain their learning well. Creating good boundaries is essential for these pups.

O Four feet on the ground.

O If your pup is jumping up, wait until all four paws are on the ground, then immediately click and reward as they hit the ground, delivering the food reward onto the ground in front of your pup. (You want your pup to stay down, so deliver the food on the ground.)

O Do this every time your pup's paws return to the ground.

O Introduce the cue: a flat hand, palm outwards, at your pup, and say 'off'.

O Click and reward whenever he is not barking, jumping up or pawing you, and has four feet on the ground.

O Teach the 'leave it' command (see the basic commands section in Part C). This is a good way to teach your pup to discriminate between appropriate behaviour (click and reward) and inappropriate behaviour (leave it).

○ Encourage good meet and greets. Your hyperactive pup is more likely to rush up and jump all over people and dogs.

○ Nothing in life is free (see the section on how you are the mentor in Part B): your pup needs to know that you are in charge of resources as his mentor. Your pup must work for everything he perceives as a reward during the training phase: freedom, food, social contact, treats, pats, going through a door, and so on. Rewards should be given for good behaviour, but never for undesirable behaviour. When treating hyperactivity, restrict your pup's access to yourself. He is only allowed to be with you when calm (a reward for calm behaviour); when hyperactive, your pup goes into his crate or onto the clip station (a form of time-out). After a period of being settled, your pup can then be allowed freedom again for his calm behaviour. Only use these methods once they are well established (at least a month after you have taught them).

○ Practise good recall. Classically, hyperactive pups don't have good recall, as they tend to be outwardly focused and easily distracted. Make sure you emphasise a good recall in your training. (See the basic commands section in Part C.)

○ Finish training sessions well. Learning is mentally consuming, and hyperactive pups tend to have short concentration spans early on and so get distracted easily. I always end every sequence with a 'Zen down', which allows hyperactive pups to regain calmness. When you finish a session, use a play retrieve (throwing a toy and then calling them back) to let your pup release any energy he has pent up after a controlled training session. Then, again, finish on a 'Zen down'. Praise your pup at the end of a session, but keep it low-key so as not to over-arouse him. Then pop him into his crate or on a clip station to rest and allow the learning to consolidate.

In very rare cases, particularly difficult pups may benefit from homeopathic or allopathic medications that have a calming effect on the sympathetic nervous system. Rescue Remedy can relax a pup, but more difficult cases can be supported by other medications, so check with your veterinarian.

There are also a number of modern toys and training aids that give pups mental and physical outlets, such as the manners minder, ball-throwing toys and the like. It is important to give your pup an outlet and a purpose.

13.12   BARKING, WHINING AND HOWLING

When comfortable, well-bonded and adapted to their environment, puppies rarely bark, unless they use vocalisations to communicate in play and conflicted situations. The most common causes of barking, whining or howling are due to separation distress, fear or threat.

The treatment
The key steps to treating this behaviour are:
O understand and treat underlying cause
O recognise if you reward the barking
O build your relationship with your pup
O teach the 'quiet' command.

Understand and treat the underlying cause
The main class of vocal behaviours I see in my clinic are separation distress vocalisations and soliciting behaviours. Go to these issues to address the underlying cause. Territorial barking and other forms come much later in late puberty and beyond, when the territorial imperative grows.

Recognise if you reward the barking
Barking is easy for pups to do and very easy for us to unwittingly reward, which reinforces the behaviour, making it more difficult to correct.
O Nothing in life is free, so make sure you give rewards only for quiet, calm behaviour.
O For example, some people give their pups a toy or something to chew on when they bark, to keep them quiet, or if their pup is barking outside and wants to be let in, they let them in. These actions continually reward your pup for barking, and encourage her to use vocalisations again in the future when she wants something. Why wouldn't she, when previous experience says it works?

Build your relationship with your pup

O Ensure you have built a strong, trusting bond with your pup, so
she feels safe and remains in a calm, learning state.

O Do lots of joining up and clip-station work, and ensure your pup
has learnt separation properly, too.

Teach the 'quiet' command

O Pups often start barking or whining in the crate quite early on due
to separation anxiety, and often we reward that behaviour, so it is
important to make sure you don't do this at this early stage.

O Attention seeking is the main driver. Review Part C on how to
teach crate training, and check that your technique is effective.
Have you tried attaching the long-line to the crate to deliver an
effective check on the vocalisation? (This acts as an interrupter.)

O If you are still getting vocalisations, you will need to move to an
intervention technique and teach the 'quiet' command.
— Move your pup to the clip station, as she will now be older than
10 weeks.

— Do your normal clip-station training as per Part C, and get the pup adjusted to the clip station and calm.

— Refer to the section on separation training, and start graduated departure by leaving the pup initially for short times, and later for longer and longer times. Click and reward calm, non-vocal behaviour.

— If the pup is persistent, introduce a long-line on a half-slip (limited-slip) collar. When your pup is being vocal, say 'quiet'. If she remains quiet for 3 seconds, click and reward. Slowly extend this to several minutes, including moving away for a short while. Avoid eye contact as you don't want to engage your pup (to avoid soliciting behaviours).

— If the pup continues to vocalise, say 'quiet', and if she is, click and reward. If not, use a 'no' command, and if she continues barking, apply an effective check. Click and reward when quiet. Continue this until the pup learns the 'quiet' command.

— Don't let the pup get anxious, though; just break it into short lessons initially.

— Slowly extend the period of quiet and separation.

Chapter 14

Proofing behaviours and fading the clicker

Learning psychology emphasises how important it is to round out our training with what we call *proofing*, and *fading* the tools and techniques used to teach the behaviours. Once the formalised training sessions are done, we need to learn how to sustain behaviour changes and translate them into the real world. This, maybe surprisingly, is one of the most important parts of the book.

I couldn't say how many times people have said to me, 'It works in the backyard, but the minute I get to the park it all falls apart.' The most common problem people face with training is that they don't do the proofing stage well (they usually rush it). If you don't do this, you end up wasting all of the excellent training time you have put in.

WHAT IS PROOFING?

Proofing is taking our training out to the real world, and practising it in a variety of increasingly distracting and challenging environments. This is done in a systematic way, allowing your pup to grow his skills and confidence gradually as the environments become more challenging. This ensures you will get to a stage where you can go out with your pup without taking tools and treats along, relying instead on just voice commands and hand signals, and praise as a reinforcer. I often still take a clicker and a stash of dry food with me, and every now and again jackpot something good. I always keep my 'no' command effective, and reinforce that at intervals, too. However, when you get to this stage, life with your pup becomes much easier and more relaxed.

By necessity, training is always started in simple, non-distracting

Proof trained behaviours in increasingly complex environments. Succeed in each environment before you proceed.

Add another dog for distraction.

Add two dogs and a child for more distraction. This is proofing in action.

environments, so your pup is able to quickly understand what is being asked of him, because he is focused and attentive to you. This extends the training into the real world, so that these learned behaviours will remain in the face of distraction and unpredictable circumstances.

Changing the environment from simple to complex is one of the most challenging aspects of training. As we know, pups have highly sensitive senses (particularly smell, and response to movement and sounds), so once you head into novel environments with lots of new experiences and social stimulation, environmental influences will hinder learning and proofing if this transfer is not done in a systematic way.

Effective off-lead command is a sophisticated level of training in a complex, novel environment, so you need to follow these steps carefully. It can be very tempting to skip the steps when everything seems to go so well in your backyard or contained space. But when it all goes wrong in the park, it can be very frustrating and demotivating. Not only that, but the inappropriate behaviours your pup is doing in that environment are being reinforced if not addressed, so he will do them again next time. Systematic proofing of cues, commands and behaviour supports your pup to succeed.

In order to do this, it helps to make a record of what has happened, when and where, and what you did to correct it. Over time, this helps you identify triggers, inappropriate behaviours, and what you have to work on. It also helps you identify successes and progress, and perhaps where another approach needs to be taken. For more detail, see the section on the diary on page 264.

You need to be diligent and persistent in the early stages of proofing — failure to do so means you are failing to hard-wire the behaviour. The more systematic you are, the more you record it, the better the results will be. Once you have successfully proofed the behaviour maybe half a dozen times, then you won't need the diary.

A couple of failures here and there isn't an issue — but when you get sustained, inappropriate behaviour (when you have given up and thrown your hands in the air) you are in trouble. Return to basics. Trust that your dedicated work will pay off — it will be worth it!

WHAT IS FADING THE CLICKER?

Fading is when we slowly and systematically remove the tools and food rewards we used to teach a new behaviour from our training. This is so your pup will follow your commands without the need for rewards. If you use a clicker and food rewards to teach 'sit', and have practised the command using these tools and rewards in lots of different situations, and are confident with your pup's response, then slowly start to remove the use of the clicker and food reward. That way, you will be able to ask your pup to 'sit' using just a voice command, and using praise or a pat as the reward.

It is very important that you never fade the food reward from the clicker: you fade them together. The *click* is always a promise that a food reward is coming, so you can never make a click and then not deliver a reward. Instead, reduce the frequency with which you are using the clicker, but continue giving a food reward each time you do click. Once the behaviour is well established you can stop using the clicker and just intermittently use the food reward.

WHEN IS YOUR PUP 'PROOFED' ENOUGH?

There is a whole complexity of theory and language associated with proofing. However, for our purposes, I think it is best to keep it simple and to establish proofing to a level that is sufficient and adequate for our day-to-day lives. If you are looking to undertake higher-level obedience, then this might be an area that you explore in more detail; go to my book *Dog Zen* for details.

For our everyday purposes, I see proofing as sufficient when your pup:

O has a well-established bond with you (the most important aspect)

O wants to be in close proximity to you — stays in contact and uses the bond gaze

O enjoys working and responding to you

O has a good level of control on-lead and off-lead, and an effective shared language

O responds consistently and reliably to your commands

O has good recall

O understands your 'no' and your 'yes' (the clicker).

How to proof behaviour

The key steps are:

O understand your pup's distraction hierarchy and triggers, including observing your pup's body language

O slowly work in increasingly complex environments (e.g. location, number of dogs and people, mix of movement and scents, busy versus quiet places, etc.) within each environment

O work through a hierarchy of tools: start on a short lead, then a long-line or retractable lead, then off-lead, if appropriate.

Here is the process I recommend going through as a way of transferring your training into everyday life.

The technique

Stage one: Understanding your pup's distraction hierarchy

The more prepared you are the better, so it is useful to list in order (from low to high arousal) what your pup's key distractors are. Of course for each pup it is different; however, here is one example: tree branches moving in the wind, interesting scents on the ground, tennis balls, traffic, moving small animals, other dogs, people.

By understanding your pup's distractions, when you move into new environments you can assess the level of distraction and therefore challenge for your pup, and manage it. (This might include going somewhere else if it is too distracting, or doing more close-contact work rather than off-lead work, or just being more vigilant.)

Alongside of this is the importance of *observing your pup's body language* and understanding his personal signals going from low to high arousal. Remember from the section on shared language that in the time between when your pup is alerting his behaviour, targeting (fixing on his 'target') and initiating the behaviour, you have a critical window of opportunity to recognise what is happening so you can interrupt it at an early stage. (Usually up to the targeting stage.) Before your pup's adrenalin rises and the primitive brain kicks in, you can make contact with your pup and get him focused on you, his mentor, so you can guide him towards making the right decision (that is, appropriate behaviour). *Looking to you* is the key: in most instances, as soon as your pup looks to you, you can intervene effectively. Always check in to see that your pup is in a learning state.

Stage two: Increasing the complexity of the environment
Determine the hierarchy of environments that you will build up to (e.g. inside, backyard, contained paddock or tennis court, quiet park, dog park). Gradually increase the complexity of the environment you are working in over time (e.g. approximately over 4 months).

O Begin working in a simple environment, such as an enclosed room or backyard. Ensure it is a place that your pup knows well, and that has few distractions — no unfamiliar smells, no other animals, people or loud noises.

O Then move to a medium contained environment, such as a fenced paddock or a tennis court. There will be more space to move, but it should still essentially be enclosed. It may have a few more distractions (such as new smells), but not many.

O Then move to a complex environment, like a quiet park with just a few people and dogs. Slowly step up to the final stage, below, within 1 to 2 months, depending on how successful your pup is.

O Finally, move to a complex environment, such as a park with lots of other people, dogs and other species, in a place your dog doesn't know so well.

Within each of these environments, run through each of these tools:

O Work your pup on a hand-held lead: this is so you have maximum control as the behaviour you are training establishes in the different environments.

O Once you are confident you have a reasonable amount of control, move to the long-line or retractable lead. You still have control, but your dog has more freedom and begins to experience the concept of being off-lead.

O Then move to the long-line dragging. (You have let go of the end, and you are following your dog so you can stand on the end of the lead and pick it up if you have any difficulties.) You still have some control, but your dog has more freedom and begins to experience the concept of being off-lead.

O Finally, after a period of time when you feel you are ready, move to off-lead — this is the ultimate test of the degree of control you have, and how well established the behaviour is. When you do start this off-lead work in the park, make sure that it is a safe, controlled place, as this stage will test you.

The smaller and more incremental the changes you make, the easier and quicker success will be. Pay attention to how your pup is doing: if he is going well, move ahead; if not, then slow down (even go back a few steps if needed) and take your time. If you have any problems with your pup off-lead, go back to using the retractable lead or long-line until you are confident. It is important that your pup succeeds, so don't be tempted to go too fast, particularly at the beginning — being conservative in your judgement is definitely preferable in this instance.

Always make sure you start each session in the park on the retractable lead or long-line to test your pup's recall around the distractions that are manifesting. Only when your pup is consistently recalling on the lead do you let him off in a safe environment. I would recommend that this is a good habit to get into on an ongoing basis: ensuring that your pup is well focused and attentive to you, making sure you have contact with your dog. Joining up before letting your pup off reinforces the bond, and reminds your pup that you have resources with you, so you should be your pup's focus even when off-lead.

How to fade the clicker and food reward

Remember that when you are first establishing the behaviours, you click and give a food reward each time your pup does the correct behaviour successfully (*continuous schedule of reward*). Then once established consistently, you move to an *intermittent schedule of reward* — randomly rewarding successful behaviour with a click and food reward — this keeps your pup motivated, as he is not sure which time he will be rewarded. Slowly over time you reward less and less, fading it out slowly.

If your pup goes backwards in his training, bring the tools back if you need to, practise again for a few training sessions, then fade again. When I have first faded the clicker and food rewards after training a pup, I still make sure I take the tools and treats with me when I'm heading out, in case I need to reintroduce it if the pup's behaviour deteriorates. Sometimes you might encounter particularly challenging situations, in which case you may decide to use a click and food reward to ensure your pup stays focused on you.

I also recommend that you occasionally do top-up sessions using the clicker and food rewards, to keep your pup learning and remembering what he is supposed to do. Definitely use the clicker and food if you are getting fall-back in your training, to help re-establish it.

Remember also that every now and then you can jackpot the reward (increase the award amount by 5-10 times) for an extraordinary performance: for example, your pup comes back when called when there are lots of dogs playing nearby.

TRAINING DIARY

Here I have provided a weekly training diary you can use to track your training sessions. You can also download the diary from www.dogzen.com/puppyzen.

As you can see (opposite), there is a space to record your training sessions each morning and afternoon. Use the blank boxes to give each session a score out of 5, so that you are tracking your progress and performance throughout the programme. I recommend you do at least 1-3 training sessions a day for 6 weeks to 3 months, as this will give you the fastest and most consistent results. This will reinforce your bond, establish your shared language and hard-wire the behaviours you seek.

Each of the early training sessions should start with joining up before you progress to the new behaviour, so that you ensure your pup is attentive to you. Remember it is fine (in fact, necessary) to do training in small bites — try to achieve too much at once and you will only confuse your pup. So just focus on one behaviour per training session to keep things simple, particularly when you are first training the behaviour.

This is a comprehensive training system, so I recommend you start at the beginning of the book and work your way through the whole programme to get the best results. The payoff is that you will build a wonderful, harmonious relationship with your dog for life, where you will have confidence in the various situations you face together. If you can't do the whole programme, then at least do Part F and cross-reference to other areas when it asks you.

You can also access our online video series; it will complement the book beautifully. Go to www.dogzen.com/products/.

This is just the beginning, creating the foundations for you and your pup. From there, who knows? Remember Hercules? He had over 145 commands! We don't expect your dog to drive the car like Monty, but at least not to drive you bonkers. So enjoy, and don't underestimate what kind of bond you can create — it comes with so much joy. Have fun and good luck.

FINAL WORDS

This brings to an end this critical part of the book. It can be tempting to skip to the practical sections. However, I really encourage you to take the time to put these foundations in place. Applying consistent, committed effort to the training foundations outlined above will enable you to effectively bond and train with your pup, and your pup will love you for it. For pups it is all contact and play, so if you take a leaf out of their book and regard training like this, then every moment together will be a joy!

In the next part of the book we will look at what you need to do to prepare for your pup. In Part F we apply these tools and techniques step by step, looking at what you do with your pup and when during his critical formative period and beyond.

BEHAVIORS	MON		TUE		WED		THU		FRI		SAT		SUN		NOTES
	AM	PM	AM	PM	AM	PM	AM	PM	AM	PM	AM	PM	AM	PM	
JOINING UP (Clip lead, umbilical lead)															
BASICS															
Sit															
Down															
Zen Down															
Wait															
Stay															
No!															
Leave it															
Heel															
Come															
Nicely															
GREETINGS															
Dogs															
People															

BEHAVIORS	MON		TUE		WED		THU		FRI		SAT		SUN		NOTES
	AM	PM	AM	PM	AM	PM	AM	PM	AM	PM	AM	PM	AM	PM	
JOINING UP (Clip lead, umbilical lead)															
BEHAVIORAL ISSUE (Please fill in – e.g. Hyperactivity)															
BEHAVIORS TO TRAIN (See the issues support document summary to help you identify)															
e.g. Calm behavior															

Preparing For Your Puppy

The work you do before you even get your pup is critical in laying down the foundations of a successful relationship. So, let's get started by choosing the right pup for your lifestyle.

Chapter 15

Choosing your pup

If you are thinking of getting a pup, it is really important that you choose the right one for you, your family and your living environment, now and for the next 10–15 years. Being clear around your needs and wants in your choice of dog will make for a high level of compatibility and a harmonious relationship for a lifetime — like Hercules and me.

A mismatch of requirements — like Charles in the preface — can lead to much suffering and stress, for both owner and dog. Examples? A strong breed like a Rottweiler or a German Shepherd matched with an elderly person who might not have recognised their reduced ability to manage the breed's strength. Inexperienced owners who love the look and uniqueness of the ancient breeds, like the Huskies, but are not able to manage the breed's natural inclination to independence, predatory behaviour and potential dominance. Border Collies, oh, so many Border Collies I have seen in clinic — bred to run, work and herd sheep — can be driven so crazy by their urban lifestyles they become neurotic, anxious and snappy, barking along fence lines, desperate to chase even cars. Choose carefully!

I know, we have all been there: that reactive, emotional decision to immediately get *that* puppy, the cutest thing we have ever seen. How can we help ourselves when our oxytocin levels are going through the roof? Nobody is immune. When you find yourself in that situation, draw a breath, pull out the list of questions below, and see whether this pup is truly a good match. It may save you lots of heartache down the road.

Let's look at the steps involved when choosing a pup:

O Consider your lifestyle and situation over the next 10-15 years.
O Choose the attributes you want in a dog, to match that lifestyle.
O Research the breed group and the specific breeds within it.

O Choose the breed for you, matching attributes to the breed group.
O Source your pup: decide where you will get your pup from (a breeder, rescue centre, retail, etc.).
O Finally, choose an individual from within the breed or litter.

Let's look at each of these in more depth.

15.1 UNDERSTANDING YOUR LIFESTYLE AND SITUATION

You need to thoroughly understand where you are at in your own life, and what you want of a pup/dog before you decide on the one you want. Your lifestyle needs will change across the course of your life, so the kind of dog you had in your teens might not be the kind of dog you get when you have a young family or as you head into retirement. Here are a few questions to ask yourself and your family to help you:

O *Are you ready for the commitment of a pup right now?*
Although the pup's formative period is short, it is significant, so ask yourself whether the timing is right to be able to commit to your pup for those 2 months right now.

O *What is your life stage and lifestyle now and over the next 10-15 years?*
Will your life support a dog over the next 10 to 15 years? That is, are there any likely dramatic changes coming up (e.g. new baby, retirement, children leaving home, merging of families, divorce, moving from a rural to an urban setting, or vice versa)? Think about how any of these might affect the type of dog you should choose. (For example, if you are in your late sixties this dog will take you through to your early eighties, so you need to consider the possible changes in your physical capabilities over that time.)

O *What are your abilities to raise a pup and support a dog?*
You don't necessarily need the skills right now, but you do need to understand what you do and do not know, and whether you are willing to upskill yourself where you need to. Your level of abilities will also impact on what type of breed you might get, and whether you will consider an older rescue pup or dog.

O *Do you have the capacity to support a dog?*
Do you have (or are willing to obtain) the time, space and financial capacity required to support a puppy intensively for those first 2 months, and then over the next 15 years?

O *Do your family or friends who live with you support getting a dog?*

Are you aligned in your approach? If not, can you reach agreement, or how will you manage the differences?

O *What do you want from a dog?*

Are you looking for an exercise mate, a lapdog, someone to help guard your property and family, or just a lovely companion for your day-to-day life? Understanding your motivations will help you work through what breed of dog might be best for you.

15.2   WHAT ATTRIBUTES DO YOU WANT IN A PUP/DOG?

Once you know the attributes you want in your pup/dog, you can then choose the breed or cross-breed that best fits these. I give a few examples of dogs that meet those attributes; however, do your own research and reflect on what kind of dog will suit your life. The relationship you have with your dog does have a big impact on your life and your other relationships, so it is worth taking the time.

Here are some attributes to consider:

O physical (size, exercise or activity level, care needs, environmental considerations)

O trainability

O sociability (people, dogs, other species)

O temperament

O health issues.

Physical attributes

Size of your pup when he is a dog

This is generally a matter of personal preference, but is also relevant to your lifestyle. What suits you: a giant breed or a small toy breed? Remember the range is from 1 kilogram to 100 kilograms or more, so consider the space you have, the size of your car, the cost of feeding a larger dog versus a smaller one, and certain breeds' predispositions to health issues, such as problems with joints, which occurs in a lot of the giant breeds. Also think about your ability to train a big, strong dog. Mastiffs, German Shepherds and other strong breeds can require a lot of strength and confidence to manage, so consider whether this is for you.

Pick the breed that suits your lifestyle.

The big and small of it – an Irish Wolfhound (1.2 metres) and a miniature Schnauzer cross (20cm). The child is about 60cm.

Exercise or activity level

It is important your dog's activity level suits your own. They all need some form of exercise, but this varies greatly from breed to breed. How much can you exercise your dog? You don't want to deprive your dog of something as important as exercise, or it may manifest into other issues later on — a well-exercised dog is a relaxed dog that is less likely to cause chaos! That doesn't mean you need to be a fitness junkie to have a dog; many breeds don't require as much activity, it is just a matter of finding the right fit. And bear in mind that size doesn't always correlate to exercise requirements. The need for exercise is largely related to the functions (if any) the breed was selected for. Hunting dogs, working dogs and terriers are all dogs that require long periods of running, catching or herding things. Working sheepdogs, for example, can run well in excess of 100 kilometres per day when working. Expect a dog that will need time and energy spent on it, who really needs a purpose, whether work, ball play, agility, obedience or flyball and the like.

High-energy dogs that need a lot of exercise include most of the hunting and working breeds and many of the terriers. Some examples are the Australian Cattle Dog, Belgian Malinois, German Shepherd, Boxer, Dalmatian, Flat-coated Retriever, Irish Setter, Jack Russell Terrier, Labradoodle, Pointer, Weimaraner, Siberian Husky, Doberman Pinscher, Border Collie, Huntaway and German Pointer.

Breeds that are less active and can adapt to a lower-energy environment include the Basset Hound, Bulldog, Bull Mastiff, Cavalier King Charles Spaniel, Chow Chow, French Bulldog, Great Dane, Old English Sheepdog, Pekingese, Pug, Chihuahua, Maltese, Pomeranian and Saint Bernard. Most of the toys and the little breeds selected for companionship are low-energy dogs. The Scottish and White Highland Terriers are quieter, but many of the other terriers are active small breeds.

Care needs
The degree to which dogs shed their coats and the level of allergies they cause are important to some people. Certain breeds do drop a lot of hair, such as the German Shepherd, Jack Russell, Dalmatian, Labrador, Golden Retriever, Husky, Akita, Chow Chow, Saint Bernard and Pyrenées Mountain Dog. Dogs that are more hypoallergenic (allergy-free) include the Basenji, Bedlington Terrier, Bichon Frise, Havanese, Irish Water Spaniel, Kerry Blue, Affenpinscher, Schnauzer and Poodle. Research this if the issue is important to you.

Environmental considerations
Consider your family size, house size, land size, other animals on the property, and whether you live in an urban or rural area. Dogs need at least a part of their property as a contained environment, particularly when they are curious, prone to wandering and following their nose. (This is especially so for puppies and for the hunter and scent hound breeds that like to follow their noses.) Obviously a larger area is better for a larger dog, and a small toy dog can be quite content with a smaller area. But that also relates to how often they get to go walking, or get out and about. Larger dogs can cope in a smaller house if they are out exercising regularly during the day.

It is worth thinking about the breeds you have in rural areas. Obviously they will have more space, but you need to have them under good control or they will wander and potentially chase stock.

It is critical to cross-foster rural dogs to chickens and stock so they don't chase them. In most countries, a dog can be legally shot by neighbouring farmers if the dog is considered a threat to stock.

Similarly, having very active working breeds like sheepdogs and working breeds in urban or suburban areas can be unfair on dogs that need lots of exercise, unless your lifestyle includes lots of walks and outings.

Be conscious of what species are around you, such as cats, rabbits, birds and chickens, as well as what species are found in your walk areas — water fowl, ducks, stock and the like. This will help you to know what species you need to cross-foster your pup onto.

Trainability

Trainability is often confused with intelligence. Most dogs are intelligent; however, this relates to what they are selected for. Trainability is found in breeds that have been selected for intimate communication between the dog and the human mentor or trainer. Dogs that are selected to work in co-operation and communication with their trainers, such as sheepdogs and German Shepherds, tend to have a greater rapport and be more trainable than breeds that are self-workers, independent hunters or work in harness. These latter dogs have not been selected for rapport with a trainer, so are less trainable as a rule.

The sight and scent hounds are selected for following their sight or smell to find prey and catch them, so they are less naturally attuned to their trainers/owners. Also the Spitz breeds were originally worked in harness, and so didn't need to work off-lead well. These classes of breeds tend to be self-workers, and don't use a lot of direction from a trainer. They are often self-driven and prone to high arousal by that drive, so they can be harder to train and command. On the other hand, breeds like the Border Collie and the Shepherd dogs rely on a subtle communication system of whistles and commands to direct them in their work, as they have been bred and selected to be highly attuned to and co-operate with their trainer. We find this level of attention to the trainer more in the retrieving, some hunting, the guard and working breeds, too.

The questions for you are: Do you want to spend a lot of time training your dog in agility and obedience, or would you rather a playful and cuddly dog? Do you want or need your dog to perform any specific tasks?

Certain breeds are thought to be more eager to learn new things, and they are usually intelligent and high-energy dogs, which means you will probably want to come up with new tricks and tasks on a regular basis to keep them stimulated and entertained. These dogs won't usually settle for snoozing on the couch all day, so if training and being really active isn't your thing, you may like to choose a different breed that is more relaxed and less active. These dogs can develop a subtle and intimate rapport with you, and will recall and learn things generally more quickly.

Stanley Coren developed a breed intelligence list (138 breeds) based on the dog's ability to learn commands. In the top 10 are the Border Collie, Poodle, German Shepherd, Golden Retriever, Doberman Pinscher, Shetland Sheepdog, Labrador, Papillon, Rottweiler, and Australian Cattle Dog (Blue Heeler). Hybrids or crosses that include these breeds also tend to be smart as well, and in my opinion are sometimes better due to hybrid vigour.

Sociability or independence

People sociability

Some breeds have been selected for greater sociability than others and make great family pets. These include the Labrador, most of the retrievers, including the Golden Retriever, most of the spaniels, including the Cavalier King Charles Spaniel, the setters, Jack Russell Terrier, Staffordshire Terrier, Collie, Greyhound, Pug, Maltese, Papillion, Yorkshire Terrier, Beagle, Boxer, Samoyed and Boston Terrier.

Remember, most dogs have the capacity to be very sociable, as it is a defining feature of dogs in general, as long as we do the right socialisation at the right time. Some more independent and not so naturally social breeds are the Shar Pei, Basenji, Afghan, Malamute, Black Russian Terrier, Blood Hound, Kerry Blue Terrier, Pekingese, Shih Tzu, Saluki, and in general sight hounds, and Spitz breeds (except the Samoyed and Japanese Spitz). These all have many special traits that owners love, but they do have this independent predisposition as a rule, so if you do get one of these breeds you would want to be experienced and put a lot of effort into socialisation and your mentor bond.

Dog-to-dog sociability

It is important to have a dog that gets on well with other dogs, and the most important way to ensure this is to socialise them with other dogs in their formative period. However, some breeds are more social with dogs than others, such as the Labrador, Golden Retriever, Cavalier King Charles Spaniel, Basset Hound (and many of the hounds, as most are selected to work together), Great Dane, Saint Bernard, Poodle and associated crosses, and Papillon. There are many more, so do your homework.

Dogs that are less likely to get on with other dogs (although all dogs can be socialised to do so) are the more independent workers, which have a higher level of gaminess if not well socialised, so are more prone to threaten or fight. The fighting breeds, selected to not respond to submission by other dogs but instead continue and attack, are the most likely to be aggressive and show potentially serious biting and holding attributes. These include the Pit Bull Terrier and crosses with other big breeds, Akita, American Staffordshire Terrier, American Bulldog, Airedale Terrier, Irish Terrier, Blue Heeler, Shar Pei, Dogo Argentino, Tosca, Neapolitan Mastiff and Dogue de Bordeaux. The other bull terriers and bulldogs are less so, but still need to be well socialised. There are also the dominant type breeds, although these are less likely to fight, such as the Rottweiler, German Shepherd and Doberman. All of these breeds need to be well socialised with people and dogs.

It is worth noting that the level of aggression that dogs selected for fighting can exhibit (if they are mal-socialised to people outside of the family) can be of a very high ferocity, given their strength of bite and holding potential. Most of these breeds can be lovely dogs if well socialised with dogs and people but, if not, their potential for harm can be great. Selecting out dogs' natural inhibition to attack when shown submission is a dangerous human pursuit in fighting dogs. It is an unnatural antisocial predisposition that is opposite to the natural selection for docility and sociability that created the dog in Nature to begin with. This selection occurs at a genetic level and should be selected out of dogs. Special care should be taken with them around children, ensuring they have good socialisation with children and babies in the formative period to ensure complete safety. They need good socialisation with dogs too, of course, and de-sexing is a good added precaution, especially in males.

The Maltese are not known for their predatory tendencies!

This bulldog cross-breed will have hybrid vigour.

Predatory — chasing and/or hunting other species

Do you want a dog that is unlikely to chase other animals on your property? In that case avoid (or otherwise cross-foster them intensely onto other species in the formative period) hunting breeds like Spitz breeds, the Husky, Malamute and Akita, or terriers (like the Airedale, Bull Terrier), Rhodesian Ridgeback, the sight hound (Wolfhound, Greyhound) and spaniels. The guard breeds like the German Shepherd, Rottweiler and Doberman also have a relatively high prey drive if not socialised well enough. However, if you would like a dog with some hunting drive, then setters, pointers, spaniels and other hunting breeds will do well here.

The least prey-driven breeds include Maltese, Bichon Frise, Cavalier King Charles Spaniel, Golden Retriever, Old English Sheepdog and the Chin. However, be aware that, although they have low prey drive naturally, they all still need socialising and cross-fostering with other species during the formative period.

Temperament

Temperament is the nature of the breed as inherited from their parents, which is later influenced by environmental effects. You need to consider a breed's predisposition to the following:

O *Confidence*: a dog that is naturally outgoing and adaptable, and learns easily, such as the Labrador, Bull Mastiff, German Shepherd, Jack Russell Terrier, Golden Retriever, Great Dane, Rottweiler, Doberman, Bull Terrier.

O *Adaptability*: a dog that can fit into many situations and adjust well, such as the Boxer, Labrador, Golden Retriever, German Shepherd, Dachshund, Beagle, Border Collie, Jack Russell Terrier, Australian Cattle Dog and lots of others.

O *Fearfulness*: some breeds have a genetic fearfulness trait in some lines, such as the English Pointer, but mainly fearfulness is due to lack of socialisation.

O *Submissiveness*: some of the smaller breeds, in particular, are more prone to excessive submission, such as the Bichon Frise, smaller poodles, Cavalier King Charles Spaniel and other small spaniels, and a number of toy breeds.

O *Protectiveness*: they have been selected for guarding usually, and to alert and protect the family, such as the German Shepherd, Rottweiler, Doberman, Airedale Terrier, Akita, Boxer, Bull Mastiff, Giant Schnauzer, Rhodesian Ridgeback, Komondor, Puli. These breeds need to learn good discrimination and to control this tendency with appropriate socialisation and meet and greets.

O *Gaminess*: originally selected in hunting dogs (chasing game) and fighting above their weight range (so to speak), they are plucky, very confident, scared of little. Terriers are the epitome of gaminess: they will take on anything and not back down. This is one thing in the hunting context, but when it expresses itself in aggression to people or other dogs it can be harmful. These include most of the terriers, Bull Terriers, the fighting breeds (Pit Bull Terrier, Dogo Argentino), including crosses with other big breeds, Akita (to a lesser degree, but still very powerful and, if not socialised well, can fight), American Staffordshire Terrier, English Bull Terrier, Staffordshire Bull Terrier, American Bulldog, English Bulldog, Irish Terrier, Blue Heeler, Shar Pei and Tossa.

O *Dominance*: this is a trait that indicates your dog may challenge you for dominance (dominance aggression), may show resource guarding and may be more dominant with other dogs. The gamey and protective breeds tend to be potentially more dominant. Entire (unneutered) males tend to be more dominant, too. Socialisation and training of course aims to lower relative dominance, and develop docility and calm, non-aggressive behaviour. Breeds that have more potential to be dominant are the guard breeds (German Shepherd, Rottweiler, Doberman), the Bull Terriers and many of the other terriers, especially the fighting breeds, and the French and Neapolitan Mastiff.

O *Noise sensitivity*: a study has indicated that about a quarter of dogs (23 per cent) are sensitive to noise. While this is largely influenced by their early exposure to noise and sound in general, some breeds seem more sensitive than others, including the Norwegian Buhund, Wheaten Terrier, Lagotto Romagnolo, Boxer, Great Dane and the Chinese Crested Dog.

Remember, breed temperaments are generalisations, and not all individuals will fit these. However, when you research what the breed was bred for it will give you some idea of their overall temperament, and it is worth paying attention to this, particularly if you are an inexperienced dog trainer.

Health issues

As a general rule, smaller dogs live a bit longer (12-plus years on average) than the large or giant breeds (approximately 8 to 10 years), with the overall average being 10 years. Certain breeds are prone to various congenital, medical and psychological problems, such as cleft palate, blindness, hip dysplasia, fearfulness and deafness, to name just a few. For example, the short-nosed dogs, like Bulldogs, Boxers and Pugs, can have nasal breathing and eye problems. Chihuahuas can have knee problems (luxating patella), and the giant breeds have a tendency to have joint and hip problems. You tend to find that the breeds that still work or have working lines, and are bred for easy care and health, often have fewer genetic defects in their breeds. Make sure you undertake good research on any potential issues, including talking to your veterinarian once you have shortlisted your chosen breeds.

Pure-bred or hybrid

Dogs' temperaments, like those of all animals, are a mix of genetics and exposure to their specific environment, and in particular what that exposure is in the formative period.

As we 'line-breed' for the pure-bred or pedigree dogs, we decrease their genetic variability and so can throw up weakening features, which breeders need to be mindful of. Docility, friendliness, trainability and health are the most important criteria in terms of our dog's wellbeing and quality of life. Looks and physical attributes should come after these.

If you are choosing a pure-bred dog, it is important to choose an excellent breeder to ensure the pup doesn't have any congenital (genetic) defects that can be associated with certain breeds. Some breeders line-breed too closely (and don't out-cross, so the dogs suffer inbreeding depression), which can cause negative recessive traits to occur. A good breeder will begin handling, house training, socialising and desensitising the pups early (see Part F), be able to give you good nutritional advice, and educate you about the breed and its qualities.

Alternatively, choose a hybrid (cross-breed) where you will benefit from hybrid vigour — more genetic variability enhances health. The advantage of hybrids is that you often get the best of both breeds (although not always). Out-crossing like this improves general health, often provides psychological and physiological benefits, and can often result in higher levels of trainability. It is generally my personal preference.

Parent dogs (sire and the dam)

Remember to ask about the sire and dam and any related individuals. I always like to see other family members if possible, as it gives me a clearer picture of the type of pup I will be taking on. However, breeds aren't like a car, in that you don't get exactly the 'model' you ordered — there is considerable variability even amongst pure-breds. However, most pure-breds have been selected with certain looks and behavioural characteristics in mind, so it helps to think about what best suits you.

15.3   BREED SELECTION

Once you have determined the attributes you want from your pup/ dog, start investigating which breed will best fit those requirements. As the dog is the most genetically variable species on Earth, you may feel like a kid in a candy shop. Getting through the complexity of so many breeds is challenging, so I find it useful to look at the breed group classification cladogram developed by vonHoldt and colleagues. They classify breeds into 10 groups (plus wolves) based on their genomes' relatedness, and I find the classifications useful in making generalisations about their traits and temperaments for the first step in breed selection. Once you pick a general breed group, you can then investigate the different breeds within that group using the attributes discussed earlier.

Below is a summary of the 10 breed groups.

1. The ancients (basal) and Spitz breeds

The basal breeds are genetically closest to the wolves. These include, for example, the Basenji (maybe the oldest of the ancient breeds), Akita, Shar Pei, Telomian (the blue-tongued dogs), the Spitz types (the Huskies, Malamutes, Chow Chow), the ancient sight hounds (Saluki and Afghan) and Dingo types. They may have been the progenitors of these other groups, as it is considered that later breeding and hybridisation led to other breeds emerging from them. These ancients are defined by being quite strong-willed, independent (even stubborn), less trainable, and less human-focused and socialised, and generally can have poor recall.

The Spitz breeds in particular — but most of the others, too — are protective and loyal to the family, fearless and confident, and are prone to be predatory. Some of the smaller Spitz breeds are somewhat more trainable and less independent, and can make good dogs for families and children, especially the Japanese Spitz, the Pomeranian and the Schipperke (ship dog).

Just like any dog, if reared properly these breeds can make lovely pets. They are very active breeds as a rule, with long, thick coats, deriving from cold regions of Eurasia, so they do better with a physical outlet.

Recommended owner: Experienced; I wouldn't recommend most of the breeds in this group for new owners. Spend time with some first, before you decide to own one.

2. Working dogs

This is a broad cross-section of working dogs, such as police dogs, livestock guard breeds, war dogs and harness dogs (excluding the Spitz ones). The group includes breeds like the Standard and Toy Poodle, German Shepherd, Doberman, Standard and Giant Schnauzer, Boxer, Kelpie, Bouvier des Flandres, Komondor.

The working and guard breeds are mostly larger dogs that have been selected to some degree for protectiveness and the ability to bond strongly to one particular mentor; although you set the family size and nature based on what you socialise for. These breeds are selected for different services and purposes, and the predispositions are suitable to each service. Some of these breeds have been selected for protection work in particular, and are then raised in a way that shapes their level of discrimination to this work. You can train a dog to guard and protect under controlled situations, and they can learn a very high level of discrimination.

These dogs are mostly large and, although highly trainable, take experience to handle. If you generalise their socialisation in the formative period, they will cross-foster onto all of them. However, if you don't, they can become highly protective, which alongside their size and strength can create issues for inexperienced handlers.

Recommended owner: Experienced and strong owners, who are assertive and confident.

3. Retrievers

Examples include the Golden Retriever, Labrador (Flat and Curly-coated Retriever), Chocolate Labrador, Canadian Retriever, Saint Bernard, Bernese Mountain Dog and Great Dane. This class of dog generally makes up the most sociable, friendly breeds, and are great with families. Generally, breeds in this group make good family dogs that can fit well into our lifestyles, and are relatively easy to care for with few behavioural problems. This is a breed class I like and recommend especially for families with children.

Recommended owner: Some great breeds in here for the first-time owner, but the giants need owners with more strength and confidence.

4. Herding dogs

Examples include the Border Collie, Heading Dog, Australian Shepherd, Blue Heeler, Huntaway, Shetland, Cardigan and Pembroke

Corgis, Collies, and Old English Sheepdog. These working sheep and cattle dogs are generally super-intelligent and trainable, and high-energy. They love to co-operate, and are very active and alert. Breeds selected for co-operativity and trainability (ability to communicate) tend to be easier to train and retain more. They have a better focus on the mentor. Generally, these dogs are fast, active, intelligent and like to work in co-ordination with the shepherds. They are some of my favourite breeds to train and work with, but you need an active life to ensure you give them what they need in the way of stimulation and activity. Some can be sensitive.

Livestock guard breeds, such as the Komondor, Kuvasz and Anatolian Karabash, are not herding dogs, as they are breeds that traditionally were reared and raised with the stock species they guard, such as sheep and goats. They are strong dogs that are self-workers, are not so trainable and like to guard. They need good socialisation, and can act as stock guards as they have been selected to cross-foster in the formative period.

Recommended owner: New owners are okay, but the key thing is you need an active lifestyle and be prepared to invest time and effort in your highly active and smart dog.

5. Spaniels

Examples include the Cocker Spaniel, Cavalier King Charles Spaniel, English Springer Spaniel, and Irish Water Spaniel. These are mostly scent-dominant hounds that point or flush as a rule, and generally work as individuals, but can work together as well. They are either scent, sight or herding hounds, which influences their hunting style greatly. As they are generally self-hunters, they are often not attentive of the trainer enough to respond to commands well (as they are being driven by their senses). They can be trained, but are not the most trainable of the dog world, as they love to put their heads down and run; they are hunters and they love it! They are sociable, friendly family dogs, although they are prone to separation distress and barking. However, if raised and trained well they are lovely companions.

Recommended owner: Fine for first-time owners, but recall and trainability can be a challenge, so be diligent and get started on your training early.

6. Small terriers

Examples include the Jack Russell Terrier, Fox Terrier, Australian Terrier, Scottish Wirehaired Terrier, White Highland Terrier, and Irish Terrier. Terriers are ground hunters and often dig out prey. They have been selected for gaminess in regard to prey, so they appear to fight well above their weight. They are spunky and can be quite stubborn. Their nose and predatory inclinations drive much of their behaviour. Lively, bossy, persistent and impulsive, they are clever and can learn, but you need to be persistent.

They aren't the most reliable to just hang with you without wandering off on a scent, unless well trained and bonded in the formative period. This is due to being keen hunters, who are often air or ground scenting, and once they get onto a scent they are hard to pull away. It is important to train them early, to cross-foster them onto all different species, and not hunt them at all unless you want a hunting dog.

Recommended owner: Some experience best, but with diligent training will be okay.

7. Mastiff-like dogs

Examples include the Bull Terrier (including Staffordshire and English), Pit Bull, Bulldog (English, American and French), Mastiff, Boxer, Boston Terrier, and French Bulldog. These breeds have been selected for gaminess, so there is the tendency for them to be more aggressive and dominant than other breeds. We initially bred this attribute so that they could hunt bigger, more aggressive prey, and, for some, to fight. They are often dominant and assertive, but they are quite sociable when socialised with other dogs, people and species during the formative period. They can be somewhat stubborn and slow to act, especially the bigger dogs, and it is fair to say they aren't fast learners. The Bulldog and Mastiff are probably the least trainable, with the Bull Terrier more trainable. However, if not well trained their hunting instincts, gaminess and fighting predisposition can be a problem.

This predisposition can manifest as aggression towards other dogs, particularly in the case of the breeds selected to fight other dogs. We see this most particularly in the Pit Bull Terriers, Dogo Argentino, and other breeds that were bred to fight other dogs. These breeds need to be well socialised with dogs and people in the formative period to make sure they don't become mal-socialised and pose a big risk.

Recommended owner: The owner needs to be strong, assertive and experienced; not normally recommended as family dogs.

8. Toy dogs

Examples include the Shih Tzu, Chihuahua, Pekingese, Griffon, Pug, Pomeranian, Papillon, Bichon Frise and Chinese Crested Dog. Most of the breeds we call lapdogs and toys are selected for close human relationships, and so generally have a sociable temperament, and can get by on less exercise and live in smaller areas. Nevertheless, they cover the whole temperament range, from fierce little guards like the Pomeranians and Silkies, through to the gentle and soft Havanese, Bichon Frise and Yorkshire Terrier, and smart like the Papillon and Schipperke.

Toys can sometimes not be trained seriously, but they need to be. Care needs to be taken to make sure they don't become over-dependent and suffer separation distress. The Papillon (linked to spaniels, too), Schipperke (Spitz type) and Silky Terrier are probably the smarter toys, and more like a big dog. The rest tend to have low to moderate trainability.

You do need to take care that when you are socialising toys with larger dogs and people they don't get stood on or treated roughly, as they can develop aversions and become fearful and/or aggressive. Introduce them carefully, but ensure you don't overprotect them either.

Recommended owner: In most cases they are fine for new owners, but remember to train them and treat them like a dog and a loved companion (rather than a baby).

9. Sight hounds

Examples include the Borzoi, Greyhound, Deerhound, Wolfhound, Whippet and Italian Greyhound. Sight hounds are some of the oldest breeds (Saluki and Afghan), and these particular breeds are included in the ancient breed group. For example, ones like the Saluki date back over 5000 to 7000 years.

The sight hounds have been selected as self-hunters and are very fast when chasing down prey. They are magnificent specimens of speed, beauty and agility, and have a strong predatory drive. They need to be raised with cats and other small species, otherwise they will hunt them. This includes toy dog breeds, as they may see them as prey, too. They are active, although they can lead a quieter life, as they are quite laid-back. They are often very sociable, although some within the group are independent. They were not selected for trainability, and tend to be less trainable than some of the other breeds.

They are generally good family dogs, including with children. They like comfort and warmth, and most, except the ancient Saluki and Afghan, can live in smaller properties. Nonetheless, like all dogs they do need exercise.

Recommended owner: Experienced owners preferably.

10. Scent hounds

Examples include the Dachshund, Beagle, Basset Hound and Bloodhound. Scent hounds are self-motivated hunters that are driven heavily by their amazing scent drive. They have the greatest ability to scent out things, but this also means they are highly driven and distracted by scents and go out of the learning state when doing so. Therefore they have low to medium trainability, and recall is a challenge.

They tend to be very sociable and can make good pets. However, because they are so driven by scent and the sociability to run with the pack (especially in the Beagle and the pack-hunting hounds), they often escape from home. They are also very food-driven as a rule, and can be predatory, so they need good cross-fostering to live with other species. The Dachshund is a good guard dog; the others less so. They also can have ear and eye issues and drool.

Recommended owner: Medium experience would be preferred. New owners are okay, given the dogs' sociability; however, you would need to understand their limitations, especially in trainability, their desire to escape the territory, and drooling and howling. Excellent early training and cross-fostering is required.

BREED SELECTION — MATCHING ATTRIBUTES TO A BREED GROUP

Your dog breed choice comes down to matching the requirements of your lifestyle and what you would like from a dog with the attributes of the dog breed (and therefore the dog's needs), to get the ideal match. The better suited you and your dog are, the happier your time together will be.

Whether you are making the choice by yourself or with others, you might find using a template useful to help you make breed decisions. You can download an electronic version of such a template at www. dogzen.com/puppyzen.

15.4   WHERE WILL YOU GET YOUR PUP FROM?

Rescue

With so many rescue pups and dogs in need of a loving home, I always like to recommend that you adopt a pup or dog from your local animal rescue shelter if you have the experience. If you want to rescue an adult dog, speak to the people at the rescue organisation to find out what the dog's personality is like, and if there are any behavioural issues you need to be aware of. You just need to consider whether you have the time and ability to train a dog if there are behavioural problems. (See my book *Dog Zen* for support if you do.)

If getting a rescue pup, I still try to get the pup as close to 8 weeks of age as possible. This will ensure that even if their start in the first 8 weeks is less than ideal, we can still make a significant difference in their remaining formative period. If the pup is older than 12 to 16 weeks, look carefully at how social she is. This will determine how much work you have to do and how much experience you might need. As long as the pup has had even a limited amount of socialisation, she is still young, so will be more malleable and trainable than an older rescue dog.

You may remember from my TV series *Pound Pups to Dog Stars* that even difficult, abused dogs are retrievable, but they can take some work and skill. Dog Zen and Puppy Zen offer you those skills, but you need to be committed to learning them. If you do, most dogs are trainable, and rescue dogs have that real desire to find a lifelong home and it seems that they will reward you with extra love. Ensure you keep within your training abilities.

Breeder and retailer

Critically, you need to choose a good breeder who will prepare your pup well. Find reputable national organisations that accredit breeders to ensure that good standards are being met. Ask to see what accreditation they have, if they belong to any associations, and do any upskilling/

Dallas, American Bulldog cross.

Maple, French Bulldog.

Fletcher, Golden Retriever.

Ruby, Cavadoodl Maltese cross

Charlie, Border Collie Springer
Spaniel cross.

Blue, Chocolate
Labrador GSP cross.

Rosie Marie,
rescue pup.

Arwen, White German
Shepherd.

training regularly. It is a field in which many different methods are suggested, so below I outline some of the areas (from a behavioural perspective) that you should ask about to help determine whether they are the right breeder for you, and your prospective pup is getting the best start she can. Aside from these behavioural responsibilities, breeders should also be covering vaccinations, diet and vet-checks, including checking for any congenital defects.

If you are getting your pup from a retailer (whether online or in-store), be aware of how old the pup is, and what time she has spent in the store, particularly. Ask the retailer the same types of questions you would a breeder, ensuring the pup is getting lots of handling, socialisation and novelty while she awaits her new home. Take care in the more unregulated parts of this market. Avoid puppy mills where they have too many pups and limited breeding stock. The standard of the facility often indicates their commitment to the pups' welfare. Ask lots of questions (as outlined earlier).

What the breeder needs to do

The breeder will have the pups during the important neonatal and transition periods, and the beginning of the formative period. This is ideally until the puppy is approximately 8 weeks old. As we have seen, this is an important development period in which critical exposure and enrichment needs to take place. You need to know that your breeder or retailer understands the importance of the formative period, and that the pup is getting worldly experience and is not shut away getting little attention and exposure to what she needs. See Part F for what we would expect of a good breeder.

Following is a general overview of what a breeder should be covering (from a behavioural perspective), and importantly the types of questions you might ask any potential breeders or retailers to ensure you get a pup that has had the optimal supportive start. This will also ensure you are supporting professional breeders, who are focused on the wellbeing of their pups. In Part F, I outline in detail what the breeder should do over the first 8 weeks. You want to ensure that your pup has had the benefit of enrichment, having been exposed to diverse stimuli to engage, interact and learn about, rather than avoid and fear.

KEY MATTERS TO COVER WITH YOUR BREEDER

O Health
- — Do any breeding and genetic considerations need clarifying?
- — Are there any medical issues, including eye check-up for progressive retinal atrophy, hearing tests, and orthopaedic issues such as joints and hips?
- — What vaccinations have been done to date, and what is outstanding?

O Socialisation
- — What early forms of contact and engagement have they done?
- — What has been done to socialise the pup with various people (age, gender, race)?
- — What has been done to socialise the pup with other dogs?
- — What has been done to cross-foster onto other species, especially cats and chickens?

O Mentor bond
- — What early work has been done? (Refer to Part F for what I would hope for.)
- — What support are they happy to do to start the bond with a new owner? Would they be happy to allow visits, introduce a piece of your clothing to the whelping den, and use a calming smell like lavender in the den?

O Shared language
- — What tools have been introduced? (Ideally collar, lead and clicker.)
- — What basic commands have been established? (Such as 'sit', 'down' and 'come'.)

O Fear and phobia prevention
- — What early exposure to smells, noises, substrates, novelty and change has been done to date? Did the pup recover from fear quickly or slowly?
- — What travel has taken place? (Including simulating some travel on aircraft if necessary.)
- — What vet visits have been done and how did the pup respond?

O House-training established
- — What method do they use, and how has it been going?
- — Have they cued toileting behaviour? (For example, using the 'be quick' command.)

○ Bite inhibition/handling
  — What have they done to desensitise the pup to handling of her mouth, ears, eyes and feet?
  — Has the pup experienced clipping/grooming, where appropriate?
○ Separation
  — Do the pups spend individual time alone?
  — Has crate training started?
○ Enrichment
  — How much have the pups started to exercise and play, inside and outside?

Once you have selected your pup from a breeder, it is a good idea to visit the pup, ideally from 3 weeks of age (once her sensory capacity is completed), to start introducing yourself to her in preparation for her moving to your home. Get your pup to smell you, see you, and connect with you and your family. Smell is their strongest memory and bonding stimulus, so you might even leave an item that smells of you to embed this imprinting and association.

I also recommend asking your breeder to use a calming smell like lavender in the whelping den, which you can then replicate at your home. By the time the pup goes home with you, she will already have an association with this smell and memory established that will help with separation. Alternatively, appeasement pheromone sprays are also available to calm the pup in a new environment.

15.5   HOW TO PICK AN INDIVIDUAL FROM THE LITTER

Once you have decided what sort of dog breed will suit your household and where you are going to find your new pup, you will need to make a choice about which puppy to choose from the litter or retailer. Whether you have chosen a hybrid or pure-bred pup, here is some guidance on how to choose. This guidance is based on the eight training activity groups (introduced in Part A) that will guide your training (outlined in Part F). It will give you and the breeder assessment criteria that will guide you on how well-adjusted the pup is, and also any issues that need to be dealt with as soon as you get him. You can use this guidance in association with the 'Puppy temperament test' in Appendix A to

Mum and 4-week-old pups in their den, with clear discrimination between surfaces for bedding, mat and newspaper for toileting. House training has started.

help assess your pup for selection. It is also useful in establishing a baseline for your training, enabling you to track progress throughout. We discuss this test in more detail in Part F, at 8 weeks of age.

Socialisation

Dog socialisation

When you first visit the litter, observe the pups' interaction with each other before you alert them to your presence. You should be looking for an outgoing pup that is neither excessively submissive nor dominant with the other pups (see the section on shared language in Part B for guidance), as these pups will be easier to rear and train as a rule. If you are more experienced, then you might consider getting the shyer, less confident pup.

Human socialisation

When you first interact with the puppies, look for the ones that approach you with their heads held high and tails wagging. These are signs of confident, socially well-rounded and friendly pups that have had the right start in life. Take your children, if you have any, and see how the pups interact with them. Have the pups had exposure to a mix of people of different races, age and gender?

Other species

Check with the breeder what has been done with any other species.

Mentor bond

The ideal pup should want to be with you, follow you around and play with you when initiated. Test to see whether he can hold a gentle gaze with you (be careful not to stare). Will he retrieve an object and bring it back to you? (This is testing co-operativity.)

Shared language

Have any of the basic commands or tools been established (use of a collar, lead and crate)? Is the pup calm and focused, or overly excited and distracted? (This is checking for the learning state.) Has the pup used a marker, like a clicker (or other, like 'yes' confirmations), at all?

Fears and phobia prevention

Reactive to restraint

Gently hold the pup down on his back for 30 seconds. Initially, he won't like it, but he shouldn't bite or react too excessively, and should relax under your moderate pressure. A pup that is not excessively dominant should relax after 10 to 20 seconds and settle down. However, don't get in a major fight with a pup if he is reactive, just let go, noting if you think he would bite. This technique is for young pups (up to 10 weeks), and does take a little skill and confidence, so be mindful. Ask the breeder if they are okay with you doing this. Does the pup recover quickly after the pressure?

Gently lift the pup up into the air and see how he reacts. You are testing the pup's emotional resilience to see how he copes with novelty and unexpected things, and how quickly he recovers. Also find out whether the pup is sound-sensitive, by dropping a pot or saucepan lid on the ground and observing how he reacts and how quickly he recovers. Fast recovery is good.

Separation
Separate the pup from his litter mates, and see how he copes with being on his own. Check with the breeder whether they have started crate training, and whether they give the pups individual time alone.

House training
Check with the breeder how this is going, and what method they use. Is there a litter box or paper in the puppy pen? Do they take the pups out onto grass and cue toileting?

Bite inhibition
Play with your pup to see what his bite inhibition is like. Does he nip, grab and bite, and will he stop if you say 'ouch', 'no' or 'leave it'? Gently manipulate his feet, tail and mouth to check that he is not overly reactive to being handled. This will differ with breed types, with terriers being more dominant, and toys more relaxed and submissive. Are they sensitive to being touched? Do they resource-guard toys or food?

Enrichment, play and exercise
Check to see whether he is playful, and whether he will engage with novel toys. Does he move freely and look comfortable, and has he been outside to play and exercise?

Health
Here is a quick list on what to look for, to help you choose a healthy puppy.
- The pups should be well rounded and have healthy, shiny coats. They shouldn't be too skinny or too fat (although rescue pups may not fall in this range).
- Examine each pup physically, and check that he does not have an under- or over-shot jaw.
- Check that the eyes, ears and genitalia are clear, with no discharge or inflammation.
- Of the 2 or 3 pups you have narrowed down, take them aside individually to test vision and hearing. This can be done by clicking, clapping or dropping something on the ground behind the pup to see if he responds. Also you can test sight by putting a treat or a toy on the ground near the pup and rolling it around, checking that the pup can see it and find it.

○ Often you will know the one with the X factor for you, but make sure you tick the above boxes, too.

A good pure-breeder should have all of the applicable papers proving the pups are in good health. However, I would always recommend a quick vet-check just to be sure, with regards to health and medical concerns. Check any breed-specific weaknesses.

In general

Unless experienced in raising and training pups, be careful not to choose the fearfully shy pup of the litter. We tend to fall for the underdog, but this fearfulness trait can be difficult to change. It is worth avoiding unless you have the skills to train the fearful pup effectively to give it confidence. Particularly avoid this type of pup if it is your first time raising a pup.

Good luck on the hunt to find your new family member — it is so exciting when you do!

Even carrying your pup out and about can provide very important enrichment experiences.

Chapter 16

Preparing for your pup

So you have finally chosen your pup, and she is due home soon — how exciting! Before your ball of cuteness and the accompanying oxytocin arrives, you need to start preparing yourself, your family and home for the new family member. This is definitely easier before the distraction of the pup arrives . . .

Here is what you need to do when you are preparing for your pup:
- get your home and equipment ready
- manage the vaccinations clash (7–12 weeks)
- prepare your family and create your 8-week plan.

16.1   GET YOUR HOME AND EQUIPMENT READY

It is very important to ready your home, get all the gear you need, and set it up before your pup gets home. In particular, you want to do the following:
- Determine your house-training approach and set up an area for it. (See Part C.)
- Purchase a crate, leads, a clicker(s), training pouch(es), collar, commercial toileting pads if you need them, suitable toys, including Kong and chew toys you can fill up with food for the pup to settle in with, and feeding and drinking bowls. A radio or other music source is also helpful.
- Set up your pup's sleeping crate. Identify a mother surrogate toy for your pup to sleep with, potentially one you can warm up; for example, a hot-water bottle or a wheat bag — but make sure this is warm only, not too hot. It would be ideal if you have something smelling of the dam and whelping den (e.g. the lavender mentioned earlier). Some breeders put soft toys in with the litter in the last week or so before the pups are re-homed, so that when each pup leaves he has a toy to take away that smells of the dam and litter mates.

We are all looking for that X factor — make sure the pup you choose suits your lifestyle, too!

○ The breeder/retailer/rescue organisation should provide you with an outline of what your pup is eating and how you should transition to your food of choice. Remember also to have high-value treats for clicker training, like roast chicken, cheese or a good-quality dog roll. There are some puppy-specific commercial treats also available, including some specifically for training, which are appealing but low-calorie.

○ Puppy-proof your house: don't leave any favourite items you love lying around that might be tempting for a puppy to chew. (You want to set your pup up for success, so don't make it too hard for him in those first few weeks.) Also tidy away computer and electric cables in those early weeks, too. Ensure kitchen and bathroom cabinets are shut securely, and that there are no potential poisons (such as bleach or rat poison) inside or outside.

16.2   MANAGE THE VACCINATIONS CLASH (7–12 WEEKS)

Remember your puppy's very critical formative period runs from 3 to 16 weeks (with the peak occurring at 12 weeks), and this is the time you need to generalise the pup's socialisation and get him used to novelty and change. This is not a time to keep your pup isolated at home. Even though this time conflicts with your puppy's vaccination period, you still need to find ways to socialise and habituate him in a safe manner.

For the first 6 weeks of their lives, the pups receive their initial immunity to the two critical disease risks, parvovirus and distemper, from their mother's immunity (if she is vaccinated). First vaccinations are then started at around 6 to 7 weeks. We want to give the pup about a week from then to establish basic immunity, after which the pup can be carefully taken out into manageable situations (see below). Therefore, from between 8 and 9 weeks you can start getting the pup out and about while managing any risk. You need to be mindful up to 12 weeks of age. After 12 weeks, when most vaccinations have established immunity, you can ease up on your careful regime.

Be wary of any instructions you might receive about isolating your pup at home until 12 or 16 weeks. From a behavioural perspective this is not good advice, and can lead to mal-socialisation issues in your growing pup. Remember, 80 per cent of euthanasia in the first 3 years of life is a due to behaviour problems, not disease.

The key is to find *safe* ways to socialise your pup.

Below the high tide mark is a safe place to exercise your young pup.

Safe places

Go to places that are less likely to have disease exposure, such as:

O the 'wet part' below the high-tide mark at beaches (the sand gets washed clean on the tide with salt water)

O friends' homes with vaccinated dogs

O reputable puppy classes (see the section below on selecting a class)

O a puppy party you can host (see next page for details).

Avoid busy parks and other places where stray or unvaccinated dogs, and potentially infected dogs, are more likely to go.

Things you can do to help protect your pup include:

O take a disinfectant (virucide) of choice, and spray surfaces beforehand if you need to

O if possible and necessary, carry your pup in your arms while still exposing him to the novelty, movement and noise of new places, and spray areas with virucide if you put him down.

Host a puppy party

Consider hosting a puppy party or an ongoing group (much like a puppy coffee group). Through your local breeder or vet, bring together some local puppy owners for playtime with your pups. This also has the added benefit of creating a support group around you. We suggest you do the exercises we recommend in Part F. Practise together.

Here are a few tips for hosting a puppy party:

- Decide the number of puppies you can host and manage safely — if inexperienced, keep the numbers low. Check out the other people's experience levels, too, trying to invite at least one experienced dog person.
- Set up a play area with puppy toys and an obstacle course — tubes, ramps, and rollers.
- Use a virucide in the area to manage infection risk.
- Have a couple of vaccinated, known and stable adult dogs to introduce to the pups.
- Each puppy must be introduced to the others using the meet-and-greet section of this book. Ensure that any rough pups get introduced to the group slowly. You must moderate and manage them to ensure they don't beat up the other pups. (See the meet-and-greet section in Part D.)
- Have crates, and later clip stations, set up to keep control.
- You can use this book and our *Dog Zen* online videos as support resources to guide some activities.
- Organise safe walking trips outside the home.
- Make it fun for you and the pups!
- Discuss and test each other on the use of your training methods and experiences.

Puppy classes

Puppy classes can be an excellent way to get your puppy well socialised to lots of different dog breeds, sizes and temperaments, which is important for your growing pup. However — and this is an important however — you need to find a reputable class that manages the complexities of lots of puppies, as one thing you do not want is for your pup to experience any form of fright or trauma. This can happen from a mismatch of the size and temperament of pups, so be particularly careful if you have a smaller or more timid pup.

When looking for a good puppy class, you should consider:
- How do they manage vaccination issues?
- How do they manage pups of various sizes and temperaments?
- Do they formally meet and greet each pup, ideally with a clicker?
  - Be wary of puppy classes that seem unmanaged and allow pups of various ages, sizes and temperaments to run around uncontrolled.

Ideally look for a class that covers:
- formative period theory, and what needs to be done when
- socialisation with lots of people (age, race, gender, clothes) and varieties of dogs and puppies
- cross-fostering with other species, if possible
- habituation and desensitisation to novel environments
- teaching separation (crate training)
- shared language and basic obedience
- basic tools, including the clicker, crate and clip station
- joining up and the follower response
- house-training advice
- play groups based on size and temperament
- providing for quiet time and rest for the pups.

Before your pup arrives home, make a plan on where and how you can safely socialise your pup. Preparing an approach earlier will help ease the stress once your pup comes along, and will ensure you make good decisions.

16.3 PREPARE YOUR FAMILY AND CREATE YOUR 8-WEEK PLAN

It is useful to make sure you and your family are prepared for your pup as best as you can, to ensure that the critical first 8 eight weeks you are together goes well. I suggest you:
- ensure family rules are in place
- practise with tools and techniques
- build an 8-week plan to guide you in those busy few weeks.

Family rules

In Part B we went through how to establish family rules for both your family and your pup, so go back and review that section. It is important that you do this together as a family to ensure your pup gets clarity and consistency, which will help build his trust with you and strengthen your bond.

EXERCISE: CREATING FAMILY RULES

Sit down together as a family and brainstorm the compulsory rules first. Look at the list together to decide which rules you need to commit to, and stick them on the fridge (or somewhere else communal).

Next, brainstorm the list of things you would like your pup and then adult dog to do, and again make decisions. If the list is too long, you might need to prioritise.

Help each other to stick to the agreed rules, knowing that this is supporting your beloved pup, so he can feel secure and trust you all, and not be confused by inconsistent rules.

Practice time

Review the importance of the mentor bond (Part B) as well as the purpose of your training tools and how to use them (Part C). Try some of the exercises from those sections before your pup arrives, so your technique is developed and you don't end up practising on your new pup more than you need to.

Try practising:

- the timing of your clicker (use the tennis ball exercise mentioned in Part C, clicking the moment the ball hits the ground)
- holding the lead, using the clicker and delivering the treat from the treats pouch
- your effective check and then timing of it — remember snappy, not a pull or tug (try on a friend's arm)
- the environmental awareness exercise outlined in Part B — do lots of this before your pup arrives home, so you get used to seeing the world through your pup's eyes and can anticipate potential risks
- reading dog language — borrow a friend's dog or hang out at a dog park and practise recognising the different states of a dog (see the section on shared language in Part B), and see whether you can recognise the orient, alert, target (OAT) sequence.

Develop an 8-week plan

It is a good idea to think through and write down some of the key things you will do in those first 8 weeks after your pup comes home, as there is lots to do and it is all important.

Here is a quick checklist for your 8-week plan:

- understand what your breeder has already started with your pup
- understand feeding and exercise requirements
- book veterinarian check-ups
- set up the house-training system, including a comfy den for your pup (crate)
- make equipment ready (clicker, training pouch, leads, toys, bowls)
- have the family rules in place
- have a socialisation plan in place
  - list of family meet-and-greets (including pets)
  - safe places for socialising your pup identified
  - puppy classes checked out or a puppy party or group organised
  - known, safe adult dogs to meet and greet identified
  - list of a variety of people to meet and greet identified
- draw up a stimuli desensitisation list
- have your training plan in place (how often, for how long, who)
- schedule your pup pick-up.

8-week planner

We have created an easy-to-use 8-week Puppy Zen planner to help you manage these critical weeks. Go to www.dogzen.com/puppyresources.

Chapter 17

Getting your pup home

We have already discussed the importance of the 7–9-week transition period and how this is the ideal time to get your pup. The following outlines how to prepare for and undertake the transition of your pup from mum and breeders to your home. Even if you have got your pup after this period, still follow the methods suggested here to ensure your pup's transition to your home is as supported as possible. If done well, your pup should settle within a week or so. Pups can develop aversions easily to new experiences (8 weeks is a minor fear-imprint period). This is a huge time of change, so it is important it goes well.

PREPARATION FOR TRAVEL

Preparation for travel should start a few weeks beforehand, so some early preparation from the breeder is desirable. There are two aspects to travel that you have to habituate your pup to: motion and containment. The sooner you can do repeated exposure to these, the better.

Containment

Ideally, use a crate whether travelling by car or plane. If flying, choose an aircraft-approved crate that can continue to be your pup's home crate. It is important to do some short periods in the crate to desensitise your pup, reinforcing their natural love of den-like places. (See Part C The crate.)

Motion

Once the pup is used to the crate, it is good to do some short practice runs, travelling for short distances to start getting used to motion and to avoid motion sickness developing.

It's important that your trip home goes well.

First trip home

○ It is essential that this trip goes well, as it will set up your pup's transition to your home, as well as set the tone for car travel in the future. So please do take care — remember how easily puppies can develop aversions.

○ Check with your breeder what they will have done before you arrive, so you can prepare a contingency plan if needs be. If they haven't started crate training, then take a little time to introduce your puppy to his crate before you head off. (See Part C The crate.)

○ Make the crate as comforting as possible, including soft toys and something that smells of the dam. Make sure the substrate within the crate is non-slip, so your pup doesn't move around during travel.

○ Secure the crate carefully with a seat belt in your car.

○ Ensure that the car trip is very calm: no loud noises (mind the radio), ensure the temperature is comfortable (not too hot and not too cold), and if you have children, make sure they do not poke or prod your pup (this will be very tempting, so take care!), and no loud noises from them.

O If it is a short trip, keep an eye on your pup to assess how he copes with the travel. If you see signs of distress, break the trip up into short sectors. If he is used to a clicker, then you can use clicking and rewarding as you travel, rewarding non-anxious, attentive behaviour toward you. (You will need a companion to be able to do this, as someone needs to keep their eyes on the road!)

O You may cuddle your pup in a towel for parts of the travel if he is particularly distressed. You are really trying to avoid him becoming anxious on this trip to your home.

O If it is a longer car trip, then break it up into 30-minute intervals. Every half hour, ensure you get your pup out and carry him around or spray a site with virucide and set him down to toilet.

O If your pup needs to travel by aircraft, it is important that your breeder desensitises the pup to the travel crate over a couple of weeks before travel. If you are picking your pup up from a plane flight, check how he has managed the flight. If your pup appears distressed, get him out of the crate for cuddles, and cleaning up may well be needed. Let the pup out onto a safe area that you have sprayed with viruscide and where he can toilet. Follow the car travel guidance as above for the trip home from the airport.

O Ensure you continue to desensitise your pup to the car travel once he has settled in, with lots of small trips with lots of positive associations and clicker work. Start with short trips, then extend to longer trips.

O If your pup develops an aversion (fear reaction) to car travel due to bad motion sickness, you will have to develop a graduated desensitisation regime to help him through this aversion. You want to develop a positive association with the car, so feed your pup his meals in the stationary car, as well as use clicker training through an increasing level of exposure and movement in the car.

O If your pup gets motion sickness, discuss options with your vet.

When your pup arrives at his new home, it will be full of unknown smells, experiences and noises. Make sure that it is a calm, relaxed atmosphere: avoid loud noises, and ensure your children (if you have any) are calm. Give your pup some calm, quiet time to settle in. Help your pup settle straight in by toileting out on a grass area, or on the paper in the crated area you have prepared. This will become the pup's toilet area, so ensure his first toileting is in the spot allocated for toileting.

Right, your pup is now home and you have done plenty of preparation — let's get started!

What to do, when

In this step-by-step guide, we will go through each of the 8 critical training activities, outlining what you should be focusing on for each day or week.

These focus points are informed by the critical periods your pup is going through, ensuring you are training the right thing at the most effective time for your pup's development.

These critical periods help define what socialisation, habituation, training and exposure we should be doing and when. Remember, if you do the right thing at the right time, your pup will require significantly less training effort.

This weekly guidance is divided into the 8 key periods your pup goes through on the way to adulthood, with a particular focus on the formative period. Also included are the associated developmental transitions, fear-imprint periods and critical periods. Have a look at the material in Part A on the formative period if you would like to review your pup's developmental stages and related critical periods.

Here is a summary of your pup's key development periods to help guide you through the details coming.

KEY DEVELOPMENT PERIODS

O Prenatal — preparing the dam
  — All about caring for mum in preparation for your pup's arrival.
O 0–3 weeks: Beginning and awakening of senses
  — Neonatal period (0–2 weeks) — milk, mum, filial imprint
  — Transition period (2–3 weeks) — awakening of the senses (calm, relax, quiet)
O 3–16 weeks: Formative period — establishing your pup's future
O 3–5 weeks: No fear
  — Developmental transition: at 5 weeks, weaning, starting to engage with the world
  — Fear-imprint period 1: at 5 weeks (minor) — poking nose out of den
  — *Critical periods:*
    • Socialisation (social behaviour emerges) — primarily canine first, but also human interaction good to start now (3–12 weeks)
    • Communication and enrichment (3–16 weeks)
    • Noise (4–10 weeks)

○ 5-8 weeks: An expanding world (social, curious, exposure)
  — Developmental transition: 8 weeks heading out to the mentors or pack (you)
  — Fear-imprint period 2: around 8 weeks (minor) — leaving the den
  — *Critical periods*:
    • Socialisation (3-12 weeks)
    • Communication and enrichment (3-16 weeks)
    • Noise (4-10 weeks)
    • Curiosity (5-7 weeks)
    • Socialisation transition to home and mentor bond (7-9 weeks)
○ 8-12 weeks: Transition to mentor and joining the family
  — Developmental transition: at 12 weeks, preparing to head out in to the world
  — Fear-imprint period 3: at 12 weeks, critical socialisation ends (early development of sympathetic nervous system preparing for closing down of socialisation at 16 weeks)
  — *Critical periods*:
    • Socialisation (3-12 weeks)
    • Communication and enrichment (3-16 weeks)
    • Noise (4-10 weeks) continues
    • Socialisation — transition to home and mentor bond (7-9 weeks)
    • Environmental awareness (9-16 weeks)
○ 12-16 weeks: Heading out into the big world
  — Developmental transition: out to the big world
  — Fear-imprint period 4: Fight-flight instinct period starts at 16 weeks — big, scary world
  — *Critical periods*:
    • Communication and enrichment (3-16 weeks)
    • Environmental awareness (9-16)
    • Socialisation — bonus period (12-16 weeks)
○ 4-6 months or onset of puberty: Juvenile — entering the big world
○ 6-12 months: Early puberty — hormones, hormones, hormones
○ 12-18 months: Late puberty — becoming an adult (sex)
○ 18-24 months: Young adulthood — establishing their role in the pack/family
○ 24 months onward: Adulthood — responsibilities and are established in the world

Below are the 8 activity groups (introduced in Part A) that we will focus our week-by-week training and developmental work on.

MB   o Mentor bond

S   o Socialisation — human, dog, other species

SL   o Shared language — tools, obedience, learning state

F+P   o Fears and phobia prevention: Priority 1: Home-related (handling, introducing family members including pets, noises, surfaces and steps/stairs, travel, veterinarian clinic); Priority 2: Outside of home (socialise — people, other dogs, other species; movement — bikes, skateboards, skates; objects, novel environments and change, roads and traffic)

TS   o Teaching separation

HT   o House training

BI   o Bite inhibition

E   o Enrichment

BEFORE YOU GET STARTED

Building your situational awareness

This part of the book is focused on what training we do and when. A crucial part of this is how you grow your own skills, confidence and knowledge. Go back to Part B and the section on the bond, particularly your role as your pup's mentor, and ensure you do the practice exercises that will help grow your skills, particularly around situational awareness.

Having an ability to read the world through your pup's eyes will help you fulfil one of your primary functions for your pup: providing trusted guidance through this human world. Being able to see risk early and predict how your pup might react to that will help you avoid your pup (and yourself) being placed in situations that are beyond your capabilities. Believe me, you will love your growing ability to truly see your pup and their world — and it will expand yours, too.

Building your reflective practice

O As training evolves over these crucial weeks, it is important that you reflect on what is working and not working, how your pup is, how you and your family are doing, what needs to change or be focused on.

O Keeping a training diary is a good way to track your progress, reflections, learnings and adaptions as you go through this critical formative period in your pup's development and will help you learn and grow with your pup.

O You can find a downloadable diary at www.dogzen.com/puppyresources.

How to use Part F if you have an older pup

If your pup is older than 12 weeks (and especially if older than 16 weeks), I recommend you do the following:

O First, do the puppy temperament test in Appendix A to identify what may and may not have been done to establish your puppy's training baseline. (We discuss this more at 7 weeks of age.)

O From there, go through this whole section from week 1, and use it as a checklist to further refine what you need to focus on.

O Some things may have already been done (like house training, introduction of the collar and lead, and resistance training), so you can move through those quickly.

O However, check whether they have been properly established: for example, does your pup have lead or collar resistance or poor house training?

O If the behaviours are not well established, re-establish them using the guidance in this book and in our online trouble-shooting resource at www.dogzen.com/puppyzen.

Primary focus

O Your first focus will be establishing your mentor bond with your pup and shaping (growing) your pup's learning state, using joining up, the crate and the clip station.

○ You will need to take your older pup back to the den, re-creating his attachment to a mentor (you) and a den-like environment (the crate and clip station).

○ This is known as the secure base effect, and enables your pup to feel calm, supported and safe with you and in your environment, allowing him to switch into a learning state and be open to training and learning new things. (See Part B The bond.)

○ Before 12 weeks you can largely train through habituation (gently exposing your pup to new stimuli).

○ However, after 12–16 weeks you will largely be using a desensitisation technique. This requires more systematic and graduated exposure of your pup to new stimuli, while using the clicker to help switch and maintain your pup in the learning state. (See Parts C and D.)

○ This helps desensitise any fear your pup has developed after the critical period, when your pup had no fear and exposure was most ideal.

○ After 16 weeks you are more likely to be dealing with fear-based issues if not much socialisation was done before 12 weeks. This is when the trouble-shooting information in our online resource will become very important to you as well (www.dogzen.com/puppyzen).

○ If your pup is older than 6–8 months and is showing significant issues, then you may need to go to my book *Dog Zen*, which is focused on adult dog behavioural issues and their treatment. (Also access the online resource at www.dogzen.com.)

Chapter 18

The breeder

Because development starts straight away after birth, we start right at the beginning. This part of the book is primarily for the breeder, most of whom have dedicated a good part of their lives to the love, care, breeding and rearing of good pups. I hope this science and experientially based guide serves you and the breeding community well, and you enjoy it.

As the breeder, you will have the pup during her neonatal and transition periods, and at the critical beginning of the formative period, where essential exposure needs to start happening and important foundations are put in place. You have an extraordinary opportunity to prepare the pup in the time of her life when she is most developmentally adapted for such interactions — at 3-8 weeks.

It is also important that as the owner you know what goes on in these first 8 weeks, so you get an idea of what and how much the breeder has done, and therefore what areas you need to focus on when you take over nurturing your pup at approximately 8 weeks. From there, you must complete the laying down of your pup's critical foundations within the remainder of the formative period ending at 16 weeks.

Below we outline what would be ideal for a breeder to do. This ideal situation will create a stable, well-rounded pup with the best foundations for life. If a breeder even does half of this, it will be a good start for your pup. What I want to do with this section is grow your understanding of how critical these first few weeks are in establishing these foundations. If the breeder commits to all or some of this work, they will have prepared your pup for the world in a way that nothing else will do.

18.1   PRENATAL: SUPPORTING THE DAM (LOOKING AFTER MUM)

It is beyond the scope of this book to go into preparing the dam for breeding and whelping. However, it is worth noting that behavioural research shows that how the breeder cares for the dam in terms of social stimulation, loving care, nutrition and their bond will produce calmer, more stable pups. The pups will be more emotionally resilient, and overall more able to live happily and healthily in our complex human world. The following sections, up to the owner taking the pup home at 8 weeks, are directed to the breeder.

18.2   0–2 WEEKS OLD: NEONATAL — MILK, MUM, FILIAL IMPRINT

The most important primary function in this time is maternal care. The newborn pups are born helpless and dependent on their mother (dam). The main focus is on supporting the dam. Watch that the dam doesn't get upset, as the prolactin and other milk and birth-related hormones may make her more protective (maternal aggression).

We don't interfere too much at this stage, just provide a little contact with the pups so that they get your scent signature and trust is initiated. Research shows that short periods of daily handling from the start can have beneficial long-term effects on a puppy's behavioural and physical development. Puppies exposed to varied stimulation from birth to 5 weeks were found to be more confident, exploratory and socially adept.

Key points at this time are:

O Newborn pups show very little activity other than simple patterns of care-seeking behaviour. They can't self-regulate their body temperature, nor can they eliminate waste without their mother's stimulation. The dam does most things, including controlling urination and defecation by licking and cleaning it all up.

O Sleep dominates as the brain unfolds. Ninety per cent of the pups' time is spent sleeping, and the rest is devoted to nursing. Sleep continues to be a critical nutriment.

O A puppy's general motor activities at this stage are limited to swim-like crawling movements, and the focus is food and mum.

O The pups are deaf, blind and dumb, but their noses are fully functioning and dominant.

0-2 weeks

○ From a sensory viewpoint, newborn pups are thermo-tactile beings (heat-seeking). They judge what to do based on what they are attracted to, such as social contact, touch and heat, while avoiding, in particular, pain and cold.

○ Their central nervous systems are developing rapidly as their senses unfold and open.

The whelping box for the first 4 weeks

It is ideal that the whelping box be in a separate and quiet place. It should be about 2 x 3 metres in size, and include a litter box defined by very low sides for your pups to go over and into once 3 or 4 weeks old. This starts their substrate-specific choice, which forms part of house training, as early as possible. The surface texture under their feet facilitates the learning of this discrimination. Keep the rest of the area clean so they can learn the difference. This is the best time to start to learn, as 3–12 weeks is the critical period for house training.

Have a low puppy pen around the den, so mum can get out or get up high to get away from the pups when she wants, to avoid getting stressed. It is critical as it eliminates too much stimulation. Let the dam guide you towards her preferred place to rest when she needs to. Keep your pups' nails clipped for the comfort of the dam.

18.3   2–3 WEEKS OLD: TRANSITION PERIOD — BEGINNINGS AND AWAKENING OF THE SENSES

This sensory transitional period is characterised by significant physical changes and neurological development. During this stage, your pup's senses are opening and he is becoming aware of the world around him. By 2 weeks, your pup's eyes start to open. By 3 weeks, your pup first 'startles' on hearing noise, which indicates his hearing is now operating. By the end of 3 weeks of age (although timing varies a little in different breeds), all of the senses have opened and are operable. The world starts to come into sensory focus.

The puppy changes from being highly protected from his environment (closed senses) to extremely sensitive to it (open senses). During this time, his environment should remain stable, because his senses are on high intake, inundated with stimuli. Keep things simple, quiet and comforting. Continue with gentle, short periods of handling and quiet background noise (e.g. radio playing).

2-3 weeks

18.4   3–16 WEEKS OLD: FORMATIVE PERIOD — ESTABLISHING YOUR PUP'S FUTURE

Critical period for socialisation: 3-12 weeks — joining our world.

18.4.1   3–4 WEEKS OLD: The emerging social being — bond, socialise, habituate

Critical periods happening at this time are:

O socialisation — first canine, then human (3-12 weeks): social behaviour emerges
O communication and enrichment (3-16 weeks): shared language emerges
O noise (3-10 weeks): introducing a range of noises to your pup at a young age so he doesn't develop noise phobias.

3 weeks old: Engaging the world, fearless, enquiring

The social being emerges as your pup's senses open by 3 weeks. The first fear-imprint period begins at 5 weeks, so up until then the pups show little fear. This means that weeks 3 and 4 are an important window of opportunity to begin introducing your pup to the world, gently and quietly, initially. Because he has little sense of fear, and his recovery response from a startle is quick, this is the best time to teach emotional resilience to stress. The more enrichment you can offer, the better to grow their brain connectivity (while remembering also that your pups are still sleeping 22-plus hours a day).

Mum is licking the pups a lot to bond and to continue initiating toileting. She will start engaging and licking them individually, each with their own smell signature. They are now ripe to start learning, socialising and habituating to the world in their pen, and soon beyond. Make sure mum can move away to a separate spot for some alone time so she doesn't get niggly with her pups. Pinning and threatening is a function of her lack of freedom to retreat. Research shows less maternal aggression equals a better adjusted pup later in life.

Mentor bond **MB**

O It is a good idea to have future owners visit the pups from now on, in preparation for the pups moving to their new homes. Get the pups to smell the owners, see them and connect with them and their family. Smell is a pup's strongest memory and bonding stimulus, so you might even let the future owners leave an item that smells of them to really embed this imprinting and association.

O I also recommend using a calming smell like lavender in the whelping den, which owners can then replicate at the new home. This will help them deal with separation when they go to their new homes.

Socialisation Ⓢ

O Start to habituate the pups by introducing a variety of children and people, calmly and quietly. Make sure you supervise this. Keep it low-key this week.

O Make sure no disease is brought in, so wash hands and spray clothes and footwear with virucidal spray. (Or have visitors remove their footwear and keep it in a separate area.)

Shared language ⓈⓁ

O At this stage the mum starts licking the pup's faces. This is different from the rear-licking, and we believe that this is the start of social signalling, and stimulates oxytocin in both mum and pup (bonding in action).

O This is the start of loving, pro-social behaviour and social communication. This social language between mum and the pup, and between litter mates, forms the basis of the shared language you are going to create together with your pup. When mum starts this, it is a signal that we can get involved, too, starting to establish our shared language by holding, gentle talking and looking, and responding to play.

O Emerging social communication is the most important thing for pups right now. The following are wired in as the social pup emerges:

— Social signalling: they can already talk, ask and give — reciprocating communication.

— Social play: they can already accept invitations to play with litter mates (e.g. play bow).

— They can solicit or ask for attention from mum, litter mates, or us (by licking and jumping up).

3 weeks

— They show an emotional response when they receive attention (e.g. wag their tails).
— There is the start of the social order: they begin to defend themselves from being hurt (fight back, growl, etc.).
— Our shared language will take advantage of these skills in particular when we introduce the clicker next week, capturing and wiring the ones we need.

Fears and phobia prevention (F+P)

O Pups start to develop the startle and recovery response in the next 2 weeks, so light noises can be introduced in this week, building up to banging pots or playing louder and louder noises in week 4, so the pup startles but recovers from the fright quickly. This is an innate switch that wires in emotional resilience and adaptability.
O We want to really develop this recovery response, to build early resilience before the fear-imprint periods kick in at 5 and 8 weeks. This is an important window.
O This is a good time to play background noises and soundtracks throughout the day, but so as not to interfere with feeding and sleeping.

Separation (TS)

O From this week on, start taking each pup out by themselves for gentle holding and talking. This is the start of separation from the litter and mum, and bonding with you.
O Pop each pup in a carry-crate briefly (with the door open), and feed the pup (a soft starter meal) in there if you have time, but only close the door if he is relaxed.

House training (HT)

O Ensure you have a separate litter box with the litter material of choice.
O This is when the pups start to learn substrate-specific choice, so start the litter tray, separated by a very low piece of wood from sleeping area.

Bite inhibition (BI)

O Teeth start coming in at 4 weeks, so no issues yet.

Enrichment, play and exercise

○ Environmental enrichment can begin by adding in new toys each day, and providing enriching experiences such as small obstacles. This helps grow brain connectivity.

○ The litter box adds a new environment and something to soil in.

○ Handling and engagement is also important enrichment time.

4 weeks old: Fearless — startle response and recovery

This is an important time to start broadening the pups' exposure to their wider environment. They are now capable of some basic learning and problem solving, so start spending time developing their communication and shared language to support brain connectivity growth. It is also a good time to start the shared language, as the pups are communicating with the dam now, so we want to teach them to start communicating with us, too. We also want them to start problem solving and learning to deal with challenges, so put some low obstacles and interactive toys in their pen. You might need to make their den bigger so they can play more and have more room. Don't forget to keep the separate litter box in the den, too, so house training is beginning.

Mentor bond

○ Continue to have future owners visit their pups.

○ Three critical training tools are introduced this week to help build the bond. They are your puppy clicker, the 'sit' command (or four feet on the ground — precursor to a stand for show pups), and the beginnings of joining up. These tools will become a critical part of the training and enrichment routine over the next few weeks. See the instructions in the shared language section below.

○ Using these tools starts to reinforce the bond gaze (the pup looking to you), which in turn helps build contact and focus. It is part of the pup being able to ask and talk to you — the start of the reciprocal shared language.

○ To train the bond gaze, put the food lure up to your face, and click and reward the pup for looking to you when she sits. She is looking to you as her mentor for direction and love, and when she looks at your face, oxytocin activates in both of you. This is even more so once your pup looks to you voluntarily, which can happen quickly, but you need to shape (train) it first.

4 weeks

Socialisation (s)

O Continue and expand habituating (introducing) the pups to a variety of children, people and well-controlled, gentle dogs, calmly and quietly. Make sure you supervise this carefully. The dogs need to be very puppy-friendly and on-lead.

O Make sure no disease is brought in, so wash hands, and spray clothes and shoes (or remove) with virucidal spray. Ensure adult dogs are vaccinated.

Shared language (SL)

O Reciprocal communication has begun already, so now we focus on capturing behaviours and shaping them by introducing your pup to the clicker and the 'Zen sit' (including the bond gaze).

O These will be the beginnings of your pup's joining up, which engages the ancient follower response, reinforcing your bond.

O It is also the start of your shared language, where your pup is listening to you and learning that you control the resources. When she knows that, she will start throwing behaviours (voluntarily doing a behaviour to get a click and reward) — in essence communicating with you and learning to ask for things.

O Teaching the pup to sit and look to you (bond gaze) to get what she wants is making her operant: that is, she is operating *on* the world — in this case by sitting and looking to you to get a reward (bond gaze). This enhances impulse control, too, with the pup learning to delay gratification. These are good things to develop early.

O The 'sit' will also switch the pup into the learning state, by calming the body and switching on the decision-making part of the brain, dampening fear so the pup is better able to learn. This is especially so with the 'Zen sit', when the pup sits and looks at you voluntarily.

O Introduce the puppy clicker (see the toolkit section in Part C).
  — Bring your puppy out from the litter, and work with her individually. She should be used to that after the first week of just playing with you.
  — Start just pairing the clicker with food from your hand (loading the clicker). Don't worry what your pup is doing initially, just feed and click together for a few repetitions.

O Introduce the 'sit'.

4 weeks

— Capture the 'sit' with the clicker and a food reward. (See Part C Basic commands.)
— If the pup is to be a show pup, click and reward four feet on the ground (which is a precursor to a stand) instead. This is okay; it just doesn't quite achieve the same control. My preference is definitely to train a 'sit' if this doesn't get in the way of future roles. (Show people sometimes don't like training a sit because they believe it might happen in the ring instead of stand in the stack. Trained properly your pup easily discriminates the difference. However I respect breeder/owner choice here.)
— See Part C for more in-depth instruction on this training.

O On-the-mat training, which is the start of clip station training, can start this week. Here we put a mat down and click and reward the pup for putting a paw on it. Throw the food on the mat as the pup puts more paws on, and click and reward again. Keep going until the pup has all four feet on the mat, then do a 'sit'. Train for about 5 minutes, then give her a 10–15-minute rest in the crate, so her brain re-organises the lessons, and she will come back fresh and further on than before she rested.

O Joining up: As outlined above, this involves introducing the clicker, training the 'sit' and encouraging the follower response. Click and reward your pup for following you (within about half a metre, on the left) and not jumping up or nipping. Deliver the food reward from your hand; ideally, as you are on the move, but this is not critical.

O Group sit: Once the pups are individually trained, when entering the puppy pen ask all of the pups for a sit before they get picked up and taken out. This is not only very useful training, but incredibly cute! Add in some distraction, so you can start to desensitise the pups to dealing with distractions and remain sitting still. For example, have a dog or an adult moving around slowly.

O Collar training: You can introduce a light collar this week. Pups normally don't worry about wearing a collar if you start early. If they worry too much, use the clicker and food to reward non-bothering behaviour (see the toolkit section in Part C).

O Introducing the 'nicely' command: When introducing your pup to people or dogs, say 'nicely'. If she is sociable and calm, click and reward (see Part C Basic commands).

4 weeks

- Subtle recall should start as early as possible — when feeding the puppy, use the feeding call (a high-pitched 'puppy, puppy, puppy!'), tap the can or container you feed her from, and start pairing this with the 'come' command, rewarding her with her dinner. This is also growing bond, contact, resilience and connectivity. (See Part C Basic commands for more detail: at this age it is off-lead and simple.)
- Remember training at this stage is without lead and relying on shaping with the clicker. This is preliminary training, so make it fun and go at the pace your pup allows.

Fears and phobia prevention (F+P)

- We started fear recovery at 3 weeks of age onwards, when the pups were in a low-fear stage, so continue doing this with background soundtracks, increasing the volume gradually over the week.
- Also increase startle-recovery training, by starting to make louder, more startling noises, such as banging pots and pans, and watch the pup's recovery. Use the clicker and food reward if the pup is reactive (that is, if not recovering quickly by herself). We want to really develop this recovery response to build early resilience before the first fear-imprint period kicks in at 5 weeks. This is an important window.
- Introduce the pups to mobile and/or noisy household items, such as brooms, vacuum cleaners and dishwashers. Click and reward calm responses. Introduce the items one by one over the week as time permits.
- Expose the pups to different surfaces, such as lino, carpet, tiles and grass. Only one surface a day, just for a few minutes. You can click and reward a calm response.

Separation (TS)

- Continue to use a small amount of a calming smell like lavender in the whelping den, which can then be replicated at the pups' new homes. This association will help with separation.
- Continue working (handling or training) with the pups individually, as well as popping them into a crate separately to continue separation training. (See Part C Basic commands.)

4 weeks

House training
Continue to develop this with ongoing crate training and the use of the litter box in the den, developing their substrate-specific choice (some will be choosing it now). Allow toileting on the grass and start the 'be quick' cue if you have time. (Refer to the section on house training in Part D.)

Bite inhibition BI
○ The dam and litter mates play an important role in teaching bite inhibition.
○ The daily handling you are doing with individual pups is also an important desensitisation to handling, and thereby bite inhibition. Spend time gently touching and manipulating different parts of the pups' bodies. You can click and reward calm responses to support this learning.
○ If nipping, start teaching bite inhibition by trading for resource guarding, and redirecting play-biting onto a tug toy. (See Part D Bite inhibition.)
○ Milk teeth emerge this week.
○ Start nail-clipping now, so you desensitise them to this very important task. This will help:
— keep the pups' feet flat and even, so their bone growth is even
— protect mum's teats
— ensure the pups tolerate nail-clipping as adult dogs (it can be a significant issue in adult dogs if not desensitised)
— learn to clip safely and not cut the quick.

Enrichment and play
○ Enriching the pups' environment and activity, and exercising motor co-ordination and problem-solving, helps grow their brain connectivity.
○ Environmental enrichment can continue by adding in new toys each day. This helps the pups get used to novelty and change, as each toy or activity has a different shape, material, way it moves.
○ Take the pups out onto grass for stimulation.
○ Include new physical obstacles for the pups to climb over, under and drag around (being mindful of safety).

4 weeks

As a busy breeder, you may not be able to do all of this with each pup, but doing as much of it as you can is still good. I want to show just how early you can start on this level of training and habituation — the more the better, and this is the ideal time to start.

By the end of 4 weeks of age
By that time, the pups should:
- be confident with various people, a few dogs, lots of novel objects and stimuli, like vacuum cleaners, brooms and dishwashers
- have started joining up and throwing (do voluntarily) 'Zen sit' when they approach you
- be able to ask, respond, show emotional signalling and communicate with their mother, peers and mentors
- rarely jump up or bite
- be able to be individually in a crate away from the litter for a short period (if you are with them still)
- start to toilet outside on the grass
- have a short startle–recovery period
- be habituating to loud sounds and other ('scary') sounds
- know and respond to the clicker, and be able to switch into a learning state
- have learnt bite inhibition by trading for resource guarding, and redirecting play-biting onto tug toys.

Coming up
By 5 weeks the first (minor) fear-imprint period, which is associated with weaning, is about to kick in, so a period of mindfulness is needed.

18.4.2   5–7 WEEKS OLD: An expanding world — social, curious, habituating
Critical periods happening at this time are:
- socialisation (primary) — canine (3-7 weeks): social behaviour developing
- communication and enrichment (3-16 weeks): well underway
- noise (3-10 weeks): startle-recovery rapidly grown in the fearless period
- curiosity (5-7 weeks): this period is about to unfold as the pups relate further to their family and pack (us and other dogs)

O socialisation — transition to the new home and mentor bond (7–9 weeks): the breeder is practising and preparing the pups' ability to bond, as early bonding is important and formative.

5 weeks old: Mild fear-imprint period

This mild fear-imprint period is associated with weaning, growing brain development and recognising novel things. (Remember this comes from the wolf pups poking noses out of the den.) Care should therefore be taken to reduce (but not fully remove) the challenges while the pups work through this minor sensitive period. Continue with socialisation and exposure to environmental stimuli to aid habituation, but take care, particularly with more sensitive pups. A couple of simple fearful events can have a big negative effect on development. This is where your clicker and desensitisation are critical.

Mentor bond (MB)

O Continue practising the element of joining up you have established, at least the 'sit'. However, the follower response and commands continue too (see below).

O Continue establishing the bond gaze. Once the joining up sequence is established, add this to it. Pups can find this self-rewarding.

O Future owners continue to visit their pups any time through to taking them home at 8 weeks.

Socialisation (S)

O Continue to introduce the pups to a variety of dogs, people and children, just being more careful during this 5-week-old period. (Choose the dogs carefully, and supervise the encounters well.)

O Don't do any cross-fostering on other species this week in case of a fright, unless going well.

Shared language (SL)

O Encourage the 'Zen sit', as it is a great behaviour to consolidate or train in this fear-imprint period, because it switches the pup into a learning state and, with the use of the clicker, navigates the pup through the fear-imprint period more easily.

5 weeks

- Introduce the 'down' and 'Zen down' commands (see Part C). Again the 'Zen down' command is an important calming command and posture, so it is good to introduce this during the fear-imprint period.
- If the pup goes from a 'Zen sit' to a 'down' or 'Zen down' voluntarily, ensure you click and reward to shape the behaviour. (See the section on basic commands in Part C.)
- You can take crate training a step further and start closing each pup in a crate for a short period (approximately 1–5 minutes), with a food-packed puppy Kong to keep her busy. Feed each pup some dinner in the crate, or click and reward the pup going in and coming out (closing the door in between).
- Continue subtle recall work. Click and reward the pups coming when you call 'come'. Also continue follower response and on-the-mat training.

Fears and phobia prevention (F+P)

- Remember, pull back a little with the challenges this week. Keep a close eye on your pups and play it safe, with not too much fear-recovery work.
- If you notice any stimulus causing early fear reactions, then use the clicker and food reward with the pup to desensitise early. (Review basic commands in Part C.)

Separation (TS)

- It is too early to leave the pups separated for long, but building a little longer in the crate each time is preparation for separation later. (See about crate training in shared language section, above.)
- The crate is also a great time for rest periods after training. Carefully extend this a bit this week, using the clicker and reward in the crate, and feeding the pups (separately) in the crate. (However, pull back for this week if a pup shows any distress.)

House training (HT)

- Ongoing crate training and the use of the litter box is developing the pups' substrate-specific choice. The pups should be going well with their paper or litter-box training in the den, choosing to go onto the paper or into the litter box often now. Also moving outside onto the grass with 'be quick' cue.

Bite inhibition **BI**
O Handle all of the different body parts of the pup's body: mouth, head, ears, neck, shoulders, feet, tail, under the tail, etc. If the pup is at all fearful, use your clicker and food to desensitise and accept such handling. Don't push beyond the pup's tolerance this week.
O Continue to develop the follower response (through joining up), clicking and rewarding pups following you and not nipping or jumping. If nipping, redirect the pup onto a tug toy or put him away. No correction at this stage, especially this week.

Enrichment, play and exercise **E**
O Continue changing up the objects and toys in the pen, and increasing social stimulation as well.

6 weeks old: Socialisation, habituating, bonding

Your pups' brains have now grown all of the neurons they will have for life; however, the connectivity of the brain is incomplete, although growing rapidly. (There is an 80 per cent volume increase through to 16 weeks of age.) It takes stimulation to turn the switches on and grow the connectivity, so enriching the pups' environment, motor activity and social experiences is critical. Remember, we are in the peak socialisation period, where the smallest amount of effort produces the highest level of results, so it is time to really ramp up social exposure. This time is your pups' highest degree of socialisation, as they approach everything readily and have the lowest amount of fear, as they are now out of their first fear-imprint period.

Mentor bond **MB**
O In these last weeks before the pups head to their new homes, it is a good time to bring in the new owners to improve their bonding through contact and smell. By also working with their pup, the new owners can pick up what you have been doing.
O Continue joining up and its related behaviours, as outlined in earlier weeks. Show the new owners how to do it.
O If possible, it is time to move to umbilical work, using a lead attached to your belt to extend the joining-up routine into everyday situations.

6 weeks

Socialisation Ⓢ

○ Continuing lots of exposure to all different types of people, dogs and other species is good from now on. Use the meet-and-greet routine, the 'nicely' cue, and the clicker and food when the pups interact and are calm and showing appropriate behaviours. (They can withdraw or be mildly interested.) Just a few exposures at a time is enough. (See Part C on cross-fostering for cats and chickens, ensuring all interactions are positive, and no checks.)

○ Puppy parties are a great idea. Here, you invite your future puppy owners and dog-knowledgeable friends to your place. Have a variety of people of different races, ages, gender and clothing. Also have them bring one or more friendly, vaccinated dogs and do some socialisation with their dogs and their kids.
  — The party should include shared training sessions with the clicker, where the puppies are each taken through the command work they have done. Ideally, do joining up, 'sit', 'down' and 'Zen down', and experience time in the crate.
  — You could make up obstacles to climb over, tunnels to go through, little ramps, mini seesaws, and big balls, flags, things that fall over — anything you can think of that will create a novel and slightly challenging experience.
  — Use the clicker to reinforce confident responses, and teach the owners how to use it.

○ Continue dog socialisation work with the friendly dogs. If a pup can go off-lead with a dog, make sure the pup has a safe place, like a low table or chairs to get under to hide if wary. Click and reward good greets. Move around to relax the pup, and manage the meetings carefully.

○ Have a fun lunch to finish, with the pups nearby hearing the happy times (more desensitisation work).

○ Start cross-fostering by simple exposure if you have chickens and cats. If you don't have them yourself, arrange to borrow some or visit a friend. (This is important work, so see what you can make happen.) For instructions go to the section on cross-fostering in Part D.

Shared language **SL**

O Crate training should have continued, and now be extended into the travel-crate training in preparation for the pups' trip to their new homes (see the phobia section, below). Use an airline-approved crate if the pup is flying to the new home. Remember crate training will also prepare them for house training and separation.

O If not already started earlier (from 4 weeks on), then this week it is a good idea to start putting flat collars on the pups to get them used to it.

O If the pup is tolerating the collar, then start lead training and the extension of the join-up. (Refer to the tools section in Part C.)

O Continue on-the-mat training, going through a 'sit' on the mat, a 'down' and finally a 'Zen down'. Work with this a stage at a time.

O Start recall on-lead. Give the command 'come', and, as soon as the pup turns to you, click and reward, and then click and reward again when the pup gets to you. Gradually only click and reward when the pup gets to you.

Fears and phobia prevention **F+P**

O Car travel: First start feeding each pup (separately) in a stationary car, building up to moving in the car by introducing short car trips, each slowly getting longer. If a pup is sensitive, use the clicker (you'll need a helper). Click and reward calm, non-anxious behaviour. Take the whole litter in a travel crate in the car, with mum beside them, if possible.

O Continue to encourage startle recovery by desensitisation (clicking and rewarding increasing levels of stimuli) so you achieve almost immediate recovery when, for example, pots are dropped on the floor. You are continuing to reinforce success and not fear, and helping pups overcome fear is important. You are inoculating against fear by allowing low-level fear and enabling the pups to overcome it and build resilience. Comfort a pup if *very* fearful; however, do not comfort with low-level fear as the pup needs to learn to do it for himself: this is contrast training in action. Some low-level stress is beneficial in growing resilience and recovery.

6 weeks

VET-CHECK AND DESENSITISATION

It is important that you carefully desensitise the pups to your vet clinic, therefore setting them and their new owners up for a life of stress-free vet visits — and keeping vets safe.

- Do some handling desensitisation at home first, mimicking vet-like handling around the mouth, ears, eyes and bottom. Be gentle, and click and reward acceptance.
- It is ideal to make the first vet visit just a meet-and-greet and desensitisation exercise only.
- Make sure the room has had virucidal spray applied before you bring the pups in.
- Click and reward pups for accepting being at the vet clinic, with its unique smells, noises and busy environment.
- If possible, have the vet team handle the pups without any procedure, clicking and rewarding acceptance. Or have only minor procedures, like hearing tests.
- From your second visit, procedures can take place. Make sure you use the clicker to keep the pups in a calm learning state, clicking and rewarding acceptance of handling and procedures. You are teaching the pups that the vet clinic is a great place to go, and both the pups, their new owners and vets will thank you for it. This might be time for vaccination and congenital issue tests.
- You are supporting the pups to have a lifetime of positive associations with vets. This is important as we don't want pups developing aversions to the vet clinic or the vet, and creating lifelong complications around getting healthcare. This can be relatively common, so it is worth putting in some effort now.
- Travelling to the vet will also help with travel desensitisation. You should ideally be travelling in the car at least twice a week, clicking and rewarding calm behaviour if possible. (You can take the full litter in a crate with mum if you have a helper.)

Separation TS

- Continue with crate training, lengthening the period the pup is being closed in the crate.
- It is time to start some clip-station preparation work, extending the on-the-mat work you started by adding some slight restraint.

Ensure your lead work to date has gone well before you start this.
○ Using a long-line through the clip on the wall of your clip station (see the clip station set-up in Part C), clip the pup onto it gently, offering lots of loose line so the pup doesn't feel too restrained to start with.
○ If the pup accepts it easily, then increase the pressure slowly. If the pup is wary, slacken the long-line to allow the pup freedom from resistance, and go more slowly until he can deal with it. Take your time and be patient, you do not want to create aversion to the clip station. Click and reward calm, accepting behaviour.

House training HT

○ It is always good to take pups out to toilet on grass as often as possible. (At an interval of 1 to 2 hours unless they have access to their crate and paper.)
○ Continue the 'be quick' command, and click and reward after completed toileting.
○ Continue crate training around the house if possible.

Bite inhibition BI

○ Continue to handle all of the different body parts of the pups — with clicker and rewards.
○ Continue to cultivate the follower response: click and reward following and not nipping or jumping. Redirect a nipping pup onto a tug toy, or put him away. Ensure no correction still.
○ Start training to discourage resource guarding.
  — The best way to teach pups not to guard is to trade them for something better (taught earlier at 4 weeks of age). See Part D on bite inhibition.

Enrichment, play and exercise E

○ Continue to enrich the pups' environment and experiences with new toys, increasing their complexity.
○ Practise the apparatus used for your puppy parties.
○ Game: Frustration barrier game. Pop food on the other side of a wee barrier so the pup has to find his way around it to get the food. Keep it simple but challenging. This is not only a good obstacle game, it also starts building the pup's tolerance for frustration and builds problem-solving skills.

6 weeks

It's critical your pup is connected and focused on you — the bond gaze in action.

7 weeks old: Preparing for the new home

This is an important week in which you are consolidating the foundations and training you have started with your pups and preparing them for the move to their new homes. We are coming up to the pups' second fear-imprint period at 8 weeks, so be mindful. The earlier work you have done on habituation to stimuli and building resilience to frights and stress (including fear recovery) is going to be important in supporting your pups' transition.

At this stage the weaning pen should be made a bit bigger to allow for the pups' more robust and active behaviour, and to accommodate enriching toys and interactions.

Mentor bond

O Ideally, a joining-up sequence with a 'sit', a 'down' and hopefully a 'Zen down', and the follower response (start of the 'heel' command), has been established. This should include the pups looking up to your eyes and face (bond gaze), establishing contact and strengthening the bond.

O Train to prevent resource-guarding issues (guarding the things they want, like food, access to their mentor, toys, their bed). See below in the section on bite inhibition.

O Hopefully, the new owners have visited by now, and their scent imprint has started to support your pups' transition. The more contact your pups and their new owners have, the easier the transition.

O Have the new owners identify how to simulate and copy your set-up where possible, as this is ideal to help your pups' transition. (It keeps things as familiar as possible during so much change.)

O Umbilical work on the joining up is advisable now, too. Try this with the new owners, too. (See Part D Joining up.)

Socialisation

O Continuing exposure to all people, dogs and other species is good from now on. Start to use the-meet and-greet routine (see Part D Meet and greet). Remember, the 'Zen sit' is the desired behaviour when anyone approaches.

O Continue cross-fostering by simple exposure to chickens and cats.

O Ideally, getting out and about would be beneficial, if this is a week after the first vaccination, and if possible, remembering to manage vaccination risk (see Part E).

O During 6 or 7 weeks of age is the best time to consolidate and practise real-life situations such as in your puppy parties. They don't have to be big.

Shared language **SL**

O Continue practising the clicker and 'Zen sit'. We are reinforcing the learning state with the clicker, which is a powerful marker to shape behaviour and shared language. In this way you are laying a powerful foundation for your pups' future owners.

O Communication is now becoming reciprocal: the pups are orienting, watching and listening to you. They are asking/speaking with their 'Zen sit' and being heard by you — a shared language is truly growing.

O Crate training should have continued. Remember, crate training will prepare the pups for house training and separation desensitisation. Lengthen the time closed in the crate with food.

O Collar training should have started by now.

O If lead training hasn't started by at least 6 weeks of age, start introducing lead training as an extension of joining up. (See Part C for further guidance.)

O 'Down' and 'Zen down' should be established behaviour or being finalised now. Continue that training. Once your pups start doing 'Zen down', it is a huge breakthrough, because it activates the learning state and calms them. It allows your pups to take in the world more clearly.

O With on-the-mat training and clip-station training, by now your pup should be sitting on the mat, then 'down', then 'Zen down'. Continue to work on this a stage at a time.

O If you have a chance, put in 3 clip stations around your place and expose the pups to them.

O By 7 weeks of age, the recall should have been started and be continuing.

Fears and phobia prevention **F+P**

O Remember it takes pups only very few repetitions to learn something when they are very young, whether positive or negative. It gets harder and harder to learn as pups get older, and, once inappropriate behaviours get wired in, we have to unwire and rewire, so prevention is better than cure.

○ Continue exposing the pups to novelty and change (floor surfaces, rubbish bins, flags, etc.) to build true emotional stability and resilience.

○ Continue to wire in a shorter startle–recovery response by creating loud noises more often, like banging pots and pans. Watch the pups' responses carefully, clicking and rewarding quick recovery. If a pup is too frightened, lower the stimuli and desensitise. (See Part D on fear and phobia prevention.)

○ Continue to set up some small challenges with novel things, like climbing over something a little difficult and getting in a shallow pool of water. While your pups might find it difficult at the start (and feel frustrated), and may have a minor fear reaction, encourage and lure them through the frustration and fear, clicking and rewarding each small effort. This builds resilience to both frustration and fear, and teaches rapid recovery from setbacks.

○ Ideally continue short car trips, making them longer.

Separation (TS)

○ Slowly increase the periods of time each pup spends by himself, being handled, playing (obstacle courses, searching for food), and being left in the crate. Extend the time in the crate from week 6. (By taking the pups one at a time away from the litter daily, and crate training and training them, you will have set the foundations of separation while reinforcing the den site attachment to the crate, too. It will also be a powerful aid in house training.)

○ Continue this work, and customise your focus based on how the pups will be travelling to their new homes. (For example, crate training is good for the drive to the new home, and particularly good if flying is involved.)

○ If you have time, extend your clip-station work by restricting the pups more and more on the long-line (see week 6). Click and reward calm responses. Once a pup happily accepts the shortened long-line, clip him directly onto the short clip-station light chain, and click and reward calm behaviours. Practise 'sit', 'down', and ultimately 'Zen down'. Focus on lengthening the 'Zen down' time.

7 weeks

The aim is to have the pup settle on the clip station for periods of time.

House training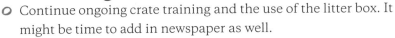

○ Continue ongoing crate training and the use of the litter box. It might be time to add in newspaper as well.

○ Take the pups outside and make sure they go on grass often. A dog door will be a useful learning experience if you have one, or you can mock one up. (See Part D House training.)

Bite inhibition BI

○ Your pups should be well on their way to being docile and gentle in their interactions, although they can play hard and rough if they want. In this situation, the pups should be redirecting that energy onto tug toys, other rough playmates, or exercise and purposeful activities like 'retrieve'.

○ Continue desensitising your pups to body handling: paw, jaw, mouth, ears, neck, etc. Make sure you have structured play sessions, and use a tug toy as an intermediary, and teach any children to stop and not move if a pup starts biting.

○ If you present your hands, a pup will bite, so use a toy instead. If the pup persists, pick him up and hold him in such a way that you have control of him, with his mouth away from you. This defuses the nipping and settles him.

○ Continue desensitising resource guarding. Increase your trading game, including lap protection, toys, beds and anything else.

○ Refer to Part D Bite inhibition for more detail.

Enrichment E

○ Rest and sleep are still a big part of a pup's life at this stage. This means it is better for a pup to have a structured activity/play-to-rest regime, with your pup being put in his crate or away in the den 70 per cent of the time to consolidate.

○ Enrichment is such an important aspect so provide toys, play, training, love, problem solving and even some pressure or stress. Make sure the pups get constructive and fun play, and enough training sessions.

○ Continue changing the objects and toys in the pen, and increasing

social stimulation as well. Rehearse all your puppy party activities.
O Hold another puppy party if possible.

By the end of 7 weeks of age

Let's summarise and check what your pups ideally should have learnt by this time, in preparation for their moving into their new homes.

O The bond will be growing, with the joining up and bond gaze going well.
O They should have had lots of exposure to lots of people of different races and ages, and to breeds of dogs and some other species. They should have learnt a meet and greet, and to voluntarily do a 'Zen sit' when meeting a person, rather than jumping up or biting.
O They will have experienced lots of different environmental stimuli, interacted with and manipulated objects, and done some problem-solving.
O They will have the basics of shared language: 'Zen sit', 'down' and 'Zen down', and ideally the beginnings of a recall. On-the-mat and clip stations will have been trained if possible.
O They should not bite or show any resource guarding.
O They will have been crated so that house training and separation will be underway (including having learnt to use a puppy door, ideally).
O Their fear-recovery response will have been established in this low-fear, high-approach (social) time. They will not be reactive to loud noises like gunshots and fireworks.
O Some car travel will have been established.
O They should be well prepared for the owners, or the show ring if a show dog.

18.4.3 SUPPORTING THE NEW OWNERS

O Ideally it would be useful to provide a short written summary of the training foundations you have put in place so the new owner can be consistent.
O Outline any commands, tools and techniques you may have started already.
O If you are interested, you can also become part of our afflilate programme, offering your owners access to our support resources. Contact support@dogzen.com for details.

Coming up

At 8 weeks of age the second (minor) fear-imprint period starts. This has its origins from the wolf, where in the wild, pups transition from the den to mixing with helper wolves. We mirror this, transitioning pups from the breeder to their new families and homes at this time. (See more in Part A on the formative period.)

The 8-week fear imprint means that the best time to transition the pups to their new homes actually ranges between 7 and 9 weeks. Because the pups are moving into a fear-imprint period at 8 weeks, extra care needs to be taken during week 8 so they don't get any frights. Being aware of this makes the end of week 7 an important time for you, the owner, to take stock of your personal circumstances and home environment, and of the particular personality of your pup. It may be that your pup is still a little anxious, or your home situation may be less settled than ideal. If this is so, and you think your breeder has the better environment and skills to handle this period, you may choose to delay taking your pup home until she is 9 weeks old. Conversely, if you have the better situation, or you need to get your puppy home for some other reason, you could take your pup home at 7 weeks, or carefully at 8 weeks.

END OF BREEDER'S TIME

Thank you to all those diligent caring breeders out there.

Chapter 19

The owner — your pup is coming home

19.1 8–12 WEEKS: JOINING THE FAMILY AND LEARNING ABOUT THIS NEW WORLD

Critical periods happening at this time are:

O socialisation (3-12 weeks) — adapt to the mentor's world and grow the extended family

O socialisation (7-9 weeks): transition to home and create the lifelong mentor bond

O communication and enrichment (3-16 weeks): the shared language is shaped

O noise (3-10 weeks): continue inoculation against noise phobias

O environmental awareness (9-16 weeks): adapt to the mentor's lifestyle and environment.

Puppy temperament evaluation and issues identification

Before we move into what you need to do week-by-week with your new pup, let's ascertain exactly where your puppy sits in terms of the skills and experiences already acquired, and his individual temperament and needs.

In Part E we talked about a puppy temperament test (see Appendix A or download at www.dogzen.com/puppyzen). We used it as an evaluation tool for you to establish the appropriateness of prospective pups you might be considering. Here, it is a very handy test to do once your pup is home, to identify:

O what behavioural attributes have already been established (creating a baseline for measuring progress over the next few weeks)

O what training tools and techniques have been established

O what training is needed over the next crucial weeks up to 16 weeks of age (training priorities).

It is a good baseline for you to have at 7 or 8 weeks of age, and is particularly useful to understand how much has been done with the breeder so you can identify what you need to consolidate or what you need to establish. Go to Appendix A and revisit the test.

You can then repeat the test at 12 weeks and 16 weeks to track progress and identify the next priorities. The 12-week test will help identify what you should focus on for the remaining 4 bonus weeks of socialisation, and the 16-week test might help identify what you need to focus on for trouble-shooting.

Priority setting
Ideally from 8 weeks we are strengthening established foundations and introducing new training appropriate to the critical period. However, if not many foundations have been established, you will need to establish them. Review weeks 3–7 using your puppy temperament test, and identify what you need to establish and/or strengthen. Your initial priority is to establish your mentor bond and your pup's secure base, so he feels safe and can maintain a learning state for all the learning and training ahead. Also prioritise socialisation.

If good foundations have been established to date, then you are in an excellent position for a steady, calm final few weeks through to the end of the formative period. Don't underestimate how valuable a good early start is. If you didn't get one, don't worry, just follow the plan we have set out for you and your pup, as you are still well within the critical formative period.

19.1.1   8 weeks old: Settle, introduce, bond (first week at new home)

In this first week at your home you want to have things calm, with not too much going on so your pup can settle. (They have enough going on!) Remember your pup is in a fear-imprint period (associated with separation from his dam and joining the pack), so be mindful of what you do for this first week, and particularly the first couple of days, in this new environment.

Even if you have got your pup later than 8 weeks of age, still ensure this first week at his new home is managed calmly and mindfully, as it is a big change for him and we don't want him to establish aversions to your home or family members.

8 weeks

In general:

- Avoid any loud noises that might frighten your pup. Instead, carefully and gradually start to introduce your pup to the noises in your household.
- Avoid having too many people around at once. Best you do not have that 10-year-old birthday party this week, although a couple of kids should be okay!
- Avoid any dramatic movement or fast, noisy activity.
- Have a quiet, comfortable area (such as your puppy crate) where you can pop your puppy if he needs to be removed away from too much stimulus. However, ensure you include your pup in your social areas often, too, for contact.
- Well-prepared pups will tolerate this change and new situation well, but still take care.

This week you need to:

- ensure you understand what has been done at the breeder's, and either continue the breeder's good work or start the work that is needed now
- settle in and calm your pup, and start or continue house training
- focus on your mentor bond with your pup, so he is building rapport and trust with you now
- teach separation (or continue to)
- introduce your pup and socialise him to your family members, including pets and visitors; doing this one at a time and keeping sessions short — about 5-10 minutes at a time, and then allowing your pup to rest to consolidate learnings
- introduce (or consolidate) some of the tools (clicker, collar, lead) and some basic commands — advanced pups will deal with longer training periods
- start or continue fear prevention, through habituation and some desensitisation.

Outcomes sought by the end of the first week

- Your pup and you are calm, happy, bonding and not overwhelmed by change.
- Any fear reactions that are occurring have been quickly identified, and desensitisation is in progress.

8 weeks

○ House training and separation are well underway, and progressing well.

○ Joining up is started or continuing. Your shared language is started or continuing.

○ Advanced pups will pick up where the breeder left off generally, although take a couple of steps back to help consolidate in the new environment.

Important note

It is important that you know not only *what* the breeder did in the way of training, but also *how* they did it. It is important that at the start you do not use different cues or techniques, but gradually move to any preferred techniques over time. Keep things simple for your pup at the start of this big transition. Integrate what the breeder did in your pup's new home environment first.

How you start sets the overall tone to your training approach. Critically, remember that what you give attention to is what you train, so you must not reward soliciting, anxious or hyperactive responses. Instead — whether by attention or actively through clicking and rewarding — you are rewarding calm, appropriate responses. You are starting your 'nothing in life is free' approach to training on this very first day. Start as you mean to carry on — your pup will learn what gets your attention fast, so make sure you are teaching your pup the right things.

Days 1–3 at home

The priorities for day 1 are:

○ settling in your pup and introducing him to his new den

○ house training

○ starting your mentor bond

○ introducing and socialising your pup to family members

○ managing separation.

Settling in and house training **HT**

○ Remember your home, the people in it, its smells, objects and surfaces are all new to your pup. He is being exposed to so many firsts. Pups and dogs can easily develop site-aversion, so you want to ensure that your pup's new home (den) feels like a place of safety and comfort. It is important that your pup doesn't receive any early frights in his new den, particular as he is in the fear-imprint period, associated with separation from the dam. Include smells from the breeder, such as lavender scent, and also any toy or cloth he has brought with him that is impregnated with the scent of his dam and litter mates.

○ Ensure you have chosen and set up your house-training method already, including your outdoor toileting site, ideally on grass and as far from the house as practicable. Follow the instructions on house training from Part C.

○ Be aware of the set-up your breeder had, and try to keep your set-up reasonably similar (assuming it was good), to help your pup feel some familiarity to this area. Use the same litter material as your breeder used (paper or toileting mats, for example).

○ When you first get home, keep it simple with just one or two of you involved. First give him lots of big cuddles and loving, then pop him out to toilet on the grass in the identified toileting area. This helps establish the surface discrimination to use grass for toileting, and gives your pup an opportunity to lay down his scent. If the weather is good, spend some time outside with your pup to get him familiar with this area (maybe half an hour or so). Let your pup smell all around the property, but ensure he gets no frights. Use the 'be quick' command for toileting.

○ Then bring your pup into the crate/pen area, so he can check it out, sniff and explore, and connect to that place. Feed your pup there; or, if on clicker training, deliver food to the ground all around the crate and click and reward. Keep the crate door open at this stage, so your pup can wander around his pen area and get familiar with it. Sit inside the pen with him and play gently.

○ If your pup needs to sleep, let him do so. Your pup is still sleeping a lot at this age. If not on the clicker yet, just use food or praise and love. Remember to start with a puppy clicker.

○ After a little while, and once your pup has toileted, slowly let your pup out into various parts of your home (a room at a time), so again your pup can sniff and smell things and explore. Watch your pup for any toileting signs, such as prolonged sniffing, stopping, circling and investigating. But allow him to relax and explore this new home. You are allowing your pup to gently get used to these

8 weeks

new things in your home by exploration and exposure, especially smell.

O Now your pup is a bit more settled, you can start quietly introducing him to other family members.

O At this age your pup is usually toileting about once an hour, and approximately 10 minutes after play, 15 minutes after food and immediately after sleep.

O Should your pup soil, don't punish him: just pick him up and take him to newspaper or outside.

O Make sure you have a cleaning mixture made up and ready to clean up any accidents and associated smells, although hopefully you are spotting your pup's toileting signals early and taking him outside to toilet. Cleaning up any messes is important, as it neutralises smells so you don't get repeated toileting in unwanted areas. (Once your pup has toileted somewhere, and the smell remains, this becomes a signal that this is a toileting area.) A recommended cleaning solution is 1 part white vinegar to 3 parts water. Some commercial cleaners are fine, too. (Just make sure they are suitable to use on your carpet and other vulnerable surfaces.)

O If you have a dog door to outside (which is ideal), you may need to tape the door open for the first few days to help your pup get used to using it. Place a stick across and under the flap, and tape it with strong tape so it holds the door open. Over the next few days, slowly lower the taped door, increasing the degree to which your pup has to push the door open, until the stick is finally lowered all the way down. Teach your pup how to go through the door, luring him with the clicker and food rewards to the other side. Some small pups might need a step installed on each side initially. Pups vary in how long this training takes.

O Once you have had some bonding time and allowed your pup to explore his new location for a period supervised, settle your pup into his crate. Hopefully the breeder has already started this process. Check the section on teaching separation and adapting to the crate in Part D to manage this.

O Remember, pups at this age have a thermo-tactile reflex that attracts them to the litter mates or mum through warmth and softness. Ensure there is something soft and warm in the crate —

8 weeks

a warm surrogate litter mate — ideally with both your scent and that of the dam on it. You are trying to replicate the situation your pup has come out of as closely as possible, so the change isn't too great. Two pups together is a bonus, if possible, as they are social animals. Note that a male and a female is an easier mix than pups of the same sex, and it's better if they are not litter mates.

O At the end of this big day, make sure you put your pup out last thing at night for toileting, and then back in his crate for around 5-6 hours. You might have to get up once during the night or early morning. (They should be able to last up till then, or longer if the breeder says so, without toileting or stress.) If you do get up, start delaying this by a further 15-30 minutes each night, so you can eventually extend it out to all night. Some pups can hold on through the night, but be careful, as you don't want your pup soiling in the crate. Don't close your pup in the crate all night if he won't last: you don't want your pup to soil in the crate or he will lose that all-important nest-site soiling inhibition. Keep the door open if necessary so he can go on newspaper.

Mentor and family bond (MB)

O Starting your bond: You are a critical aspect of trust and support, so it is important that this starts off well so your pup grows his trust in you. (Your first test on building trust is managing this week well.) This is the right time for you to be stimulating the ancient bonding behaviours between pups and sub-adult helpers (mentors) that form attachment relationships.

O As described above, spend a couple of hours settling your pup into the new environment. Help your pup explore the area, with lots of sniffing, smelling and touching, and lots of cuddles and talking from you. Get your pup used to you, your smells, voice and calm energy.

O Preferably, your pup's main den should be close to your central family area. If this is not possible, you might also want to establish a mobile crate for your pup, so you can pop him into that and bring him into your social area. It is good for your pup to have plenty of social contact, and be able to see and hear you going about your day. You are stimulating your pup to have controlled contact with you. If your pup starts soliciting for attention and not

8 weeks

settling, you might pop him back into the main pen area to settle down.

○ If the breeder hasn't already started some basic training, start now — it is a lovely and productive way to spend time and bond. Your pup will love you pairing up the puppy clicker with food!

○ Work on the 'sit'. Start by just throwing food on the floor, and click as your pup eats it. Then draw him to you with a food lure, and click when he is near you but not on you. Next, start to lure to shape a 'sit', or just mark anytime they sit. The aim is to shape (train) the 'Zen sit'. This should become your pup's default state when he approaches anyone, especially you. Refer to week 4 with breeder for more detail, as that was the ideal time to start it. Remember with 'show pups' you might prefer to do a stand four feet on the ground, due to the show stack issue.

○ If you have not established the family rules with the family before your pup arrived, do so now. Then remind all of the family members of the rules, and be consistent in applying them.

Socialisation ⓢ

○ For the first couple of days, focus on introducing your pup to family members, including your pets, through exposure and habitation (hanging out together). Let your pup sniff, lick and be touched and be held by family members. Don't over-stimulate your pup, and watch for his reaction. Some pups will take lots of this, others only so much, so notice when your pup might have had enough. For more anxious pups, just go slow and take your time, ensuring everyone is quiet and calm. Particularly supervise any children, so they don't prod, poke or frighten your pup, including making loud noises. Use play and happy, upbeat tones as you introduce your pup. Use the meet-and-greet techniques set out in Part C, once you get clicker training going. Advanced pups will be more robust.

○ When introducing other dogs, ensure the adult dog is on a lead and is carefully moderated. Again, allow your pup to sniff and explore, watching the other dog's reaction to ensure they don't get too rough, too early. Your pup will lick the other dog's jowls and jump up, so moderate the adult dog with a lead, and check if needed. Use the clicker and meet-and-greet method outlined in Part C. Make sure your pup is able to get under a low table or somewhere to get away from the older dog if you take the dog off-lead. Keep it relaxed and informal at this stage, making it safe and positive.

○ If the adult dog is likely to be reactive, ideally you have done some clicker work with the adult dog beforehand, and taught her a good meet-and-greet routine so the greet goes well and is controlled. Your pup's first meet and greets with people and dogs are critical, so ensure they go well and your pup has a positive experience.

○ When you introduce your cat to your new pup, either pop the cat in a crate or hold your cat so you can manage this first greet. It is unlikely your pup will be aggressive or scared at this stage, so all should go well. Be careful if your cat hasn't met a pup before (or has and didn't like it). In this case, manage your cat's reaction carefully. See Part D for guidance on cross-fostering.

○ If your pup is anxious in any of the meet and greets, don't persist with introductions. Instead, focus on introducing your pup to the clicker so that you can then use a more graduated desensitisation approach, as outlined in the meet-and-greet processes provided in Part D. Using the clicker will help keep your pup in a non-anxious learning state and reinforce appropriate responses.

○ Plan and book puppy classes for the next week or two — your local vet might have suggestions.

Shared language **SL**

○ If not started by the breeder, start your clicker training straight away on day 1 or 2, as it is such a powerful learning tool. (See the toolkit section in Part C for how to introduce your pup.)

○ Remember to be mindful as you introduce your pup to the clicker for the first time, just in case he is sensitive to the noise. Use a puppy clicker, which has less volume.

○ In this settling-in phase, make sure you start pairing up (loading) the clicker with food rewards, so that you can switch your pup's focus onto you and switch his nervous system into a learning state and get the 'Zen sit'. (Review the section on the learning state in Part C: it is a critical aspect of training.) Continue any more advanced training the breeder has established such as 'down', 'Zen down' and joining up.

8 weeks

O Start shaping your pup's learning state early. Your pup is still sleeping approximately 75 per cent of the day (3:1 sleep:activity in the day), but this will change considerably over the next 2 months. Ensure you give your pup his rewards when he is calm (attention — pats and cuddles, talking to him, letting him out, click and food rewards), but not when he is being solicitous, vocal, anxious or hyperactive.

O Start practising reading your pup: observe your pup's language and begin to learn your pup's personality and idiosyncrasies. Begin observing how your pup communicates when he wants to go to the toilet, is hungry, is thirsty, is frightened, is calm and confident, is focused and in a learning state. (See the section in Part B on shared language for guidance.)

O By day 3, introduce your pup to a collar, if the breeder hasn't done so already. If the breeder has already established a flat collar, then I would recommend changing to a half-slip collar in preparation for training. Again, go to the Part C toolkit for instructions on how to do this carefully, so you don't give your pup a fright and develop any potential aversions. Start on a limited-slip collar now that he is 8 weeks of age.

Fears and phobia prevention (F+P)

O Your pup is taking on so much in these first couple of days that it is best to focus on bonding and socialisation.

O Ensure you identify any potential issues, and protect your pup from any fear-inducing stimuli (such as loud noises) until you start slowly to expose and desensitise him to them. Play 'sounds scary' audio from YouTube or iTunes.

O Check the list you have made of the things you will be desensitising your pup to over the next few weeks, as part of the 8-week plan you prepared in Part E. If you have not already made the list, do so now in preparation for later in the week. Watch for any of the 8-week fear-imprint sensitivities, and if you observe them use click and reward to desensitise (see Part D).

Teaching separation

O Remember, arriving at his new home is your pup's first real experience of separation from his dam and siblings, unless the

8 weeks

breeder has (ideally) already started the process. This is the critical period for separation, so needs to be done properly.

○ As your pup will be experiencing some separation distress, he will be vocalising and jumping up on the side of the crate. You need to ignore this behaviour, so some tough love might be required. Although doing so might feel difficult and painful right now, you are actually saving your pup far more stress later by avoiding him developing separation distress, so stay strong. Both you and your pup will be thankful in the long run for your patience and persistence. See the section on teaching separation in Part D. Cover the crate with a blanket at night to settle your pup, and you can have music playing too.

○ The important thing is to set your pup up for success. Remember to set up the crate with something that will remind your puppy of the whelping den. Maybe something smelling of mum and litter mates, as discussed earlier. Include soft, warm things that comfort your pup.

○ Rehearse a few play sessions with the Kong and other toys to get your pup's interest in them, then leave him with these items for enrichment and to help him settle.

○ Remember not to reward vocalisations by returning and attending to your pup. You will be rewarding the wrong behaviours, and thereby increase the vocalisations. After your pup has rested for 15-30 minutes or more, wait until he is quiet, and then go to him. Click and reward him just before you open the crate. Try to get the 'Zen sit' and bond gaze, before starting to play.

○ It is ideal to graduate your pup's separation. If you are at work it is more difficult to gradually ease your pup into separation for longer periods. Ideally, you want to have someone home for this first week or more, or at least coming in at intervals, so that they can help establish this graduated departure. Remember your pup is used to having his dam and litter mates with him a lot of the time, so this is a big change.

○ Have a smaller travel crate to bring out beside you as you watch TV or do other normal activities, and give your pup time there, too. You may have another little puppy pen out in the living area, too, but remember to put paper down on the floor, maybe with plastic under that.

8 weeks

Bite inhibition BI

○ This is unlikely to be a problem at this stage, but if your pup is starting to bite already, review the guidance provided in earlier weeks for breeders (check what your breeder has already done) and see the bite inhibition techniques provided in Part D.

○ Start teaching 'gentle' and using joined-up walking, and click and reward when he is not jumping up or nipping at you.

○ Also use a tug toy to redirect your pup's attention. Pick your pup up, pointing his head away from you. If your pup is over-aroused and nippy, put him away to calm him down. No correction is used at this stage.

Enrichment and play E

○ The purpose of play this week is to help introduce your pup to his new home and the associated smells, places and things in the home. Take care with noisy things.

○ Suggested games might be gentle tugging games, and chasing things if your pup is interested.

○ Assess what your pup likes to play with, and trial toys. Don't overdo this, though. Have fun!

Days 4–7 of week 8: Settle, introduce, bond

Mentor bond MB

○ Check in with your family rules to see how you are going as a family and what might help guide your training.

○ The number one task is to continue to form a healthy bond. Spending happy, calm time with your pup is critical this week. I recommend as a minimum 2–3 15-minute sessions each day of training and/or play, with rests in between and after.

○ Play is a good way to bond. If your pup is sociable and happy, just let her play and enjoy your growing bond. Remember, one of the main functions of play is to rehearse behaviours your pup needs to learn. Use tug toys to redirect biting.

○ If your pup is at all anxious, use the click-and-reward process, as the clicker will encourage calm behaviour. Using clicker training to introduce the basic commands — 'sit', 'down', 'Zen down' — can be a lovely way to bond and spend enriching time together.

○ If not started by the breeder, start lots of joining-up practice, as this teaches your pup 'watch me', 'follow me', 'trust me' and 'listen to the clicker', which become the basis of your deeper relationship. Access to food and social contact are both powerful reasons for your pup to follow the mentor — you.

○ Start joining up without the lead. For now, use a food lure to start entraining the follower response in your pup. Click and reward as your pup starts following you (within half a metre, on your left side, ideally), then practise the 'sit', 'down' and 'Zen down'. If the breeder has progressed to a lead, use it.

○ Do the joining-up ritual around 2–3 times/day, for around 5–10 minutes at a time. Watch your pup for fatigue, as your pups will have different needs around training times. Remember to pop your pup in her crate for a 15–30 minute period of rest and consolidation of learning after training; she will come back fresh and advanced.

○ Around day 6 or 7, introduce the lead and limited-slip collar for joining up (if not already done). (See Part C on how to introduce the lead if that has not been done already.) To start with, ensure there are limited times of pressure on. What you are aiming for is that when you stop, your pup sits and looks up at you. If you are there for a while, your pup will lie down, and in the end adopt 'Zen down'. You are aiming to have them start to do the 'Zen down' voluntarily. They are truly turning to you for guidance now — a milestone moment. Celebrate when you achieve it! Wag your tail and play.

○ One of the most important parts of training your pup is understanding what and how you are communicating to her, including your posture, eye contact, pressure on the lead, orientation (body position) to your pup, and the intonation you use. Review the section on shared language in Part B.

○ Start paying real attention to your pup. See how your pup changes and responds as she adapts to her new world. Grow your awareness of your pup's idiosyncrasies and personality so you can start to develop an awareness of what/when your pup might react to something, and of how sensitive and confident she is.

○ Cultivate your situational awareness by practising looking at the world through the eyes of your new pup. What things might be

8 weeks

new to her that you might need to desensitise her to or withdraw her from at this stage? What might give her a fright, and what just needs a good introduction? Try the situational awareness exercise in Part B.

○ Your situational awareness includes being aware of yourself, which is critical to good training. Be aware of your level of confidence, and ensure you don't project onto your pup any anxiety or sensitivity, but instead appear calm, relaxed and engaged.

○ Review the 'nothing in life is free' section in Part B. It outlines how you are *always* training, which is why it is so important to be aware of what behaviours you are rewarding. For the next 2 to 3 months make it a rule that you ask for a command ('sit', 'down') before your pup is rewarded with anything — except if it is playtime, then she can relax! Use a release command when finished (e.g. 'that'll do').

Socialisation (human, dog, other species) Ⓢ

○ Continue socialising to any family members you haven't introduced your pup to yet, including friends who regularly visit.

○ If your pup has already met them, then continue socialisation by getting them to do some basic clicker work with your pup (otherwise establish this now). See Part D Meet and greet.

○ Ensure you go through a meet and greet for any visitors (people and dogs) to the house, to start a good routine that you continue as your pup grows. Invite people — especially children (in small numbers). Ask guests to bring their vaccinated, friendly dogs. Disinfect human hands, and spray virucide on clothes and shoes.

○ Ensure you manage interactions well (particularly with dogs you don't know), so your pup doesn't experience any fright or trauma at this stage. Allow your pup to move away or retreat under a table for example.

Shared language Ⓢ⃝Ⓛ

○ Once you have paired the clicker to food rewards, you can start teaching (or continue establishing) the basic commands of 'sit', 'down' and 'Zen down'. These are great commands to begin with straight away. Also encourage 'Zen sit'.

○ Once your pup is regularly going into 'Zen down', then she is often

8 weeks

in the learning state, and is alert and ready for your next cue. This
will get your pup focused in on you as the source of information
about the world, how safe it is and how to grow the shared
language you both rely on.

O Continue regular daily training sessions doing joining up —
around 3 sessions a day of 5-15 minutes is enough to start with.
Make them fun for both you and your pup, so they become part of
developing your trusted bond.

O This is the time to start more formal training, so from now on
whenever you are training your pup you should have your tools
with you — your food pouch with food rewards, and clicker.

O Even if you don't go out and about, plenty of play and exercise
sessions around the house are necessary. Remember the golden
rule of training: start simple. (Review the golden rules of training
in Part C.)

O If not already done, introduce the lead on day 5 (or at least by the
end of this first week). Being on the lead might be your pup's first
experience of resistance, so like all new experiences go slow and
be mindful of your pup's reactions. See Part C on how to skilfully
introduce your pup to the lead, as you don't want your pup to
develop any adverse reactions to such an important training tool.

O If you haven't already, set up your training diary, and start to
set yourself some training goals so you can order your priorities
correctly.

Fears and phobia prevention **F+P**

O Remember that there are lots of new experiences happening for
your pup, so a very important focus this week is to ensure your
pup doesn't get a fright. Practise your situational awareness so you
identify any potential issues early on.

O It is good to start with a low level of exposure first, to test whether
or not your pup is reactive (and so avoid any major frights). If
you see any reactions, establish a more formal hierarchy of the
stimulus, from low to high, and start with the low. Click and
reward for calm responses as you increase the stimuli. Take care
and keep an eye on your pup's reactions — don't go too fast.

O Initiate early active desensitisation with the clicker. First, identify
what this week's desensitisation priorities are, based around the

8 weeks

It's important that you introduce your pup to people of various races.

house. Identify what the stimuli are, and then set up a learning experience for them. (See Part D.)

O I recommend, in order (advanced pups will have done these already, in which case just test and reinforce):
  — body contact and handling, desensitising the mouth, head, ears, feet, tail, etc.
  — household noises and objects — vacuum cleaners, brooms, dishwasher, etc.
  — different surfaces — slippery floors and stairs, etc.

O Remember you are using both habituation and desensitisation, gradually and systematically exposing your puppy to stimuli, depending on how your pup reacts to the items. Use the techniques of habituation and desensitisation outlined in Part D.

O For this first week, start with approximately 3 new objects a day — don't rush too much. Be mindful of watching your pup's reactions and going at his pace.

O Generally, as your pup is in the peak time for learning new things, he will approach everything with friendly enquiry, so these

8 weeks

introductions should be relatively straightforward (habituation through general exposure). The use of the clicker will ensure that associations stay positive and keep your pup in a learning state so that they wire in.

○ Continue playing tapes with any potentially scary sounds in the background at low volume. Click and reward calm, appropriate behaviour. Do not drop dog plates, etc., until next week, unless the breeder has done this work already and your pup is relaxed.

Separation (TS)

○ Separation should be going well by now if the breeder has started this. Hopefully, your pup is calm and settled in his crate and doesn't vocalise, and can tolerate 1-2 hours in the crate and pen without fuss. If not, start working towards this, see Part D.

○ You will be starting to know the idiosyncrasies of your pup by now, so it is time to tweak the situation if vocalisation is occurring. Identify any problem vocalising, and work on it. (See Part D on barking.)

○ Make sure you let your pup have some downtime — particularly in these new and exciting first few days when we can be tempted to play with your pup all the time. Your pup still needs a lot of sleep and structure.

○ Be particularly mindful of this if you have got your pup during the holidays when you might be at home more, or if you have taken the first couple of weeks as leave from work to support your pup. Make sure your pup gets some time alone each day.

○ Remember dogs are a very social species. So make sure you are using social contact as a reward for quiet, settled behaviour in the den. Only let your pup out when he is non-vocal. Do not pay your pup any attention when he is vocal, and do not reward vocalisation with access out to the yard. Leave chewable toys and a packed Kong for enrichment and support.

○ After each training session, remember to pop your pup into the crate so he has time to consolidate the learning and rest.

House training (HT)

○ Adjust the toileting area to reflect how your pup is getting on. You will have observed whether your house training area is ideal by how your pup is using it.

8 weeks

○ If successful and going outside or on the paper or pad, start reducing the newspaper area from the nest out. If not being successful, continue to keep paper all over the puppy pen.

○ If your pup is toileting largely outside and away from the house, you are well on the way— however, don't expect it to be that quick.

○ If your pup is soiling in the crate, we have a problem. Cut down the unpapered area to just your pup's bed size, then cover the rest of the area with newspaper or other toileting substrate. Ideally, your pup only has the option of going on newspaper in the pen, or can access outside through a dog door.

○ Try to work out how long your pup can last, and then start to orchestrate a walk out to the edge of the garden (to long grass, ideally) to toilet your pup when you think he is about due. Say 'be quick' as you get there. After he has toileted, click and reward. Carry on this training until you see that the 'be quick' cue is effective. This cue is much easier to train, the earlier you do it. You are now starting to entrain your pup's toileting behaviour. Advanced pups may have this already.

○ If your pup is still going on the appropriate surface (e.g. paper), that's good, too. Make sure you keep some choice on the substrate (i.e. paper in three-quarters of the area and the rest as, say, bare lino close to the crate) so your pup has a choice each time he toilets. We want your pup to continue establishing his substrate-specific choice: choosing to soil on substrates that are not house-flooring substrates, like paper, pet toilet substrates, grass or bark. Start closing your pup in his crate for short periods, and extend the time with a bone or nice treats.

Bite inhibition 🅱️

○ Biting — especially when pups have their sharp milk teeth — needs to be addressed early and curtailed; the sooner you start, the better.

○ Your pup learns not to bite too hard from the dam initially, then from the pack early on in socialisation. That becomes your role as the pup moves into your home.

○ Teach your pup that he is hurting you by initially saying a simple 'ouch!' loudly. Don't pull back and make a tug game out of it, as then you are teaching him the wrong message. Make sure you stand still.

8 weeks

O Start with the 'ouch' response for now. Once your pup gets more confident as he builds bonds and establishes himself in the new environment, he might start to jump up and nip more, with his little sharp milk teeth (until 4 months). This is the time to start teaching the 'gentle' command.

O Start some tug-toy games to redirect nipping onto play objects (if not already).

O Walk with your pup beside you in joining up, and click and reward when he follows with no biting or jumping up.

O If your pup persists in nipping, pick him up and hold him with his head away from you, so he can't bite you. Let him relax and move back towards you, place him on the ground and click and reward. Then do joining up with the clicker, and end with a 'Zen down'. Review the bite inhibition section in Part D and follow it regularly.

Enrichment, play and exercise E

O As we know, play is an important part of your pup's day, as it is where your pup rehearses and practises lots of future adult behaviours. Your pup often practises these in parts and out of context: that's the function of play — to help put the foundations in place.

O Your pup needs to learn to play with the family, so start with teaching a retrieve and play tug. With children, make sure it is low-level activity and keep it structured, so that you can control any nipping.

O The demand for exercise increases with age, and it is very important to good physical development. However, be careful not to overdo it when your pup is young, especially in giant and large breeds.

O Exercise/play at least 3 to 5 times a day for 15-30 minutes. Include a couple of trips out in the car during the week, carrying your pup around outside the home. This includes early joining up and basic command training sessions, as these can be good opportunities for exercise, too.

O *Game: Rocking board.* Ideally the 'rocking board' game is introduced from 4 weeks on, but you can start it now. Cut a solid rubber ball in half, and nail it to the middle of the base of a 50-centimetre square of board. (Make sure the nails are flush

8 weeks

with the board, or recessed, so they cannot hurt your pup.) Glue a non-slip mat on the top side. It should now resemble the sort of wobble-board you find at the gym. With this game, you are encouraging your pup to get onto the board and tolerate the movement. To start with, place your foot on the top of the board to make it stable, and click and reward your pup whenever his paw touches the board. (Lure him with food if you need to.) Slowly encourage your pup to get all four feet on the board — click and reward. Gradually release your foot pressure so that the board moves, clicking and rewarding your pup for accepting the increasing levels of movement. This is teaching your pup motor co-ordination and building resilience to movement. This is helpful when your pup is out and about on surfaces that might move (e.g. stones). If your breeder has started enrichment games, make sure you know what they are and do them, too. Don't start yet if your pup is fearful this week.

8 weeks of age reflections

By the end of 8 weeks of age, your pup should:

- have a strong mentor bond — feeling safe and happy with you, looking to you for direction and responding well to your arrival, with joining up and 'Zen sit' well underway
- be socialising well with the family and other pets
- be accepting the crate, sleeping longer through the night, and not whining or soliciting when left (or at least stopping quickly)
- be responding well to the use of the clicker, collar and lead
- be going well with basic command training
- be calm and often in a learning state when training
- be toileting well on paper and starting to use the grass, and beginning to toilet on cue
- be playing appropriately, with you managing his bite inhibition with 'ouch' and the 'gentle' command, and starting the resource-guarding trade game.

Advanced pups will be well ahead of this and may be wanting even more stimulation.

8 weeks

19.1.2 9 weeks old: Bond, socialise, habituate

You are getting settled with your pup, and she should now have adjusted to your home and her crate, and house training is set up. She should be over the fear-imprint period, especially as she settles and bonds with you. However, you might be seeing a few issues arising; separation might be getting harder as your pup gets attached to you but the clip station hasn't been established yet to manage that. Your pup might be starting to get over-excitable and hyperactive as your bond gets stronger, so it is important that you don't reward those responses, but direct that energy into constructive behaviours, such as joining up and toy play. Focus on developing the 'Zen down' to help shape your pup's calm learning state. Ideally, your pup should be starting to do the 'Zen down' by the end of this week, if not already.

This week focus on:

O consolidating house training
O generalising your mentor bond to the rest of the family
O extending separation
O continuing socialising to new family members and visitors, including pets
O continuing to familiarise your pup with the training tools and with basic commands
O continuing desensitisation to the vet clinic when visiting the vet.

Mentor bond (MB)

O Check to see that your pup is connected and focused on you, looking up to your face. As you do joining up, draw your lure hand up to your left shoulder to direct her eye line towards yours — and click and reward gentle eye contact.
O Continue with daily joining-up sessions, and start extending this to the umbilical lead if things are going well. When using the umbilical lead, take care not to trip over or stand on your pup. See Part D.
O Spend time relaxing and playing together.
O Try to get your pup's retrieve started. Play with your pup's favourite toy or ball, and call 'Fetch!' When your pup brings the toy or ball back to you, click and reward. Initially, don't try to take it; just pat her and say 'good girl'. If she drops the ball/toy, click and reward. Repeat, then start adding the 'give' command, and

click and reward if your pup gives you the toy/ball. It is like a trade. Put the toy on a string if it helps.

Socialisation

O Start increasing the number of people, dogs and other species your pup is meeting. You are in the critical period of socialisation, so you need to use this time wisely. Those pups that haven't had much yet need to do a lot before 12 weeks.

O If you are feeling comfortable, start getting out (with your virucide) to friends' places with people, vaccinated dogs and other species, like cats and birds. Maybe even a farm visit, or a visit to a café or garden bar.

O Plan your puppy class, so you can take advantage of lots of people and pups. Take your tools. Your pup needs to be 1 week out of first vaccination.

Shared language ⓢⓛ

O Remember, pups are highly adapted to reading our cues and gestures as they try to relate to us and establish a place in the family order — so know what you are communicating. Remember the importance of tone and body position in training. (See the section on shared language in Part B.)

O Continue lots of joining up, and clicker and lead work (2–3 times a day for 10–15 minutes).

O Extend the follower response into a 'heel' command, and introduce the verbal cue.

O Hopefully 'down' and in particular 'Zen down' are established. Aim to have your pup throw 'Zen down' often, as it will switch her into a learning state.

O Introduce the 'wait' and 'come' commands. Recall is critical to establish early.

O Start some recall work now, and introduce the long-line and retractable lead, too. See Part C.

O Wear your rewards pouch and carry your clicker as much as possible. Notice how your pup's attention and focus are on you when these are present. She has now made the association between them and food, and so is wiring in these positive associations with training and you. You are starting to train her

9 weeks

learning state, switching it on merely with the presence of these tools.

O Increase the experience of pressure on and off, in preparation for teaching contrast training next week. Do this by creating more 'corners' in your joining-up routine, making the circle more square-like or doing 180-degree turns.

O Start playing hide-and-seek around your property or house.

O By the end of this week you should have some basic commands and joining up established: 'Zen sit', 'down', 'Zen down', 'wait' and 'stay'. Recall should be started. These basic commands prepare your pup to focus on you when you start moving out into the world more next week.

Fears and phobia prevention (F+P)

O Your pup is coming out of the fear-imprint period, so if she hasn't started showing fearful responses to things she should start to stablilise now. If your pup is showing any anxiety or fear, then identify the sources now and start desensitising her to them. Continue your noise desensitisation particularly, mapping out the order of stimuli (hierarchy from low to high). Continue to drop loud things to improve your pup's startle recovery.

O You can start to take your pup out into controlled, safe places. It is important to get her out and about, to habituate her to the world and to desensitise her socially and in the environment. Take your virucide with you and use it, and manage things carefully (e.g. spray the area around you in a café and put her down on-lead).

O As you prepare to start heading out more with your pup from next week, check in to see how your pup's confidence is going with regard to novel, noisy and moving things. Desensitise her to anything she fears, ensuring you set up your hierarchy. (See Part D Fear and phobia prevention.)

O Next week (10 weeks of age) you will be coming to the end of the noise-critical period, so make sure you have done plenty of noise desensitisation work with clicker training. Include louder noises now, even recordings of low gunshots, fireworks, thunder, construction tools, motorbikes and the like.

9 weeks

Separation **TS**

○ By the end of this week healthy separation should be established, with your pup being able to stay by herself in a crate, pen or yard for a couple of hours without any major fuss. If the breeder had already started this, maybe even for 3 or 4 hours.

○ Your pup should have puppy Kongs and toys in her crate for enrichment and support, and be chewing and enjoying them. Also soft bones if you use them.

○ Remember not to reward any vocalisation. Start to introduce the 'quiet' command, and click and reward increasing intervals of quiet (3, 5, 10, 20 seconds). Refer to the barking section in Part D.

○ Your pup will be eager to get your attention when you return home, so make sure you set your pouch up near the crate so that she can see you grab it, then click and reward a quiet meeting with you. Aim to have her sitting watching you intently and quietly. Use 'sit' and 'Zen down' to get your pup settled. If your pup is in her crate, ideally take a bit longer to open the crate so she hopefully throws a 'Zen down'.

House training **HT**

○ This should be becoming established by now. Check in with your progress. Is your pup toileting on the paper? How often is the paper being used (most days, hardly ever)? Or does she soil outside sometimes/always/never? Keep progress details so you see what you need to support.

○ Some pups can take up to 3-4 months for this to be established, but it is possible for it to happen earlier.

○ Start reducing the paper coverage towards the toileting corner if your pup is going on the paper consistently. If your pup is toileting in the corner of the puppy pen, reduce newspaper coverage to that corner only. You might be able to pop a small bit of carpet under the front of the crate, so she chooses not to go on this but go on the paper.

○ If you have a dog door, by now you can stop taping it open, and have it in the closed position and being used. If your pup is not using it, spend more time training this: luring her through by feeding her on each side of the door to get her used to it.

○ This is a good time to check again that your backyard remains properly puppy-proofed, as pups become more keen on getting out from now on.

○ Continue taking your pup out regularly for toileting and cue the 'be quick' command.

Bite inhibition

○ As your pup gets more bonded and confident, nipping can develop. Make sure your training is effective, as it gets harder as your pup gets bigger.

○ It is useful to encourage your pup to express her mouthing tendencies on suitable objects. Play can be very helpful. Encourage tug games, ensuring you end the game with a 'leave it' command. Try to make the games interactive, like 'fetch'.

○ Do lots of clicking and rewarding when your pup is not biting. Redirect her onto a toy or put her away in the crate to settle if the biting is persistent.

○ The 'gentle' command and redirection onto a tug toy should be established by now.

○ Do the techniques in order of priority, as laid out in Part D on bite inhibition.

○ If your pup continues to nip, you may have to step it up and use the jaw pinch or lip roll (see Part D).

○ For very rough pups that still persist, it might be time to start contrast training with the long-line and slip collar. Normally we wouldn't start this work until 10 weeks, but we introduce it sooner for these more pushy, rough pups, as they will have the resilience for it.

○ You can also get teething rings and toys that your pup can use.

Enrichment, play and exercise

○ Increase both play and exercise, as your pup is growing quickly and maturing now. Get her used to exercise and ready for getting out more.

○ Focus on retrieve and tug toys. Use them to play, allowing your pup to pull and have fun. Both become a form of enrichment and burn off that young puppy energy.

○ Add in other enrichment toys that help your pup problem solve. Put your pup behind a puppy pen panel and place food on the

9 weeks

other side, so she has to work out that she has to go around the panel to get the food. This helps her control her frustration and work out how to find a solution and get the reward.

o Playing with other dogs is important, too — especially other young pups, so puppy parties or puppy classes are good.

o *Game: Tug.* Tie a rope onto something relatively heavy for your pup, and teach her to pull it. Click and reward as she slowly moves the object. This is teaching your pup a behaviour that has effects, and is interactive and fun for both of you. Later, tie the rope to a door handle to make it even more fun. Use clicking and rewarding to train your pup to first hold the rope and then pull it. Use a bungy rope if this is easier for your pup.

19.1.3   10–11 weeks old: socialisation, habituation, noise

The sub-critical period for noise is ending, so make sure that as your pup's environmental awareness grows you have desensitised her to environmental stimuli found around the home (vacuum cleaner, dishwasher, music, loud laughter, etc.). Increasingly, the clicker becomes a critical tool to help desensitise your pup to things she is frightened of.

Start (or continue) getting out and about outside the home for generalised socialisation (at 12 weeks).

This is the time to consolidate your shared language and proof it outside the home, as well as your tools and basic commands so you can establish boundaries, particularly before your pup becomes more externally focused after 12 weeks.

Mentor bond (MB)

o Continue with daily joining-up sessions. Ensure all family members are practising joining up and controlling resources, so that your pup looks to them for direction as well.

o If anyone in the family is being left out by your pup, make sure they control some of the resources. Make sure they have a pouch, clicker and some tools available, as your pup will recognise these training tools, which will help create positive associations and switch your pup into a learning state. They could take over some of the feeding, too.

o All the training you have been doing should be building your pup's confidence and focus on you. Your pup should trust you well by now, and the bond should be strong.

O Continue proofing your joining up at other people's places, cafés, and the like. In these situations, your pup should be looking to you, focused and attentive.

Socialisation Ⓢ

O Continue broadening your pup's social boundaries to other people, dogs and species. Make sure you do lots of baby, toddler and children socialisation.

O If you haven't already, then this week definitely start to take your pup out and about in safe exercise areas.

O Try to get a day out on a friend's rural property (or vice versa: go to the city if you live on a farm). Be aware that if you live in a quiet, rural area you might be limiting your pup's socialisation. If so, consider extra trips to town in this period to ensure your pup has broad exposure.

O Visit friends who have dog-friendly cats. Cats that grow up with dogs are best, as they will be less frightened and reactive, so you can trust them with your pup.

O You should have started puppy classes or formed a puppy group to provide lots of socialisation opportunities.

O If your pup has had limited social contact up until now, then this is the time to really focus on socialisation.

O Do another puppy party with obstacles and problem-solving toys. Socialise, rehearse training exercises, and have dog-to-dog socialisation.

Shared language ⓈⓁ

O It is now time to introduce the clip station (see Part C). Take care and go slowly, as you want the introduction to this to go well. Having this established will be greatly beneficial to your ongoing training.

O Both the crate and the clip station create the secure bond effect, which strengthens your pup's attachment to you and your home.

O 'Zen down' should be going really well, and your pup is switching into a learning state well. You should be able to see the change in her body posture and overall demeanour. Do lots of 'Zen down' practice on the clip station.

10-11 weeks

○ Ensure you have introduced the limited-slip collar by now. If you have a particularly big, strong or rough pup, you may find that the limited-slip isn't effective and doesn't change your pup's behaviour. If this is the case, consider introducing a full nylon slip collar. See Part C.

○ *Game: Hide-and-seek.* Continue playing hide-and-seek at the park now, so that you are teaching your pup to look for you, rather than you looking for your pup! Make sure you are safely away from traffic, possibly on a drag-line.

○ Start proofing behaviours: see Part D on proofing.

Fears and phobia prevention (F+P)

○ You are now extending your environmental stimuli desensitisation to outside the home, so if you haven't made a list of what you need to desensitise your pup to, make it now.

○ Remember to go carefully at first to see how your pup reacts and if she has any sensitivities. If you identify any, use a graduated desensitisation approach, using the clicker and food to reward calm, accepting responses.

○ You are in the middle of the environmental-awareness critical period, so you need to get out and about as much as you can.

○ Continue graduated exposure, experiencing trucks, traffic and lots of varied situations. Click and reward calm, accepting responses.

○ Café visits are a great opportunity to expose your pup to lots of people, noise and movement (and probably other dogs)!

Separation (TS)

○ This should be well established in the crate, and you should be able to leave your pup for 2 to 4 hours, hopefully more, with no barking or fuss.

○ If the crate is well established, you can now start the clip-station training.

House training (HT)

○ You should be going pretty well with your house training, with your pup now using outside more, if not all of the time (high-achievers!).

○ If she is still reliant on newspaper, it should be down to the corner by the dog door (or the door), and you might put some newspaper just outside the dog door, too. Slowly start moving paper away to the grass, 1 metre at a time.

○ The 'be quick' command should be becoming effective, so use it all the time, and click and reward when your pup is done. Do this when away from your property, too, if possible.

○ We can now start using the clip-station house-training technique to support generalising toilet training to the whole house (see Part D). Start to clip your pup up on 2 or 3 different clip stations around the house. Freedom around the house under supervision can increase too. Move slowly out.

Bite inhibition **BI**

○ She should be going well on this training. Continue with the 'gentle', 'leave it' and 'no' commands, lifting and pointing her head away if needed. Ensure resource-guard training continues.

○ If children are having issues with your puppy biting them, make sure they use a tug toy to redirect her. Check the children are standing still, and you may need to moderate with a slip collar and long-line. (See Part D Bite inhibition.)

○ If persistent, try using the jaw pinch or lip roll.

○ As you get the slip collar and long-line working, you can start the check if your pup persists in nipping. (See Part D Contrast training.)

○ Start discrimination training to teach your pup the difference between toys and inappropriate items like cushions and shoes. Now and over the next month, as teething happens, destructive behaviour can increase.

Enrichment, play and exercise **E**

○ As your pup gets older you can increase play and exercise. Lots of visits outside the home are happening now, which helps.

○ You can start to use tug toys to reward good training sessions with some fun play afterwards. However, don't use toys or play to shape (train) behaviour, just to reward successful sequences of behaviour.

○ Pups can often prefer to play with a human, so make sure they develop and continue to broaden their social skills and play with dogs outside their family group.

10–11 weeks

Ten-week-old pup being desensitised to passing traffic.

○ Your pup's locomotion and co-ordination should be developing and improving. She should be enjoying playing and running with other dogs now, building confidence around adult dogs. (Note: these should be dogs of good temperament.)

○ *Game: Chasing bubbles.* This is a cute game to practise the 'get it' and 'leave it' commands. It also allows you to control play sessions through switching off play sessions (which is particularly important for hyperactive and obsessive pups).

— Get yourself a good bubble-making kit (children's ones are good as they are non-toxic). You can also get flavoured bubbles (e.g. liver).

— Blow a bubble and ask your pup to 'get it'. If she has a natural interest, she should jump up and get it — click and reward. If your pup needs encouragement, click any part of your pup's orient/alert/target sequence to start shaping the behaviour, slowly moving to rewarding only when jumping up and getting it. Take care with growing joints, and don't overdo it.

— Remember this is practising your 'get it' command, so say

this each time you blow a bubble.
— Once 'get it' is well established, you can start the 'leave it'
  command (which has already been taught outside of this
  context).
— Blow a bubble and say 'leave it'. The moment your pup looks
  away from the bubble, throw a piece of food in that direction
  and click and reward for leaving the bubble. At this stage use a
  lure away rather than a correction to reinforce 'leave it'.

11 weeks of age reflections

Next week we are heading in to the last formal week of socialisation,
so hopefully your pup has been out and about, enjoying meeting lots of
new people, dogs and other species.

O Your pup should be comfortable in these situations, showing
  confident, calm behaviour, and not being overly hyperactive,
  fearful or showing weariness or aggression.
O In this environmental-awareness phase, your pup should be
  getting lots of exposure to noise, movement, surfaces, objects,
  novelty and change. Again, your pup should generally be
  accepting all of this with calm, confident behaviour.
O You might see a small amount of fear/startle, which is normal, so
  just use a graduated desensitisation approach with the clicker to
  help your pup accustom to the situation. In general, though, your
  pup should be tolerating most things well.

19.1.4   12 weeks old: Socialisation consolidation

This week is a very critical week, as it is the last week for socialisation
through habituation, so double-check you have done enough varied
social and environmental exposure.

In a week's time a significant fear-impact period starts, and will grow
over the next 5 weeks for pups that haven't been socialised before 12
weeks. For these pups this coming period signals the emergence of the
fight-flight reaction, so they will develop more sensitivity to novel and
fear-inducing stimuli. Research shows that these pups will likely be mal-
socialised, however Puppy Zen with its desensitisation and counter-
conditioning tools can help pull this back if you work hard now.

Those pups who are well socialised and have followed the advised
plan will have a powerful fear-recovery response in place already, which

12 weeks

will now turn this period into a bonus socialisation period instead.

Continue to ensure your pup has a wide understanding of who is in his pack and so should be friendly with, and hard-wire the extended family.

For those who have just got their pup or this book, this is a critical week to make up for lost time and do as much varied socialisation as you can — of course at a pace your pup can tolerate.

Mentor bond (MB)

o The mentor bond should be strong by now, with your pup attentive and focused on you. You should have solid joining up, bond gaze and 'Zen down'. (If not, focus on this.)

o A good bond and control should be shown across the whole family.

o Joining up may be starting to be effective on the umbilical lead, and even going well off-lead with the clicker. This is especially so for those pups who got intensive training from the breeder when 3–8 weeks old.

o Review your family rules and check that they all are well established. Focus on any that might need strengthening.

Socialisation (S)

Here is a quick checklist to see what you might need to do this week:

o People
  — age range, particularly children (varied across babies, toddlers, older children)
  — gender (particularly men, who can be more intimidating for a pup)
  — race (work on extending beyond your normal social group), remember some cultures don't have a history of dogs as pets in the family, and tend to be more fearful and reactive, so your pup must be desensitised to this reactivity
  — different clothing (e.g. hoodies, hi-vis vests, caps, sunglasses).

o Dogs
  — lots of different breeds, colours, sizes and temperaments.

o Cross-fostering
  — lots of species, particularly ones your pup is likely to be exposed to as an adult — cats, chickens, birds, sheep, rabbits, stock on farms.

You need by now to have exposed your pup to multiple people, dogs and other species multiple times (at least 3 to 5 times for each individual type). If not, it certainly must be done before they are 16 weeks and out of the formative period. This might sound like a lot, but a quick car trip to your local café can tick numerous boxes in just one outing and visiting a friend's farmlet can tick many more. Puppy parties of course can bring them all to your home and help a lot too.

If at any stage your pup, once over 3 months (or a confident, robust younger pup), shows overt interest and starts lunging at another species, you will need to do the cross-fostering technique outlined in Part D. Get onto this now, as you don't want this behaviour to establish itself, as it is very difficult to treat in adult dogs.

Shared language 🆂🅻

○ Your pup should be throwing 'Zen down' often now, holding a good 'sit', 'down', 'wait' and 'stay'. Do lots of this practice. Review Part C.

○ Your pup should be able to maintain a learning state for good periods of time when training, staying focused and attentive on you.

○ Practise your contrast training, which should be establishing well by now. Once contrast training is well established and your pup has learnt 'no', you will see their learning potential speeding up rapidly, as pups (like all of us) learn best by contrast. It allows critical boundaries to be put in place easily, so master the technique.

○ The 'leave it' command is important at this time to be able to stop pups doing things they shouldn't be doing. It also reinforces the 'no' command, and will allow you to firm up your 'come' command.

○ Discrimination training should be started to teach your pup to discriminate between toys and cushions, shoes and the like.

○ Check off your basic commands in Part C, and see how you and your pup are going. Work on the less-established commands, and continue to consolidate those that are going well. Work on your proofing in a variety of situations. (Remember to step this up slowly, so you succeed in increasingly challenging environments — set you and your pup up for success.) This is important before

12 weeks

the next fear-imprint period begins next week.

O   Keep crate and clip-station training going for a long time; in part, for life.

O   The good news is, if you have done a good part of what we ask of you above, you will fly through the next month, as your foundations are well established and your pup has developed good emotional resilience.

O   For those just getting started, let's start putting in the foundation work. It might be worth reading Amber's case study (see page 415) for an encouraging real story to help you understand how to get started at this age.

Fears and phobia prevention (F+P)

O   With the third (and most critical) fear-imprint period beginning next week, consolidate your noise and environmental desensitisation work now. This fear-imprint period is related to finalising relationships with you and your extended family. It is also an important stage for environmental exposure and habituation.

O   Make sure you spend this week getting your pup out and about a lot, consolidating his tolerance for change and novelty, and rounding off his emotional resilience.

O   Review the list of things you wanted to desensitise your pup to, and ensure he is exposed to any that have yet to be covered. Make 2-3 exposures to each of them this week — particularly if they will play an important part in your pup's future life.

O   Do tests (carefully) on items that you have already exposed your pup to, checking effectiveness. For example, get your vacuum cleaner out, put on the radio and dishwasher, drop a pot and check your pup's reactions. Note which items might need some extra work. Make sure you have your clicker and food to reward calm, appropriate responses, and do some graduated desensitisation work if your pup is reactive.

Separation (TS)

O   Separation should be going really well, with your being able to leave your pup in the yard or kennel 4-plus hours without him barking. He should be confident on the clip station and good in

12 weeks

the crate for an hour or more. All pups develop at different rates, though.

O Your pup should be sleeping through the night (or close to it) without barking.

O Do lots of clip-station work around the house and out and about (at cafés, etc.).

House training HT

O You should be starting to phase out the newspaper to the outside (if you haven't already), and house training should be close to completion in the better pups.

O Keep working on it if your pup is a bit slower. Remember this behaviour is largely involuntary, so it is about creating structure and routine to establish control. It is about setting the environment up so your pup can succeed.

O Continue using clip stations to generalise to all of the house. You may be letting your pup have more freedom throughout the house, working from the den area out, a room at a time. To help your pup succeed, keep doors closed to rooms downstairs or away from where you spend most of your time. Your pup is least likely to toilet in areas near to you.

O The 'be quick' command (or whatever your choice of cue or command) should be going well. Remember the earlier you start, the quicker you capture it.

Bite inhibition BI

O This should be well established by now, but head to Part D for trouble-shooting if you are still experiencing issues and your pup isn't responding to general training.

O Keep rehearsing and testing resource-guarding potential and do the trade game.

O Use the 'leave it' and 'no' commands, moderating with a long-line if needed.

Enrichment, play and exercise E

O At this critical time, make all play and exercise related to socialisation and environmental desensitisation, so you are getting plenty of graduated exposure.

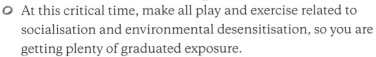
12 weeks

O Play and exercise with lots of different people — get them to throw ball, play hide-and-seek, blow bubbles. Have fun and grow your pup's social group.

O Let your pup enjoy lots of walks and (controlled) playtime with lots of different breeds of dogs.

O Your puppy parties and puppy classes should be happening regularly now.

12 weeks of age reflections

By the end of week 12, your pup will:

O have a strong bond with you (and other family members), and be focused and attentive

O be confident in greeting new people and dogs of all variations and types

O be non-reactive around other species he has been introduced to

O be well established in the basic tools and commands, including recall and contrast training, joining up, 'sit', 'down', 'Zen down', 'wait', 'stay', 'leave it', 'no', 'be quick'

O be calm and responsive in novel situations, and quickly recover from frights

O have house training established (potentially still extending to the rest of the house)

O have completed bite inhibition, and generally be gentle and reliable with children, too

O be playful and engaged, able to retrieve and offer up his ball/toy when asked.

Your puppy temperament evaluation

This is a good time to redo the puppy temperament evaluation test, so you can review how your pup is going and identify what you might best focus on in the next 4 weeks — the critical bonus period of socialisation. This bonus time is an excellent time to consolidate what foundations you have put in place and work on any weaknesses.

For those just starting, this test is critical to establish your baseline, so be diligent and clear. Have a trainer or experienced friend assist, or go to our online community. Go to Appendix A for the test.

Coming up

The third fear-imprint period comes as the rapid development of the sympathetic nervous system starts closing down socialisation at 16 weeks. Remember this was Nature's way to assist wolf pups to be wary as they go out into the big hunting world, and this last month provided time to develop hunting skills, and deepen bonds and co-operativity, readying them to take a role and serve the pack well.

19.2   13–16 WEEKS: BONUS PERIOD OF SOCIALISATION (PREPARING FOR THE WORLD)

Critical periods happening at this time are:

o communication and enrichment (3–16 weeks)
o socialisation — bonus period (12–16 weeks).

19.2.1   13 weeks old: Consolidating the foundations

We have reached the end of the important critical period for socialisation. If no or limited socialisation has happened to date, this can lead to mal-socialisation and problems. However, as long as some foundations have been laid down, we can take advantage of the next 4 weeks, the bonus period of socialisation. Carry on with the good work of socialisation, exposure to environmental stimuli and laying down the training foundation. This training will help extend your pup's prime time for learning and adapting to our world.

Hopefully you have done your puppy temperament test (Appendix A) to see what your training priorities are for the next 4 weeks. It is good to start this week with a clear, strong focus for your good training foundations, so you can make optimum use of these critical bonus weeks.

From 12 to 16 weeks your pup will become increasingly more independent, so focus on recall, joining up and growing your bond gaze (your pup looking to you for direction). The dominance hierarchy in your pack (family) might begin for those more dominant types of pups, so they might start pushing boundaries — make sure you provide clear direction and make it clear you and the family control the resources.

If the foundations have been well established, you might want to start your pup off into more purposeful training. You might start obedience or trick training to extend your pup (if that's what she needs). Do lots of extension work, like retrieving, swimming, off-lead recall, and proofing in increasingly complex environments, both on-

13 weeks

and off-lead. This will stretch and challenge your pup, enriching her work and building her confidence, abilities and fear resilience, and growing her emotional intelligence.

Just got your pup?

If you have just got your pup or you haven't done much socialisation, then do the pup temperament test in Appendix A to see what issues might be emerging in your pup. It is likely that you will have to do lots of desensitisation work, as your pup might have less emotional resilience and less experience.

First, establish clicker training as quickly as possible, and get started with lots of joining up to establish a good bond. These will become very important tools in the desensitisation process. Review all of the earlier weeks, and do what you need to catch up. Using your clicker and food rewards and the strong bond from joining up will allow you to take your pup 'back to the den' and re-create the early learning state inherent in that formative period. With these tools and desensitisation (instead of habituation), you can retrieve the situation well. Go online to our dogzen.com/puppyresources for more help if you have just got your pup and she is showing signs of emerging issues that aren't covered in this book. Also check out Amber's case study (see page 415) for guidance and comfort that it is still doable at this age.

Mentor bond (MB)
O This should be deepening and strengthening every day, and should be a source of great joy seeing this wee one grow her connection and trust in you.
O Ensure that other members of the family or friends get to train your pup, too, so the commands are generalising to others. This is important for your pup.
O Continue to commit to lots of joining-up sessions (3 times a day) over the next 4 weeks to consolidate the bond. This can be happening out and about often now.
O Clip-station work is important, so do 3 sessions a day, with lots of focus on 'Zen down'. Take a portable clip station with you when you go out, and use it. (For example, at a café or a friend's home, take a mat and tie your pup to something secure — a chair leg or maybe your own leg.) Using a clip station is a good way to

introduce your pup to the places and homes you are visiting without her toileting inappropriately, especially if there are existing animal smells.

○ Find a purpose for you and your pup — maybe canine good citizen qualification, puppy sports, beach walks or retrieve in the water.

Socialisation

○ Continue to use the meet-and-greet and 'nicely' techniques, and continue with lots of socialisation across the board.

○ Reflect on what types of people, dogs and species you have covered so far, and identify where you might have gaps. Make the time to extend your pup's socialisation based on those gaps.

○ Continue desensitisation to environmental features. Get your pup out and about, getting used to novelty and change. Click and reward calm, appropriate responses.

○ Make sure you visit lots of different environments: town, beach, farm, cafés, inside buildings, escalators and lifts, and busy, crowded spaces like gatherings and sports events. Take care, and use your clicker to keep your pup in a learning state, rewarding calm, appropriate responses.

○ You are increasing the variety and intensity of exposure as your pup's resilience grows while still within the formative period. Use your situational awareness to identify any stimuli your pup is reacting to, and pace the interaction if needs be (the hierarchy of exposure).

○ If you have got your pup later, or she is showing reactive responses, you might have to pace your interactions, taking more of a graduated desensitisation approach. (Go to the section on fear and phobia prevention in Part D.) If you see symptoms of mal-socialisation, such as wariness of strangers, different races, other dogs, or children, or even threat or aggression, act now and be proactive in meet and greets. Go online to our trouble-shooting resources for emerging problems (www.dogzen.com/puppyzen) or my book *Dog Zen* for serious cases.

Shared language **SL**

○ Do lots of practice of the basic commands and use of the tools. Particularly work on your recall, 'wait' and 'stay'.

13 weeks

- Proof all basic commands in increasingly complex environments, on- and then off-lead.
- Start extending your intermittent schedule of reward, reducing the number of times you click and reward successful behaviours. This is the beginning of fading the clicker. Determine how fast you do this by monitoring how well your pup is succeeding: if your pup starts to fail, you are going too fast. Continue to carry these tools with you so you can bring them back if needs be.
- Generally, recall will be one of the last behaviours you will fade the clicker on, so leave this until all of the others are well established and past 16 weeks of age.
- Your pup should be throwing 'Zen down' in many relaxed situations, and 'Zen sit' when meeting people. Watch whether this is happening; if it isn't, make it a priority to practise. Use your meet and greet, and cue with the 'nicely' command.
- Look to see how your pup is maintaining the learning state: is it often, and is she calm in most situations, or is she anxious and reactive? If the latter, keep focused on joining up and the basic commands, particularly 'Zen down', and meet and greets.

Fears and phobia prevention F+P

- Keep building your pup's confidence and growing her exposure to novel and potentially frightening stimuli, such as lawn mowers, trucks, diggers, alarms and fire engines.
- This work will pay dividends, as it creates a stable, happy dog that has emotional resilience in all situations. Keep committed — only 3 weeks of intensive work to go! Go back to your list and check things off.
- You are hoping that your pup's startle-recovery response rate is getting quicker and quicker, so your pup can tolerate novelty and change and grow emotional resilience.

Separation TS

- This should be well established by now. If not, go back to Part D or refer online for help.
- Continue to use the clip stations and crate regularly. Leave your pup loose out in the yard or in a kennel, for those who choose to have them in a kennel, which is a good back-up.

13 weeks

○ By now you should be able to leave your pup for 6 to 8 hours in the yard or a suitable place that is escape-proof. In necessary situations, this can be longer.

○ Using puppy daycare or a puppy walker is a great option to help graduate separation. Research these people carefully, as it is a big responsibility. Get references or referrals if possible.

House training

○ If you are having trouble, go to Part D again or online for more help.

○ Some pups will still be failing at times, which is okay. Remember, don't punish; just keep the structure and routine and, if failing, go back a step or two.

○ Use clip stations a lot, because your pup won't soil on this and it helps generalise to the rest of the house.

Bite inhibition (BI)

○ This should be well established by now (unless you are just starting).

○ Go back over your techniques and improve them. Remember, teething is going to happen at 4 months old (as your pup's milk teeth are replaced by mature teeth), and this can continue for some time in oral dogs. Structure and good techniques will prevail.

○ If you are having continuing problems, thoroughly review the in-depth methods in Part D, and if still having issues go online or to *Dog Zen*.

Enrichment, play and exercise (E)

○ Your growing pup still needs lots of playtime, which is also great for your bond (and your own wellbeing). It never ceases to amaze me how much joy I get out of my dogs and pups playing; I smile and feel good when I see that play bow and tail wag, and research shows it benefits us both greatly.

○ Make sure you utilise your walks as training sessions. Take your tools and remember, training is enrichment.

○ You are still working on 'nothing in life is free' in this intense training period. Your pup has to work for all rewards — food, attention, freedom, etc.

13 weeks

○ *Game: Go to a mark.*
  — It is always good to throw in some fun or purposeful things for your pup to learn, so you might want to try this fun trick that we train for film work: 'go to a mark'. (The mark is normally a piece of flat wood on the ground.) This game allows you to work your pup into an allotted spot and be in focus (which is good for camera shots).
  — Do this the same way you shape behaviours like 'sit' and 'down': lure the pup with food. The same can happen with 'on your mark'.
  — Lure your pup up on to the mark, and click and reward as soon as any of your pup's paws touches it. Slowly shape 2 feet on the mark, by click and rewarding first 1 foot, then both, until your pup finally gets them going to the mark. Then try sending your pup to the mark from a distance. Use 'mark' as your cue.

19.2.2   14–15 weeks: Consolidating and proofing

We are in the last weeks of the bonus socialisation period, which closes down at 16 weeks of age. So these weeks are fully focused on consolidating and proofing the foundations we have put in place, and identifying any gaps and getting them filled.

Dog-to-dog aggression can grow in the bigger breeds during this time, so focus on socialising with other dogs, in particular with the more dominant pups.

Do lots of exercises that keep you and your pup interacting, and reinforce your pup's socialisation and extend his environmental exposure. Lots of dog walks, beach and café visits, and puppy school or parties, as well as group puppy walking and puppy daycare.

Mentor bond (MB)
○ Review your family rules and see how you are going. Are they well established, or are there some gaps?
○ Is your understanding of your pup growing? Watch your pup's demeanour and personality in different situations: is he confident, aware, responsive, co-operative, affectionate? If not, work on your joining up and the training outlined here.
○ Continue lots of joining up, starting to proof off-lead in increasingly complex environments.

O How is your pup's relationship with all family members? Do any of those relationships need extra work? If so, get that family member doing joining up and controlling the resources.

Socialisation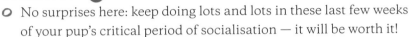

O No surprises here: keep doing lots and lots in these last few weeks of your pup's critical period of socialisation — it will be worth it!

O Stretch and test your pup in increasingly complex environments with his meet and greets. The 'nicely' command should be switching your pup into a learning state well by now.

O Keep working on the priorities you set last week and ticking them off.

Shared language SL

O Continue consolidating and proofing all of the tools and basic commands.

O Focus on lots of proofing work on your recall, on the long-line and retractable line.

O Practise reading your pup's body language. Grow your ability to recognise early your pup's orient, alert, target (OAT) sequence. What are your pup's trigger situations, and how do you avoid them or control them?

O How is your situational awareness going? Do you understand your pup's triggers, and can you identify risky situations? This will become increasingly important after the 16-week period.

O Practise your contrast training, effective check and 'no' if you find yourself in situations where your pup is not listening to you. Make sure you address these situations early, so your pup doesn't learn he can win over you!

O Make sure your check is effective: not too hard (so you frighten him), and not too soft (so nothing changes). Make sure you are always providing positive contrast with click and rewards and lots of praise and love.

Fears and phobia prevention F+P

O Again, keep up your pup's exposure to novelty and change: click and reward calm, appropriate behaviours.

O Have you noticed your pup's growing resilience and calm, and his ability to stay in a learning state in increasingly challenging

14-15 weeks

environments? Check his 'Zen sit' and 'Zen down' are well established.

O Have you identified any stimuli or environments that your pup is particularly reactive to? If so, make sure you focus on these and do some structured desensitisation work.

Separation TS

Established by now. If not, go back and review Part D, or try our online trouble-shooting resources.

House training HT

Established by now. Remember to go back to the early set-up and keep good structure and disciplines. If having issues, go to Part D again or go online.

Bite inhibition BI

Established by now. If not, go back to Part D, or again online trouble-shooting is available.

Enrichment, play and exercise E

O Training and proofing are brilliant opportunities for exercise.

O Have a good play session after training as a reward for your pup: there is lots of learning going on here, so reward with play. Then have your pup rest in his crate or on a clip station to consolidate the training.

O *Game: The retrieve game.*

— One way to make play constructive is playing retrieve games.

— For example, throw a tug toy on a light nylon line and say 'fetch' or 'get it'.

— When your pup has it, say 'bring it', and when he gets to you don't take it away immediately but pat him and praise him. (Remember, possession is nine-tenths of the law for dogs, so he won't really want to give it to you.)

— Keep patting and not competing or grabbing for the toy.

— Then do some trading for a high-value food reward as you say 'give it'. (Ideally, giving it to your hand, but you might have to work up to that and start on the ground first.)

— Click and reward once he gives it, then give him praise and get him excited again and repeat . . . He and you will love it!

O Remember to let your pup rest and sleep; ideally on his clip station or in his crate after training sessions, so his brain can consolidate the learning. This is important, so don't underestimate this.

O *Game: Copy me.*
   — The purpose of this game is to encourage your pup to follow and mimic you, developing co-operation and co-ordination.
   — Do something like jumping over a log, rolling over, running to a corner, climbing under a table, or going through a tube.
   — Say 'copy me!' in an up tone. When your pup follows you a little way, click and reward, then further and further until he completes the behaviour.
   — Do the next behaviour, your pup mimics you, click and reward.
   — You aren't so much teaching your pup how to do something (shaping behaviour), but rather you are teaching your pup to watch, follow and mimic you — strengthening your connection and bond, and looking to you for direction.

19.2.3 16 weeks old: Graduation week!

Well, here we are in graduation week, the end of the formative period. This is when you need to put up some little tests for your pup, to see whether she is ready to graduate: whether your bond is well established and you have a clear shared language, you can say your family rules are well established (or close to it), and you can trust your pup in all social situations, and trust her ability to manage novelty and change.

Remember for those pups who have followed this whole course and even those that started at around 8 weeks, the learning door has opened and you can take your pup easily to the next level. By doing what you have done you have created the pathway to greater neuro-plasticity — well done!

For those who have started late, using the clicker, joining up, desensitisation and the other tools we have given you, will still create excellent foundations for your pup.

Mentor bond **MB**

O Your mentor bond is deepening and generalising; that is, other members of your family or friends can work your pup, too, so we know that the commands are generalising to others.

16 weeks

○ Your pup is focused and connected to you, and checking in with you regularly on walks.

○ If not, this week focus on lots of joining-up and clip-station work.

○ Your recall is going well, off-lead in challenging environments. This is one of the strongest tests of your bond: your pup is choosing contact with you over the exciting temptations of the outside world. If not, do lots of practising, ensuring you are taking your time to proof it well: increasing environmental complexity slowly, ensuring your pup succeeds in each situation well before moving to the next stage.

Socialisation Ⓢ

○ Meet and greets with other dogs, people and other species are well established and effective.

— Your pup can do the 'Zen sit', 'wait', touch the visitor's hand on command, and interact sociably without jumping up, or at least responding to your 'off' command. However, the 'Zen sit' should be his go-to behaviour now.

— Your pup should be settled around people, and sociable with all people (and children) of all ages, different races and gender, and should not react. Your pup is accepting of all variety of people, including different clothing, those in wheelchairs, and so on. Keep putting up new challenges.

— Your pup should be cued by 'nicely', or only need a human in front of her for the 'Zen sit' cue to be done properly.

— Your pup can meet and greet dogs calmly and sociably. You can moderate her play and excitability so as not to annoy older dogs. Your pup can do the dog handshake — remember, there are appeasing/calming pheromones in this area.

— Cross-fostering: your pup is friendly to cats, chickens and birds, and ideally sheep and stock, particularly if you live rurally. Your pup does not stare, chase or bark at them.

○ Continue lots of practice to consolidate, focusing on increasing the complexity of the environment, social stimuli and learning skills.

○ If your pup is showing overly excitable or potentially aggressive responses, head to Part D for trouble-shooting, and spend this week doing lots of meet and greets with your clicker and food rewards. Go online or to our videos or to *Dog Zen* if you need help.

Shared language **SL**

Your pup should be able to:

O do all 10 basic commands

O respond quickly to your 'no' and 'leave it' commands

O do a joining-up routine, 'heel', look up to you for direction, not jump up, stop and sit when you stop, look up to you, and do 'down' and 'Zen down' if you are waiting

O walk on the 'heel' cue without pulling on the lead, in easy to moderate situations

O relax in 'Zen down' (throw it or do it if asked for), and hold a 'wait' or 'stay' as directed for 1 minute at least

O have good recall in a variety of situations, and respond to 'no' if failing

O understand discrimination (good toys, wrong items) and contrast training.

The following are now your training priorities:

O You are on an intermittent schedule of reward with your clicker. Start to fade the clicker on most of the basic commands (except probably recall). Your other resources (pats, praise, attention) will then become important reinforcers of good behaviour.

O If the basic commands and the bond are well established, then you can start to ease off on 'nothing in life is free' (see Part B on being a mentor), although it carries on for life, just as learning does.

O Continue proofing the basics out into the world in increasingly complex environments (see the section on proofing in Part D). It is important that proofing is well staged, so that you get success at each stage before you move onto the next challenge. Success will depend on your diligence, consistency and your pup's distractibility. Lots of long-line work will help.

O Do lots of training on the commands and techniques that are not as well established.

Fears and phobia prevention **F+P**

O Your pup should be generally calm and confident, normally in a learning state.

O Your pup can tolerate change and novelty with little reactivity but good responsiveness.

16 weeks

O If not, identify what your pup's triggers are (i.e. stimuli and environments). Head to Part D for trouble-shooting, and do lots of desensitisation work, using the desensitisation hierarchy and the clicker to switch and maintain a learning state. Do this work as early as you see the need.

Separation

Although these should be established by now, I would like you to test these things.

O Your pup is able to stay on his clip station and/or crate without problems, and be able to be left at home in the house or yard without barking or destructive behaviour. See Part D if this is still an issue, or go online.

O Your pup is able to be left in the house without issues for a couple of hours at least, and ideally for longer periods. Leave him in a social area like the sunroom (though ensure it is cool).

O If this isn't happening, then do lots of crate and clip-station work through graduated departure. Head to Part D for trouble-shooting.

House training HT

O Your pup should be able to last all night without toileting, and be able to cruise the house without any mistakes 90–100 per cent of the time. Congratulations, and keep up the good work to fully consolidate.

O If not, head to Part D to trouble-shoot, or go online.

Bite inhibition BI

O This should have been addressed by now, otherwise it needs some serious focus to sort it out. Go thoroughly through the techniques in Part D, and step up a level if need be.

O Your pup should have a soft, gentle mouth by now.

O Your pup should have learned to discriminate what are his toys and what are household items, and leave the latter alone.

O If not, head to Part D, trouble-shooting, or if serious issues go online or to *Dog Zen*.

Enrichment, play and exercise E

O Your growing pup needs lots of play and exercise to help embed the new behaviours he is growing for adult life. Repeat and practise games from earlier.

O In this last critical week before socialisation fully closes down, getting out and about is critical, so incorporate play and exercise in the big outdoors, with lots of socialisation. Use your walks as training sessions, taking your tools and treats, and utilising them in each situation. Practise hide and seek at the park or forest.

O Your puppy loves to play, but is well mannered and not overly boisterous. He can self-moderate his play, is respectful of other dogs, and is mindful of other dogs' responses. If not, then see Part D, practise further moderation on the long-line and 'no'.

O Consider whether you can find an exercise outlet that suits your pup if you are away a lot during the day. Remember a dog walker or doggy daycare is good if you are urban-based and restricted for time. (However, do ensure the people involved are well skilled and reputable.) Your pups and dogs are social, and love contact and interaction with other dogs and people as a rule, so find it for them if you are limited with time. Organising or joining a dog-walking group is a good idea.

O Remember you need exercise, too, so that's a great thing about dog owners: they get out and about, so join up with other dog owners, too.

16 weeks of age reflections (end of formative period)

By the end of 16 weeks of age your pup should be able to:

O Have a strong bond with you (and other family members), and be focused and attentive. He will hold the bond gaze regularly and trust you. He will follow you and find you in the park if you hide. He can do a lead or off-lead join-up easily. He knows both your 'yes' and your 'no'. He loves you and greets you with enthusiasm, but 'Zen sits' as well.

O He adopts 'Zen down' when you are waiting or talking, and throws it often.

O He is confident in greeting new people and dogs of all variations and types. He knows and responds confidently to your 'nicely' cue, and can do a hand touch if unsure.

O He can meet people at the door and gate without any fuss or aggression.

16 weeks

○ He is non-reactive, even friendly, around other species he has been introduced to.

○ He is well established in the basic tools and commands, including recall and contrast training, joining up, 'Zen sit', 'down', 'Zen down', 'wait', 'stay', 'leave it', 'no', 'be quick' and 'gentle'.

○ He is calm and responsive in novel situations, and quickly recovers from frights.

○ House training is established (although potentially still extending to the rest of the house).

○ He has completed bite inhibition, and is generally gentle and reliable with children, too.

○ He shows no resource guarding, and so dominance issues should have been prevented.

○ He is playful and engaged, and able to retrieve and offer up his ball/toy when asked.

○ He enjoys playing with lots of toys, and is able to discriminate what he is allowed to chew and what not.

○ He is comfortable out and about in cafés, shops, on different surfaces and in the face of challenging noises and traffic. He can travel, and deal with a farm situation, swim at the beach, go to daycare, and stay away from home.

○ He can stay on the clip station, crate, backyard and/or kennel for reasonable times quietly.

○ He is not a problem barker.

○ He has started some purposeful activities, sports or games.

○ He is already a well-rounded individual and a joy to be around.

Your puppy temperament evaluation

This is a good time to do the test again, so you can review how your pup is going as socialisation is about to fully close down and their fourth fear-imprint period is about to begin. This fear-imprint period is designed ancestrally to safeguard and prepare the 4-month-old wolf pup for going out to the hunt and leaving the den. Similarly, the dog pup is heading out to the complex human world, where challenges abound — traffic, sheep, cats, strange people wearing hoodies and/or hi-vis jackets . . . Is your pup prepared for this weird and wonderful extravaganza of life? This test will help you answer that!

It will help to identify continued training priorities, and what emerging issues you might need to address now before they get too established. (Part D and the trouble-shooting sections are designed to help you address these emerging issues.) Go to Appendix A for the test. Go online for more help if needed.

Coming up
The fourth fear-impact period — the flight instinct period (4-8 months). Although the primary focus of this book is on the formative period, some of the key transitional times for your pup as she grows into adulthood are outlined below, along with guidance on how to navigate them.

19.3   4–6 MONTHS: JUVENILE STAGE — ENTERING THE BIG WORLD

Fourth fear-impact period — the flight instinct period (4-8 months).

The juvenile phase is normally from 4 to 6 months of age, or up to the beginning of puberty, which might extend in some dogs to around 8 or 9 months. Looking back at the ancestral wolf, this time is often described as the start of *hunting school*, where the wolf pup would leave the relative safety of the den with the pack, to follow the migrating herds and start hunting. This transition is a critical and dangerous time in the wild. The wolf pup is still growing and learning a lot, guided by helpers, but your pup is on the move now, engaging with a whole new world.

By now the wolf pup needs to know who her social pack is, and importantly who isn't. The wolf pup's fear response to novel things increases to ensure she is cautious in her expanded, riskier world. In the wild, the pack would give the pup lots of structure as it grows from being a young pup learning the ropes of hunting and pack living to being an adult with clear responsibilities.

The pariah dog ancestor became a scavenger and was more dependent and adapted to the human (or at least our ancient world), which makes the dog more adaptable than the wolf was. However, modern people have made such rapid and extreme changes to their world (e.g. cities, traffic and much more) that the dog puppy needs to be adapted to these different environments and social diversity. Therefore this period is still challenging and requires habituating and/ or desensitising.

4-6 months

This is the beginning of the fourth fear-imprint period, also known as the *flight instinct period* (4 to 8 months). This period can last for a few days or several weeks. This period is also called the fear of new situations period, which is self-explanatory!

In your pup, this transition is not so dramatic, but it is built on the same premise and drivers. Heading out into the world from the safety of her den (primarily your home), she, too, is more sensitive and cautious in this expanded world. Yet your pup is also more outwardly focused. She needs to have already learnt who is in her pack and who isn't, as well as built up her resilience to novelty and change and a wide diversity of environmental stimuli. It is a time when your pup will 'test her wings' and wander further away than before. You might notice that your pup becomes a bit unsure or even fearful of new things, or even of familiar things that move more than before, although well-adapted pups will be less sensitive.

Although your pup's independence is growing, she is still relatively naïve, and is reliant on you, as her mentor, to help her navigate this transition and guide her. This world can be counter-intuitive to some of her natural instincts; for example, don't hunt! Your pup will start to get more outward focused, and may start running off to explore things. So the key priorities are:

O reinforcing your bond

O strengthening your basic commands (particularly recall)

O maintaining good rules and boundaries.

The juvenile phase is the consolidation phase. It is very much the same training established in the formative period, however you are consolidating and proofing. Your pup will be easily distracted, so it is important to be patient with training sessions! You need to keep your pup structured and focused while she stretches her boundaries.

At the beginning of this period, given that it is also a fear-imprint period, you may need to wind back the challenges for a bit if she shows too much fear or sensitivity. You want her to appear to do the slightly fearful action herself, but you don't want her to be too fearful in doing so; rather, coax, lure, and click and reward her through it. Remember the principles of desensitisation and a graduated hierarchy. If she shows fear, then go back a couple of steps and set up exposure incrementally. Only comfort your pup if her fear is extreme; if it is not, don't comfort

4–6 months

(as you don't want to reward this state), just wind it back a bit and take her through the graduated hierarchy. In the end you have to support your pup in a systematic, structured way that enables her to make her own decisions, otherwise she is not wiring in the learning.

Mentor bond

O Your pup's independence is growing, so her bond to you is critical.

O Lots of joining up practice will continue to reinforce the bond in this time of change, and also ensure your pup continues to look to you when she is unsure. It will also provide her the important secure base effect (security and trust) that she needs in this transition.

O Reinforce looking to you for guidance: click and reward her looking up to your face. When your pup is unsure and weary, you need to reinforce her looking to you as her mentor and ally, letting her know you are assessing the situation and will help her navigate it. Your 'nicely' command is important here, too, cueing the learning state.

O Make sure the whole family has a good bond with the pup. If anyone is having problems, focus on them, and then get them to do a couple of weeks of formal training with him, and let them take control of the meals and some of the care. This can include any children over 6 or 7 years. You may need to control the clicker initially if they aren't consistent. Ten-year-olds and older, if confident and motivated, can be encouraged and given pouches and clickers with guidance to do basic training.

Socialisation S

O Be aware that there is a sensitivity at this time, so actively using your meet and greets and clicker will keep your pup in the learning state and allow her to adapt and learn quickly.

O Continue to give your pup lots of new experiences and socialisation with plenty of people, other species and dogs, really consolidating this as she becomes more outwardly focused, ensuring you have good control of greetings.

O You should be able to meet almost any person or dog now (although of course still be very aware in case something unexpected emerges). If you have any issues, address them

4–6 months

early before they get hard-wired in. Go to Part D for guidance if required, or online or *Dog Zen* for more.

O Now is the chance to do those things you were wary of doing in the vaccination phase, such as getting your pup to dog parks, although be careful she doesn't get frightened. Remember that the rear-present is your best defence if you are faced with an overly exuberant adult dog.

O Moderate your pup's rough or soliciting licking behaviour with older dogs by using the long-line and slip collar to check your pup as if the correction is coming from the other dog.

O Remember, as long as you have done a reasonable amount of socialisation during the formative period, this will effectively extend your pup's openness and learning state into this period too.

Shared language **SL**

O As this is a key fear-imprint period, you might have challenges with maintaining your pup's learning state, so watch carefully and, using the clicker, switch her back into it as soon as you notice her going out of the state. Use 'Zen sit' and 'Zen down' to calm her.

O Here, I want to emphasise the use of the clicker as a marker and as a learning state changer. The clicker is the best tool to effect that kind of change, as it is cued in now to switch state. Keep your tools on you (rewards pouch and clicker). This will focus your pup into a learning state, too. (She knows what they mean by now!)

O You should be proofing what you have taught your pup, so you need to use the clicker and maintain a learning state as you increase the complexity of the training environment. See proofing in Part D.

O Your pup is still young, but is growing her understanding of her place in the world. Lots of structure and guidance are still needed. Also plenty of rest and sleep.

O Reinforce all of the basic commands in the shared language you have taught her, specifically your 'no' command, recall and contrast training, to ensure you retain good contact and control with your pup as she grows older and more independent. Recall will be harder to establish now if not well established already, so get in lots of practice.

O Also continue to establish consistent rules and boundaries. Use natural consequences or apparent natural consequences, so you don't get associated with any corrections. (See the explanation of contrast training in the Puppy Zen toolkit section in Part C.) Do it sparingly, though. At this age we are still shaping behaviour rather than correcting it, so there is much less need for checks and other corrections (unless issues are already emerging, in which case go to Part D for guidance). We are mainly using the contrast of 'pressure on' and 'pressure off' to teach your pup resistance and joining up. There is an emphasis on positive reinforcement.

O Continue reinforcing 'nothing in life is free' for the next month, getting your pup to work for all rewards by obeying a command first.

O Check in with your family rules to see that they are all well established.

O This is the age that your pup can start getting over-excited, pulling on the lead and jumping up, if you haven't nipped it in the bud yet. It is important to reinforce four feet on the ground with the clicker at this stage. 'Zen sit' and 'Zen down' are important to maintain calm behaviour.

Fears and phobia prevention 🅕🅟

O As mentioned, due to the fear-imprint period at this stage, it is important to keep your clicker and food rewards on hand to desensitise any reactivity (see Part D for techniques).

O A well-socialised puppy that has been meeting people in an outgoing manner may start to show apprehension or fear towards people and things during this period. Continue to give your pup lots of novel and new experiences, but be aware if she shows any signs of fear, and be prepared to take a couple of steps back, in terms of the speed of training, if it is too much for her.

O If early habituation wasn't enough or your pup has new fear responses, identify them early and treat them with a systematic approach. (See Part D for guidance if issues are emerging.) Getting your pup out and exposing her to many varied stimuli is critical to identify these fears early and to deal with them.

O Ensure you graduate your pup's exposure as she continues to adapt to the world out there.

4-6 months

Use a backline to help introduce your pup to the clip station.

Separation TS

O You should be able to leave your pup for extended periods of time now, say up to 6 to 8 hours in the yard or in the house unrestrained.

O You should also be able to leave your pup outside or on a clip station, or in the car (windows part open, in shade, and for only a short period) without any fuss.

O If you are still struggling with being able to leave your pup, you need to treat this with a graduated departure technique, so head to Part D.

O Remember, pups are the most prone to separation distress if you spent most of your time with your pup during the formative period. Make sure she has alone time.

House training HT

This should be well established by now. If not, head to Part D, and set up a more structured environment. Go online if you need more help.

Bite inhibition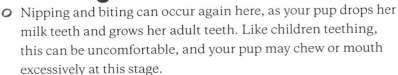

O Nipping and biting can occur again here, as your pup drops her milk teeth and grows her adult teeth. Like children teething, this can be uncomfortable, and your pup may chew or mouth excessively at this stage.

O If you are having difficulties, then review the bite inhibition techniques in Part D. You may need to use and emphasise contrast-training techniques if persistent. If you are only starting the resource-guarding technique, take more care when trading. Sometimes I put the traded item on a string for safety and the pup on the clip station, so I don't get bitten.

Enrichment, exercise and play E

O Play continues to be an important part of how pups learn and practise their adult behaviour sequences, so they need to play. Continue the games you have learnt.

O Pups tend to be very playful through this stage, and the games get more active and rough, especially in the bigger, stronger and more dominant breeds. Be mindful of how you match up your play buddies. Your puppy classes should continue if possible. Use your moderating long-line work if your pup is a pushy type.

O You can continue to take advantage of well-run daycare services, too. Review these carefully, though, to ensure your pup will not receive any trauma there. Ensure they are good at matching up pups in particular. See my earlier suggestions for puppy classes; these criteria are similar.

O Your pup is about 70 per cent of her adult size, and the growing ends of her bones are still relatively soft and still developing. So, particularly with large and giant breeds, take care you don't overdo exercise or extreme rough activity, which might compromise your pup's growing bones. Full-on exercise starts after a year old for bigger breeds.

O Learning to moderate play is important so that your pups don't get beaten up. Excessive licking of jowls and jumping all over an adult dog will lead to growling and snapping or worse by the adult dog. You can help moderate play with a long-line and slip collar, offering up a moderating check on the lead as required. Take care that the long-line does not get caught up around the other dog.

4-6 months

O Utilising tug toys and play items to exercise and reinforce successful sequences of behaviours is important.

Summary

O *Major physical developments*: Your pup is 70 per cent of adult size, but there are no sex hormones yet.

O *Developmental behaviour*: Your pup is investigating outside of her territory and developing social relations, but is wary of novel things, yet ripe to adjust to them with the right techniques. Your early preparation in our programme will prepare her.

O *Social orientation*: She has an outward focus: while still engaged with the mentor and family, your pup is easily distracted. She will be more engaged with other dogs now.

O *Learning focus and capability*: Your pup is distractible, particularly due to environment; however, keeping your training consistent will help minimise this.

O *Separation*: Make sure you are extending your pup's ability to be separated: your pup should be able to be alone for 6 to 8 hours by now. However, daycare, puppy classes or some stimulation is still necessary and advisable. Doing puppy parties are also a great idea.

O *Bite inhibition*: Your pup is dropping her milk teeth for adult teeth, so she may want to chew again and mouth, so reinforce the bite-inhibition techniques.

O *Training focus*: There should be a focus on socialisation with more people and dogs, and cross-fostering work, reinforcing boundaries, focusing on recall, the basic commands and contrast training should be continued, and the mentor bond maintained.

O *Fear*: Desensitise any noticeable fear responses, especially early in this period.

Older and rescue pups

O Some exposure during the formative period, even minimal, will effectively lengthen the period of socialisation, and so you can continue exposure and building that shared language into understanding all the family rules.

O *Secondary socialisation*: The wolf moves from the natal pack to her next pack at around 1 to 4 years, so a secondary socialisation

It's important you desensitise your pup to handling — click and reward calm responses while pulling on the collar . . .

. . . and when handling the mouth and muzzle, feet, tail and groin area.

period is wired in. Therefore, rescue dogs that go late into a home can adjust again. The use of the clicker and the techniques we teach allow this transition best. Part D, on trouble-shooting, might be useful for you if there are any emerging issues, or go online or to *Dog Zen*.

19.4   6–12 MONTHS: EARLY PUBERTY — BECOMING AN ADULT

The period from 6 to 14 months is a fear-impact period (also called the 'fear of new situations' period), and is similar to the juvenile period and its issues. Your pup may now become fearful of new or old things that move more. A well-socialised pup that has been meeting people in an outgoing manner may start to show apprehension or fear towards people and things during this period. This stage is believed to be related to a cognitive recognition of fear, which means your pup interprets fear on an intellectual level in addition to an emotional one.

This is the time when our pups go through the first half of puberty. Sex and dominance order can become an important focus, but de-sexing can help with this. I recommend de-sexing males by 6 months before they start leg-raising and dominance issues appear. (And the operation is easier, with fewer potential complications.) It is best not to let testosterone (and other androgens) kick in unless you are breeding the dog. I recommend that bitches go through their first cycle, allowing them to become feminised, and de-sex after their first heat. There are many opinions on this.

Female behaviours are less of an issue compared with the problems that male behaviours can develop. In high-density dog living, sexual drivers often cause problems and stress, so unless you are breeding, it is easier on the dog and you to de-sex him. As a general rule, de-sexed dogs are much easier to manage, especially males. This of course also prevents unplanned puppies in a world where we have lots of unwanted dogs already. If you choose to breed, make sure you know what you are doing and understand how to select breeding dogs. Also make sure you know how to rear pups, supplying each puppy and owner with the right information and a genetically sound and docile dog. It is not something to do on a whim.

If you keep your dog entire (don't de-sex him), be aware of some of the issues that might result. In males, for example, you might experience more marking (micturition), possible dominance and fighting, roaming and hypersexual behaviour, including mounting people and dogs. As a rule, entire male dogs are bigger and stronger, and harder to train and control than neutered dogs. In females, you might experience heightened aggression from the bitch towards other females when in oestrous (heat), and towards people sometimes at this time. Managing your pup through the 3 weeks of heat is messy (bloody), and takes care and containment, as males will smell the bitch from a long way away and try to get to them and mate with them. Know what you are doing if you choose to take your pup through oestrous.

Early puberty can be a challenging time, because the hormones — especially in males — do change their behaviour significantly. De-sexed individuals still develop similarly to entire dogs, but their behaviours are more relaxed and less driven, and they are more focused on you and the family. Once sexual or predatory drivers kick in they can dominate the dog's attention and focus. Even more effort in your training will be necessary, especially your meet and greets, as the dog may get more dominant and your recall and commands will be challenged more. As puberty kicks in, the smell and the sight of other dogs starts to pull your pup away from you. Even if your pup is sociable, he will be keen on wanting to run off and meet them. Your meet and greets will get harder for a while, and you will need to focus effort in this area. (See the meet and greet section in Part D). This isn't to say don't have an entire male dog, as they can be lovely and doing this programme will prepare him well, it will just be more challenging so ensure you are prepared.

Mentor bond (MB)

O Joining up and creating a shared language help strengthen your rapport with your dog. Although your bond should be strong by now, external stimuli will become important and distracting through this phase, and so proofing is important.

O Make sure you extend the bond to all family members and people who may be walking or living with you and the dog. Get out and about to proof your bond.

6-12 months

Socialisation Ⓢ

○ Socialising with people, dogs and other species should all be going well by now if you have done the early work. However, as your pup gets older the drivers can get stronger.

○ By mid-puberty (12 months) we can start to see the territorial imperative kicking in, and that grows through later puberty and into adulthood. Catching it early is important, as is doing lots of meet and greets with whomever your pup seems to be targeting with aggression, and doing work in the contexts in which it is occurring (e.g. at home, at the gate, in the car). Do controlled greetings initially (see Part D Meet and greet), so you can ensure success, and then extend it (proof it) into everyday situations.

○ Dog-to-dog aggression often starts to show at around 12 to 18 months, but it can show signs of starting from 8 months. Like the human meet and greets, do controlled meet and greets with dogs, and then, as you succeed, move into everyday situations. Males, especially entire dogs, are more prone to inter-male aggression at this stage. Address it early: don't let it get established. De-sexing is recommended if this behaviour starts. Go online or to *Dog Zen* for more difficult issues.

○ If you haven't done your cross-fostering work in the formative period, predatory behaviour may start to get serious in this phase. Check out Part D to trouble-shoot, if this is happening. Address the behaviour as early as you see it, otherwise more serious techniques will be necessary.

Shared language ⓈⓁ

○ Each day that you put some time into clicker training, you will be building and reinforcing your bond through this challenging time. Fade the clicker once you have the behaviours effective in novel situations, keeping it handy along with your pouch.

○ This is a good time to look for enriching experiences that the dog can do regularly (depending on your dog and his needs) like obedience, flyball, trick training, and the like.

○ The 10 basic commands should be in place by now, and you should be proofing them out into everyday situations. By the end of this phase you should be consolidating and finalising all of your basic commands. By 12 months, your shared language should be firmly established and the young dog quite stable.

O The longer you leave establishing the basics or addressing any emerging issues, the more challenging it becomes, as you then have to modify established behaviours rather than just shape new behaviour. Nevertheless, the dog is still young, so you can still teach him — just get onto it now. It is best to get the basic commands in place by 12 months. By 18 months, your pup is much more like an adult dog. I think of 12 months as the consolidation age and a good time to fine-tune.

Fears and phobia prevention (F+P)

O It is still important to get your pup out and about, to habituate him to the world and desensitise him to anything he may fear. Take the chance to generalise and proof commands, especially get the recall in place while on walks and in parks.

O Do the desensitisation work as issues arise. Don't let fears or phobias develop: nip them in the bud as soon as you notice them. New reactive responses can pop up, and need to be identified and treated immediately.

O Take care with fireworks, back-firing cars and other unexpected loud noises, ensuring your noise desensitisation is well established.

O It is a good precaution to put a GPS tracker on dogs that are escape artists.

Separation (TS)

O Your pup should be able to stay by himself in the yard for the day by now if you are working, as long as he is getting plenty of contact and exercise outside of that time. It is always great if you have social contact for your dog, if possible, and/or an enriching environment to leave him in. Daycare is a good option to stimulate.

O Mix with neighbours' dogs when you are both away, if they are compatible.

O Plenty of contact, exercise and enrichment is critical to balance time alone.

O It is good to have had your dog spend a day or a weekend at a good boarding facility by now, to adjust him to that.

6–12 months

House training **HT**

This should be established; otherwise head to Part D.

O Entire males from about 8 months on may start to leg-raise and mark in the house (micturition) if you are not careful. Make sure you use a clip station in areas that have been marked on or are at risk of being marked on. If he does mark, clean the site immediately with the water-and-vinegar solution, move a clip station right on top of the spot once dried, and clip him there regularly for at least 30 minutes at a time, a few times a day. You are establishing this as a den (sleep) site, so he shouldn't mark there again.

O Neutering will stop marking in most cases, so do this early if marking looks like a problem in the making.

O If there are problems with marking outside, you can use the 'leave it' command to interrupt inappropriate toileting (e.g. on car tyres) and redirect to an appropriate spot. However, entire males will do it unconsciously in response to smells and the sight of other entire males.

Bite inhibition **BI**

O Your dog is getting much bigger now, and so nipping or biting is more serious. Go to Part D trouble-shooting for help, or *Dog Zen* and online.

O Review and test resource guarding and destructive discrimination techniques. If necessary, reinforce them and practise them.

Enrichment, play and exercise **E**

O You can start to build your dog's exercise into longer and more energetic sessions, as his bones and tendons are maturing and able to take more demands, dependent on the breed.

O Take your dog out often, and include him in all of your enjoyable activities, like swimming, running, visiting dog parks and so on. (Again, consider breed needs.) Find the dog a purpose if you can. For example, sled breeds can join harness clubs; others might be agility, obedience, flyball and the like.

O Play continues to be an important part of your dog's development, so make sure he gets lots of contact with other dogs, as well as playing with you and family and friends.

O Continue the games described in earlier weeks.

6–12 months

Summary

- *Major physical developments*: The dog's secondary sexual characteristics are developing, and hormone levels rising.
- *Developmental behaviour*: The young dog escalates sniffing and marking behaviours, shows an interest in the opposite sex, and may start mounting.
- *Social orientation*: As your pup hits puberty, he may challenge members of the pack or the opposite sex, and older competitors.
- *Learning focus and capability*: Although trainability is moderate to high, the dog becomes increasingly distracted by sexual hormones and growing his territory.
- *Training focus*: Firm up your bond and the basic commands, and embark on sophisticated advanced training.

19.5   12–18 MONTHS: LATE PUBERTY — ESTABLISHING A ROLE IN THE PACK/FAMILY

Territory is more important now, so your dog might be involved in guarding and protecting territory, as she is sub-adult and starting to take more responsibility in the pack. (And dogs get increasingly territorial up to adulthood.) Recall can be a bit more challenging. Issues of dominance might start arising here, particularly in the bigger guard breeds, like Rottweilers, Pit Bulls, big terriers, and Spitz types. Good generalised socialisation will help, and a strong bond with the mentor who is keeping control of resources. Your dog is at her optimal peak at this time and so is eager to learn, and is physically at her peak and raring to go. Males are more territorial as a rule, too.

Between 12 and 18 months is the optimum time to finish off proofing the dog's basic training, so that she grows into a stable, well-rounded adult.

Think of human teenagers aged 10 to 16 years old: they know how life goes and what to do, but are still learning their role and place in the world. Dogs are the same: they will already know most behaviours and will now have some independence, but it is still good to give them guidance as they mature, and keep them well bonded to you. Your dog may possibly start to challenge the position of older dogs she is interacting with, and in difficult cases dominance aggression can develop. Their territorial imperative also grows through this time, so being well socialised helps here. By 18-24 months some dogs will certainly be challenging. (This is more likely with males, particularly entire and more dominant males, and especially those in the bigger guard and powerful breeds, such as German Shepherds, Rottweilers and Dobermans.)

It is good to continue to focus on recall at this stage, because if males are entire they start competing for bitches. Entire dogs are likely to be trying to roam, and will possibly fight more and become more dominant. I recommend you de-sex your dog unless you wish to breed.

Mentor bond (MB)

- Keep up your strong bond work with lots of joining up. Remember, you converse through postures, gestures and cues by now. The young dog's focus moves outward and other males or females become more interesting and challenges can start to take place.
- As hierarchy and dominance can become more obvious, you need to make sure you control resources clearly, set clear boundaries and your 'no' command is effective.
- Entire males and the bigger, dominant breeds may start to ignore younger, less assertive family members, so don't let this happen. They must do training and be seen to be controlling resources. Keep testing resource-guarding potential and don't allow that to develop. Look online or in *Dog Zen* if this is an issue.

Socialisation (S)

- Your dog should be well adjusted by now, but the territorial behaviour may be on the increase, so lots of meet and greets at the front door and gate and around the car.
- Get out and about with people, dogs and other species. Strangers and people (especially other races) can become threats, so socialise well.
- Daycare and kennels need adjusting to. Dog sports are a good option or an outlet.
- Keep up the visits to cafés, shops and sports games, and join a walking group, perhaps.
- Keep up training and exposure to children and babies now that the dog is bigger and can cause more damage, so keep this work up regularly, especially if you don't have children at home.

Shared language **SL**

O Your shared language becomes more subtle, and your relationships more sophisticated and rewarding. Start to grow some other outlets for your dog's energy, such as dog sports, agility, obedience, Rally-O, a canine good citizen certificate, sheepdog trials, bird dog trials, scent work and harness work — whatever might suit your breed.

O Check in with your family rules, and ensure that they are well established and being maintained. Keep your long-term commitment to these.

O With joining up well installed, it is a matter of expanding the language beyond the 10 basic commands, depending on what your need is. Your dog is ripe for learning anything now: you don't need to teach her to drive cars or fly aeroplanes, but a dog with a purpose is a happy dog.

O You may have faded your clicker, but it is great to periodically reinforce it with behaviours like recall and meet and greet, as you continue to proof in increasingly complex environments, particularly off-lead.

Fears and phobia prevention **F+P**

O If or when you find issues, do the desensitisation work as soon as you notice an issue: the earlier the better, before things get hard-wired in. (See the section on desensitisation in Part D.)

Separation **TS**

O Your dog should be able to stay by herself in a crate, pen, kennel or yard without a fuss by now, and be welcomed into the local kennels or daycare and friends' places.

O Make sure the environment is enriching, and if she has access into a human social area through a dog door she will be much happier.

O Remember, though, dogs like to be close to your social areas, so ensure you give appropriate amounts of contact — dogs are social beings after all.

O Make sure your fencing is stronger and higher now, especially for entire dogs and the escape-prone breeds such as Beagles, Basenjis and the Spitz breeds.

House training **HT**

This should be going well by now. See Part D to trouble-shoot if there is a problem. It is still not too late to go back to basics if soiling is happening.

Bite inhibition **BI**

O Your dog should not be biting or nipping at this stage. If she is, you have a significant problem, so I suggest you go to Part D for support, or to *Dog Zen* or online.

O The aggression treatment options start to become more specific in these stages and harder to treat. Hopefully your ground work will have prevented these, but if proving difficult, don't delay going online or to *Dog Zen*, or seeking professional help early.

O Assess resource guarding, and check out with strangers and children to make sure your dog is still docile. Work on meet and greets if there are any issues at all.

Enrichment, play and exercise **E**

O The need for play continues. Although it is starting to decrease, it is still an important part of a dog's development. Make sure your dog gets plenty of opportunity for play, as this maintains your bond, your dog's confidence with other dogs, and her social skills and sensitivity. Finishing successful training sessions with praise and playtime with a tug toy is ideal.

O Your dog is in the most active phase of her life now. Her bones and musculature are nearly fully mature, and she needs fitness and exercise to develop to her full potential.

O Your dog is also needing to combine her learning with physical outlets, so purposeful activities grow her motor co-ordination and skills. She is craving for outlets too, so give them to her. This is the age most of the competitive dog sports encourage you to start. Other outlets are things like pet-facilitated therapy dogs, Bark NZ (taking dogs into schools), community service roles such as visiting retirement homes, and so on.

Summary

O *Major physical developments*: The dog's final secondary sexual characteristics are developing and hormone levels are rising. Full adult size is reached by 2 years in smaller breeds, and 2.5 years with larger breeds. Entire dogs develop quicker and grow bigger.

O *Developmental behaviour*: Typical behaviours at this age include sniffing, marking, interest in the opposite sex, and mounting.

O Joining up, control of resources and resource-guarding trade training needs reinforcing.

O *Social orientation*: Members of the pack, the opposite sex, or older competitors may be challenged. Do lots of meet and greets, socialisation and contact with lots of dogs.

O *Learning focus and capability*: Trainability is moderate to high, but the dog is becoming distracted by sexual hormones and the prerogative of growing her territory. Keep the bond and bond gaze strong, and notice orient, alert and target cues.

O Have interrupter strategies, such as 'leave it' and 'no' commands, and ensure they are effective.

O *Training focus*: Firm up your bond and the basic commands, and embark on sophisticated advanced training. Find a shared purpose or sport.

O Exercise can increase, as your dog can participate and keep up with you running or almost any sport, but take care with chasing bikes, motorbikes, etc., as this requires training.

We are now getting out of the puppy stages and into the area my book *Dog Zen* covers, so I will make just a few remarks here, and suggest you go to *Dog Zen* to complete the picture.

19.6   18–24 MONTHS: YOUNG ADULTHOOD — RESPONSIBILITIES AND ESTABLISHMENT IN THE WORLD

Dogs are now nearly at their full size and in the peak of their life. They are feeling their power, and are starting to teach the other adults/dominants in the pack to define where their new status is. Therefore, they are likely to be more dominant, and possibly assertive, particularly in the larger, more dominant breeds, or if they are entire.

Territory is more important now that they might be involved in guarding and protecting territory, as they are sub-adult and starting to take more responsibility in the family.

Recall can be a bit more challenging. Issues of dominance

might start arising here, particularly in the bigger guard breeds, like Rottweilers, Pit Bulls and big terriers, and the Spitz types.

Good generalised socialisation will help, and a strong bond with the mentor who is keeping control of the resources. Being at their optimal peak at this time, dogs are eager to learn and are physically raring to go.

Again, an important time for your dog to have an outlet and purpose with lots of exercise. Getting involved in family activities and having lots of things to do is important.

Summary

- O *Major physical developments*: By the end of this period, the dog will have reached adult size (perhaps 6 months more for giant or large breeds).
- O *Developmental behaviour*: There are expressions of dominance, protection, sex if entire, and family stabilising, with the dog taking more responsibility now.
- O *Social orientation*: The dog enjoys both family and external stimuli, and responds to territory and to family dynamics.
- O *Learning focus and capability*: Trainability is high, although previously learnt behaviours have an influence (make sure they are good!), and so may challenge the mentor a little at this stage.
- O *Training focus*: By now, it is really good to move on to advanced training. Also a clear purpose and outlet for your dog is important and the family can get involved.

Review the puppy temperament test (Appendix A) to see if your older pup going into adulthood reaches the criteria you would like and to identify any issues early if they occur.

19.7   24 MONTHS ONWARD: ADULTHOOD — RESPONSIBILITIES AND ESTABLISHMENT IN THE WORLD

By now you should have all of the basics established for a mature, stable dog that is well connected and bonded to you. You know this if your dog exhibits focus on you, keeps close, but is relaxed. The basic commands and shared language are now more a conversation, and routines and rituals are established. Your dog has mature sensibilities and is able to read you, and you him. The bond starts to synchronise and flourish.

It is hoped that you and your dog have an outlet or purpose together — that is, something to stretch him and keep him learning. This might be obedience, agility or some form of advanced training. Many of our own dogs are animal actors: after a day on-set, you can see they have had a full day and look contented and happy.

A dog is always changing and learning, so it is important to keep reinforcing training with regular sessions, especially joining up and basic commands. This is also a good way to keep the bond strong between you, to keep you connected and playing. It is great stimulation for your dog, too — they will enjoy the time with you, the mental stimulation, and of course food rewards.

Summary

- *Major physical developments*: Generally complete.
- *Developmental behaviour*: The dog will be a stable adult, and it is time to mate them if entire. There is potential for the dog to be in charge biologically of the dog pack. If there is going to be a dominance aggression issue — aggression towards family members and/or other dogs — it will most likely start from 18 months onward. This is particularly so for entire males and the more dominant breeds, but will be unlikely if you have socialised the dog well and he has a good bond with you. The dog will be mature in his decision making.
- *Social orientation*: The dog will be socialised to the family and taking responsibility. The dog will be aware of external stimuli, and can mate if entire.
- *Learning focus and capability*: This is developed and mature.
- *Training focus*: Joining up and basic commands remain core activities, and play continues. This is a time to start consolidating some purposeful activity, such as a sport or competition, otherwise lots of interactive play.
- Again it is good to finish here with the puppy temperament test to review your successes and pat yourself on the back (or pick up any issues, the earlier the better).
- Go to *Dog Zen* or our online programme, and join our online community to keep up with what we are doing and what we offer.

24 months

IN CONCLUSION

If you are getting your new puppy, I am so glad you are reading this section. You have an opportunity to do the right things so that you have a wonderful friend for life; one that is attuned to you, has a great personality and isn't troubled by behavioural issues. Put in the work during this time and you will have an incredibly rewarding and happy life with your dog.

Of course, just like us, dogs can experience trauma at any time of their lives, which can disrupt their development and stability. These could include attack by another dog, animal or person, an intruder entering the house, the owner suffering a trauma (injury or sickness), or the dog getting lost or left somewhere or suffering a severe fright (such as a bad thunderstorm, close gunfire or being hit by a car). Dogs with a powerful bond will deal with these traumas more easily, as they have established coping mechanisms and resilience, and look to their mentors at the right time for help.

Enjoy the bond you have created with your pup, it will reward you a hundred times over as you move through life with your well-adjusted, loving companion, that is fully adapted to this human life. Walk with your mate, live in this wonderful moment with her. Love is understanding. You have grown to love, play and train together in ways that fulfil her as well as you.

24 months

Chapter 20

Case study: Amber, the Irish Terrier

Now I would like to share with you the story of a 13-week-old pup that was experiencing some emerging issues. Through this story I will show you how the information in this book comes together to guide older pups as well. It is possible to teach older pups new tricks, although doing the right thing at the right time is definitely best.

Amber, a gorgeous 13-week-old wire-haired Irish Terrier pup came to visit with her lovely owners, Marian and Chris. They got Amber at 9 weeks old, and her nickname was already 'Naughty'! She was the last puppy left of the litter, and up till that time her behaviour had been strongly influenced by her dam, her grandmother and another dog.

Diligent, intelligent and caring owners, Marian and Chris had really done their homework. They had laid some good foundations with Amber. However, with a recent parvovirus flare-up in their district and following some related advice, they had ended up limiting Amber's socialisation and introduction to novel environments during her critical 3–12-week socialisation period. On the positive side, although a number of emerging issues were becoming evident, there was enough of a foundation in place that at 13 weeks of age there was still time to support Amber into becoming a happy, stable dog.

Amber is a typical Irish Terrier, with the potential to be strong-willed and very dominant (especially with other dogs), predatory, hyper-vigilant, difficult to keep in and with limited recall. It is one of the most dominant terrier breeds, with poor impulse control unless you train them correctly. It is definitely a breed that needs solid foundations, a good, firm hand, and plenty of work through to the

end of her formative period at 16 weeks and beyond. The issues were varied, and largely due to her missing out on exposure in those critical first 12 weeks.

Amber sat at a behavioural crossroads. If left, she was heading down the distressing track that Charles, who we met at the beginning of this book, ended up on. However, still within her critical formative period, she had the potential to follow the path of Hercules and lead a very happy, productive life.

So how did I go about addressing Amber's emerging issues? Let's go through these step by step.

OBSERVE

First I needed to understand what was going on, so I observed what was happening:

○ What was Amber doing, and how was she behaving? Was she calm, hyper-aroused, sensitive or aggressive?

○ What were Marian and Chris doing, and how were they with Amber? Too firm, too soft? Did they have the tools?

○ What was their relationship like? Were they connected, was Amber focused and in contact with them? Did Marian and Chris provide direction and confidence?

I observed that Amber was hyper-aroused, distracted, outwardly focused, not fully connected to Marian and Chris, and was reactive to novel people, dogs and things. Their relationship was loving, but not fully connected due to Amber's distractibility and outward focus. Amber had the potential for strong-willed independence and dominance, so she was definitely a pup that required firm, clear direction that was consistent and that she could trust. Let's have a look at these across the 8 critical activity groups:

Mentor bond (MB)

○ There was a loving bond with no extreme separation distress, although contact with Marian and Chris (looking to them for direction) could be strengthened.

○ Amber was outwardly focused with the potential to be dominant and strong-willed, so they needed to firm up a little with her, using their tone, body language and an effective remote check.

We explore how to balance this with her strong need for mental and physical stimulation in the enrichment, play and exercise section below.

Socialisation (S)

O *Human*: Amber's human socialisation was poor to average. She reacted to my partner Kim coming up the stairs and when presented with a camera. Chris and Marian weren't sure of her reliability with children — there had been only limited introductions to date, and Amber had been a little reactive. (They had tried once or twice with children, which is not enough.)

O *Dog*: Reasonable, but a little protective and unsure, showing recumbent submission and inappropriate behaviours in play with my dogs.

O *Cross-fostering*: Predatory signs were emerging — no surprises there. Amber loved to chase seagulls, chickens, and birds generally. Marian loves her chickens and they have wildlife near their home, so this would need to be addressed quickly.

Shared language (SL)

O Amber had been introduced to the clicker, which was excellent, and had learnt a 'sit', but no 'down', 'Zen down' or other commands.

O She couldn't be trusted to stay on their property, with no reliable recall.

O She had started some resistance training, but was pulling on the lead and jumping up.

O She was prone to bark-soliciting (barking for attention), especially when we started the clicker work.

Fears and phobia prevention (F+P)

O Amber was reactive to novel noises, which occurs when a pup has not been exposed to much novelty and change during the formative period.

Separation (TS)

O There were some limited signs of separation distress (barking when in the kennel). Chris and Marian were worried about leaving her in her kennel for longer periods of time (more than 1 hour). However, she needed to learn separation, and that this would not be harmful for her if done in a graduated and careful manner.

O Amber needed clip-station training and more systematic separation.

House training **HT**
O Was well established.

Bite inhibition **BI**
O Amber's bite inhibition was limited, as she was biting them in play (sharp teeth!), and was showing emerging dominance aggression by defending objects like toys and food (resource guarding).
O She demonstrated destructive behaviour, and had no discrimination of right from wrong objects to chew.

Enrichment, play and exercise **E**
O She was high-energy and playful, so needed strong mental and physical stimulation. However, these needed to be well managed so she didn't get hyper-aroused and out of a learning state.
O She needed to be allowed to play, but also needed to know when it was time to finish. Teaching the 'leave it' command would be important to manage her high play drive.
O The plan was to click and reward her returning to Marian or Chris, and trading the reward for her toy. Then they could move into a short training sequence ('sit', 'down', 'Zen down'). If she was still highly aroused, they should pop her in her crate or on her clip station to help settle her.
O More enrichment would help her to settle and recover more quickly from being startled as well.

This is a long list. Although the degree of each of these issues was not bad, it certainly indicated emerging difficulties ahead if nothing changed, especially with Amber heading towards the latter end of the formative period, and having passed its peak period at 12 weeks. However, there were still 3 weeks left until the next fear-imprint period was due to start at 16 weeks. Given Amber had the social foundations in place, and with the use of the clicker allowing us to extend her learning state through counter-conditioning and desensitisation, we had the tools and window of opportunity to firmly establish Amber's foundations.

PREPARATION

Particularly given Amber's outward focus and distractibility (but important for all early training), we needed to establish a simple, distraction-free environment (see The essential rules of training in Part C) so she could focus and switch into her learning state.

We then had to ensure that Amber, Marian and Chris had the right tools:

O Amber had a flat collar, which provided no training information around 'yes' and 'no' (pressure off, pressure on), so we first popped a half-slip collar on, and later a full slip as the work progressed. Onto that we added a good training lead, and later a long-line.

O Of course we had our clickers, a good variety of food rewards of different values, and our training pouches.

O We then had to pair the clicker up with the food rewards. Amber had already had some clicker work, so this didn't take long, just a few click-and-rewards so she connected the click with a food reward.

O Later on through the training we also introduced contrast training, the clip station and the basic commands.

LAYING DOWN FOUNDATIONS

Now that the training environment was conducive to learning and we had our tools together, the next step was laying down the training foundations so that we had all of the things we needed to address Amber's emerging issues. We focused on the following:

O *Joining up*: Establishing our bond and contact, so Amber would look to us for guidance and direction through reinforcing the follower response. We also started contrast training, with pressure on (collar tightened as she moved away) and pressure off (collar loosened as she moved back towards us, click and reward) reinforcing that safety and comfort meant being close to the trainer.

O We introduced our basic commands through our joining up, to build our shared language and enable decision making: moving her from the reactive part of her brain into her pre-frontal cortex, which helped calm her.

O Most critically we quickly developed her 'Zen down' to shape a calm learning state. This was a very important milestone for this hyper-aroused, outwardly focused, distractible pup. As we have discussed earlier, the 'Zen down' position activates the vagus nerve, calming a pup's body down. As I clicked and rewarded Amber for being in the 'Zen down' position, she started to associate the clicker and food reward with calmness. Once she started throwing (voluntarily doing) the 'Zen down' position, we could see her actively relaxing, becoming more focused and able to learn. This was a very important switch in her learning state.

O Achieving the 'Zen down' is a critical milestone in your training, and to succeed you need to get this right. Amber changed her postural demeanour 180 degrees: she went from posturally tense, outwardly focused, and unmalleable to posturally calm. She was focused on me, listening and watching eagerly. She was trying to shape her access to the food and clicker by working out what was needed (she was asking). My real indicator that she had clicked onto the role of the clicker in training was when she started to throw 'Zen down' (ask). This is the prize behaviour you are after: it tells you she is connected and focused on you and her training, and for the first time communication is reciprocal. She asks, you reply (*click*).

O We reinforced her 'Zen down' and the basic commands on the clip station as well, to develop the site-specific aspect of her bond.

Once we had achieved that state, we knew we could then proceed to addressing her behavioural issues.

As a novice trainer and pup, you should practise the above routine 3 to 5 sessions per day for 3 to 4 days before moving on to addressing specific behavioural issues. Importantly, you are strengthening your bond, capturing the pup's learning state, building your shared language and basic commands, and practising contrast training.

Critically, at 13 weeks of age we needed to get these in place quickly given the short period of time left of her bonus critical period (12 to 16 weeks) so intense training was needed.

SOLVING ISSUES

Once Marian and Chris were confident that, by working together with me, they had laid down their foundations with Amber, they could move on to addressing her emerging issues back at home on their own. They are all covered above, so I will just highlight the key focus areas I gave them:

O *Socialisation (dog and human)*: Practise lots of varied managed meet and greets (especially with children), particularly in this bonus socialisation period up to 16 weeks of age.

O *Predatory* (cross-fostering using the desensitisation technique above): Gradually introduce Amber to all of the important other species she needs to be friends with, slowly increasing the level of stimuli from still to active.

O *Fears and phobia prevention* (addressing Amber's reactivity): Desensitise Amber's reactivity to a gradually increasing level of stimuli, clicking and rewarding calm responses. Do this across a wide range of stimuli. This work helps build her fear-recovery ability and emotional resilience. Get her out and about a lot, so she gets used to novelty and change while retaining her learning state. Maintaining the learning state when out and about is a result of good basics being wired in at home, then systematically proofing these in increasingly complex situations. You will slowly grow Amber's ability to be calm (stay in a learning state) in distracting, high-arousal environments. This has to be built up through slow, increasing exposure. If she can't maintain a learning state, then you have increased the complexity of the environment too fast. This is a patience game with more-challenging, hyper-aroused pups.

O *Bite inhibition and destructive behaviour*: For destructive behaviour, use contrast training to teach her what is an okay item to play with, and what is not. Use the bite inhibition techniques to ensure this is nipped in the bud. Also use the resource-guarding trading technique in Part F to reshape this.

O *Barking*: Never reward this behaviour. Use of the 'quiet' command. Click and reward increasing periods of quiet on the 'quiet' command. (In our session, we had used a check on the 'no' command after she failed to be quiet: because she had been doing this for a while, she needed the contrast.)

PROOFING

Marian, Chris and Amber need to practise, practise, practise as they slowly increase the complexity of the environments that Amber is exposed to. Marian and Chris need to start in quiet environments so they and Amber can practise their techniques, then slowly increase challenges (for example, invite people over before heading to the beach). It is really important that everyone gets a chance to practise.

The challenge is always taking hard-won training wins from the backyard to the busy distracting outside world! It is important that they stage this carefully, going slowly, so Amber and they have a chance to succeed in increasingly challenging environments, building their confidence together and encouraging themselves to keep going through success.

If at any stage they feel their work with Amber is falling back or not succeeding, then it is likely that they have increased the complexity of the environment and training challenge too fast. They should go back a couple of steps and reinforce successful appropriate behaviour.

We also encouraged them to do lots of work with older children first, slowly coming down the age groups, using meet and greet and clicker and food rewards. We also encouraged lots of dog socialisation and meet and greets.

PROGNOSIS

Amber is a super-smart puppy, and enough of the critical foundations were laid down in her critical period of socialisation (3-12 weeks) to ensure she has the potential to grow into a wonderful dog. With the use of the clicker to shape her learning state, plus the opportunity of the bonus period of socialisation (12-16 weeks) to consolidate and expand her socialisation and habituation to environmental stimulus, she has every chance of becoming a gorgeous companion and a happy, stable dog. Consistent and concentrated effort in that 3-week extra socialisation window is critical.

I am looking forward to watching Amber grow into the wonderful companion she can be, and to seeing the huge benefits Marian and Chris will receive from the efforts they put in now — the enormous amount of love and joy this bundle of gorgeousness will bring to them.

Final words —
bringing together our hearts,
heads and hands

Puppy Zen

Wrapped in a young pup's wagging tail,
is its loving smile.

And that warm lick on your face?
Its asking, its talking, its desire to be heard.

Listen with your whole being.
Engage this loving pup with your heart,
head and hands.

Reply with your body and smile back,
with understanding.

Breathe.
Be present, be patient.
This is the language of love.

We have been on a long journey involving our heads, our hearts and our hands in this book. I have deliberately asked you to stand a little apart from the emotional ties with your pup, so that you can build the knowledge and skills you need to grow your pup into a beautiful dog and create your bond for life.

So let's now again revel in how gorgeously endearing these beings are; how they arouse such a sense of love, joy and play in us, igniting our love hormone (oxytocin) at levels akin to what we feel for our lover, children and family. And they feel it, too!

What an extraordinary and unique bond we have, this bond between us and our pups, not even replicated with our closest ancestors, the chimps and orangutans. Our pups look into our eyes for direction, understanding and love. They read our gestures, pheromones, our subtle tones, understanding us at a level that no other animal on Earth does. This shared language has been built from 40,000 years of living with each other under the stars, in days when we were much closer to them and our own animal nature.

How strongly I feel the need to protect and enjoy our long history together, a special gift offered to us from Nature herself. This relationship is in our DNA and definitely in theirs. It is not some recent event, but has grown over tens of thousands of years of being together, a collaboration and inter-species bond unique in the animal kingdom. Dogs are for us often one of the last vestiges of the wild in our lives. If we lose touch with them, what then do we have left?

Our pups and dogs enrich our lives and the communities we live in. Often, as I walk my dogs on our local beach, we are stopped by travellers who ask if they can pat our dogs, a moment of joy and connection with strangers. A dog-sick traveller gets to remember their beloved animal at home, and our shared love of these beings creates a moment of connection across cultures and worlds. Yet even as I write this, I see petitions created by concerned dog owners worried their beloved pups will get pushed further and further out into the corners of our communities and society.

As responsible dog owners, we have a critical part to play in this. We have to first start with ourselves, ensuring we grow our own abilities to raise gorgeous pups. And from there we must influence organisations to focus on education so that our pups and dogs are welcomed into the heart of our communities where they belong — helping grow empathy in our children, assisting the blind, rescuing the fallen and, importantly, being loving, happy companions.

The 'Zen' in 'Puppy Zen' reminds us to cultivate in our pups (and ourselves) calm, attention and focus. From that place, we can unlock our pups' amazing neural plasticity and potential, switching on the right genetic switches so our shared language unfolds into a deep bond. We, too, learn from our Puppy Zen masters how to live fully in the present moment, to love, enjoy and experience this natural world. We, too, can learn to be present, mindful, compassionate and enjoy this deep friendship of love and joy.

Our pups are such vulnerable beings in our hands. So malleable, so naïve, so open. Placed into our hands by a quirk of Nature that changed the wolf from hunter to scavenger, turning its gaze to us and what we could offer. Instead of this vulnerable pup being held by the wolf dam and her pack, it is we who now hold these fragile beings in our hands. It is to us they turn to for direction, guidance and love.

It is our hands that hold their future: sitting at a crossroads at this critical juncture of the formative period, a time of such enormous potential and growth. It is our responsibility to bathe our pups in the living experience of our lifestyle, extended family and unique, complex world. We hold the fate of these small ones in our hands, heads and hearts.

We have told three stories in *Puppy Zen*: Hercules, who got the best start; Charles, who was so loved, yet he missed so much; and Amber, caught in time, now with a wonderful life ahead of her and her family. Your pup and you stand at this crossroads; which path will you take?

Appendix A: Puppy temperament test

Use this template to support:
- Part E: Help pick your individual puppy from the litter
- Part F: Set baseline and priorities for training (8 weeks) and track progress (12 weeks and 16 weeks)

1. **Socialisation (including the pup's idea of who his pack is)**

   Do the following test for people (various ages, genders, races, types of clothes), dogs and multiple species:

   a. Does the pup approach in a manner that is:

Social (confident, friendly posture)	Always	Sometimes	Never
Fearful (avoiding, submissive, withdrawn)	Always	Sometimes	Never
Aggressive (barks, hackles up)	Always	Sometimes	Never

   If friendly or okay, consolidate that behaviour; if unfriendly, prioritise training to rectify.

   b. Is there a particular type of person/dog/species that the pup is sensitive to?

   Choose the pup that is best in this test unless you are experienced. Focus training on what the pup is sensitive to, while consolidating the ones the pup is friendly with.

2. **Mentor bond** (love/contact/social gaze/looking to/roles/co-operativity)

   Which ones of the following does your pup do?

Follows mentor	Always	Sometimes	Never
Looks up to mentor	Always	Sometimes	Never
Join up is established	Always	Sometimes	Never
Retrieves and releases for mentor	Always	Sometimes	Never

Consolidate training if always, prioritise joining up if sometimes or never.

3. **Shared language** (tools, obedience/skills/learning state)

Can the pup accept resistance/ confinement?	Always	Sometimes	Never
Can the pup accept a collar, lead and crate?	Always	Sometimes	Never
Does the pup respond to any basic commands?	Many	Few	None
Does the pup respond to a marker (e.g. clicker)?	Clicker	Other marker	No
Is the pup in a learning state?	Always	Sometimes	Never

Prioritise training for weaknesses.

4. **Fears and phobia prevention** (emotional stability/resilience/recovery)

Reactive to restraint (hold 30 seconds)	Yes	A little	No
Ability to recover from fright/resilient	Fast	Medium	Slow
Reaction to elevation (lift in air)	Good	Okay	Poor
Sound sensitivity	Good	Okay	Poor

Build the pup's resilience and emotional stability by increasing graduated desensitisation to stimuli (particularly ones the pup shows fear towards). Increase the pup's general exposure to novelty and change.

5. Separation

Can the pup be in crate or away from the handler without reaction?	Always	Sometimes	Never

Focus on crate and separation training if the answer is sometimes or never.

6. House training

Does the pup have a nest-site soiling inhibition?	Always	Sometimes	Never
Does the pup have any substrate-specific choice (e.g. paper, grass, wood shavings)?	Always	Sometimes	Never
Does the pup respond to a toileting cue (e.g. 'be quick')?	Always	Sometimes	Never

Prioritise house training if the answer is sometimes or never.

7. Bite inhibition

Does the pup nip/grab/bite when you run?	Always	Sometimes	Never
Does the pup continue the behaviour if you say 'no'/'leave it'?	Always	Sometimes	Never
Is the pup touch-sensitive? (You can't handle the pup's muzzle, ears, head, neck, feet and tail.)	Always	Sometimes	Never
Does the pup guard resources (food, toys)?	Always	Sometimes	Never
Does the pup discriminate between appropriate and inappropriate objects?	Always	Sometimes	Never

Prioritise if sometimes or never answers, and consolidate always.

8. Enrichment

a. Will the pup engage with novel toys?	Always	Sometimes	Never
b. Is the pup's locomotion ability to run good?	Always	Sometimes	Never
c. Is the pup playful?	Always	Sometimes	Never
d. Does the pup rest when tired or stay vigilant?	Always	Sometimes	Never

a. *Consolidate if always; actively engage if sometimes or never.*
b. *Consolidate if always; observe and consider a chat with the vet if you think there are issues.*
c. *Consolidate if always; actively engage if sometimes or never.*
d. *Consolidate if always; work on joining up, particularly 'Zen sit' and 'Zen down' to activate learning state if sometimes or never.*

References

This book is written for everyday dog owners, so the scientific references are noted as 'research says' or something similar to ensure readability and simplicity rather than being cross-referenced in detail. The researched facts are important to help reveal and explain the broader story of the origin, intelligence and relationship capacity of the dog, as well as showing how the training paradigm of Dog Zen was created.

Ainsworth, M.D.S., Blehar, M.C., Waters, E., and Wall, S., *Patterns of Attachment: A psychological study of the strange situation*, Lawrence Erlbaum Associates, 1978.

Beck, Alan M., *The Ecology of Stray Dogs: A study of free-ranging urban animals*, Purdue University Press, 1973.

Bekoff, Marc, *Rewilding Our Hearts: Building pathways of compassion and coexistence*, New World Library, 2014.

—*The Emotional Lives of Animals*, New World Library, 2007.

Bekoff, Marc, and Pierce, Jessica, 'For a model of fair play, look to dogs',

Scientific American, Sept 2015.

Belyeav, D.K., 'Destabilizing selection as a factor in domestication', *Journal of Heredity*, vol. 70, no. 5, 1979.

Bowlby, J., *Attachment*, Penguin, 1972.

Bradshaw, John, *Dog Sense: How the new science of dog behavior can make you a better friend to your pet*, Basic Books, 2011.

Coppinger, R., and Coppinger, L., *What is a Dog?* University of Chicago Press, 2016.

Coppinger, R., and Feinstein, M., *How Dogs Work*, University of Chicago Press, 2015.

Corin, Stanley, *The Intelligence of Dogs*, Simon and Schuster, 2005.

Fox, M.W., *Behaviour of Wolves, Dogs and Related Canids*, Harper & Row, 1972.

— *The Dog: Its domestication and behaviour*, Garland Press, 1978.

Hare, Brian, and Woods, Vanessa, *The Genius of Dogs*, Dutton, 2013.

Horowitz, Alexandra, *Inside of a Dog*, Scribner, 2009.

— *Being a Dog*, Scribner, 2016.

— 'Attention to attention in domestic dog (*Canis familiaris*) dyadic play', *Animal Cognition*, vol. 12, no. 1, 2009.

Killion, Jane, *Puppy Culture*, DVD series, 2017.

Klinghammer, Eric (ed), *The Behavior and Ecology of Wolves*, Garland Press, 1979.

Lorenz, Konrad. *Man Meets Dog*, Routledge Classics, 2002.

Mech, L.D., and Boitani, L., *Wolves: Behavior, ecology and conservation*, University of Chicago Press, 2003.

Mech, L.D., et al., *Wolves on the Hunt*, University of Chicago Press, 2015.

Miklósi, Adám, *Dog Behaviour, Evolution, and Cognition*, 1st and 2nd ed., Oxford University Press, 2015.

Pryor, Karen, *Don't Shoot the Dog*, Bantam USA, 1999.

Scientific American Special Collector's Edition, *The science of dogs and cats*, 2015.

Scientific American Special Collector's Edition, *The story of us*, 2016.

Scott, J.P., and Fuller, J.L., *Genetics and the Social Behaviour of the Dog*, University of Chicago Press, 1965.

Stewart, G., *Behavior Adjustment Training*, 2nd ed., Dog Wise Publishing, 2016.

Thich Nhat Hanh, *The Miracle of Mindfulness*, Parallax Press, 1976.

Thich Nhat Hanh, *The Sun My Heart*, Parallax Press, 1988.

Topál, J., et al., 'Attachment behaviour in dogs (Canis familiaris): A new application of Ainsworth's (1969) Strange Situation test', *Journal of Comparative Psychology*, vol. 112, no. 3, 1998.

Vette, M.A.G., 'The onotogeny and genetics of sheepdog behaviour', The University of Auckland (unpublished thesis), 1980.

Von Holdt, breed cladogram in Miklósi, *Dog Behaviour, Evolution and Cognition*, 2nd ed. Oxford University Press, 2015.

Wilson, E.O., *Biophilia,* rev. ed., Harvard University Press, 2011.

Acknowledgements

The first person I want to thank is Kim, my fiancée and co-practitioner in Dog Zen. Her belief in me and our Big Idea that we can transform dog behaviour in New Zealand within 10 years, inspires and pushes me forward. Kim has helped me grow, carry and express this vision through her ability to find the story, edit out the clutter and to ask the critical questions to point the compass. My deep gratitude to dear Kim.

Marie Manderson, an expert dog trainer and Puppy Zen co-practitioner, who has been with me for 20 years. She has been a constant companion and support to me and our team forever! She contributed her fine mind and skills to peer review and improve this book. It was in our workshops and clinic that we learnt these lessons together.

Jazmin, my daughter and trainer extraordinaire, has been steeped in Dog Zen and Puppy Zen for 35 years and is a hands-on doer. She is wonderful with people and animals, and her experience, wrangling and beauty are present in this book and my life. I love her!

Nalu, Jazzy and Russo's daughter and my granddaughter, helped us show you our methods with her training demonstrations that have been captured in the photos. She's the youngest Puppy Zen Master in the book!

Thanks too to Alisa and Koan, for helping online with Dog Zen, and Bo, Suzie, Russo, Gordy, Catch, Karl and Ngaire for sharing time, space and ideas to help us bring Dog Zen to the world.

To my human teachers and friends: the late professor Erik Klinghammer; John Paul Scott, the father of Critical Period theory in dogs; Marc Bekoff; and Michael Fox and Adam Miklósi, leaders in canine behaviour. To my dear friends Alex Walker (vet specialist); Megan Alderson (GP vet) and Professor John Craig, respected ethologist, for their time and constant support.

And to my special friend and internationally renowned animal photographer Rachael McKenna, who brought us the lovely images that are laced throughout this book. Also, my heartfelt thanks to my publisher Margaret Sinclair at Penguin Random House whose gentle care helped us bring this project to life.

Finally, my gratitude to my true Dog Zen Masters — all the dogs and puppies in my life who have taught me what unconditional love is.